THE HIDDEN
SELF

THE DIAGRAM GROUP

Editor	Denis Kennedy
Contributors	Susan Bosanko
	David Harding
Art director	Richard Czapnik
Artists	Suzanne Baker
	Joe Bonello
	Alastair Burnside
	Brian Hewson
	Paula Preston
Illustrator	Graham Rosewarne

First published in Great Britain by
George Weidenfeld & Nicolson Ltd
under the title *Who Are You?*

This 1992 edition published by
Chancellor Press
Michelin House
81 Fulham Road
London SW3 6RB

ISBN 1 85152 119 4

Printed in Portugal

THE HIDDEN
SELF

MAYA PILKINGTON & THE DIAGRAM GROUP

CHANCELLOR
PRESS

Contents

Chapter 1

YOUR PREDESTINED SELF

Chapter 2

YOUR PHYSICAL SELF

Chapter 3

YOUR
REVEALED SELF

Chapter 4

YOUR
SOCIAL SELF

Foreword

Who Are You? is an unusually comprehensive selection of information and activities that will give you greater self-knowledge and understanding. It combines ancient methods tested by time and modern approaches that have been validated statistically. All the practical exercises designed for knowing yourself have been updated as a result of modern findings about the nature of human personality.

In compiling this book of self-discovery, the artists and editors of the Diagram Group and the author, Maya Pilkington, together have created a new dimension within the familiar Diagram Group style. **Who Are You?** is a manual for your personal use, integrating text with illustrations and carefully planned spaces for your own responses. Here you can explore yourself from many different points of view.

Who are You? will guide you through a new experience of yourself even if you choose not to participate, but, if you do, you will make this book your own. There are questions to answer, preferences to select, diagrams to complete, measurements to make and a variety of practical ways to explore more than 100 fascinating aspects of your life, your personality and your relationships with others.

The sections of **Who Are You?** can be used in any order; each double page spread gives step by step instructions and clear explanations. The final choices remain always with you. Because it is recognized that self-development and growth result from your active involvement in the process of self-discovery, this is not a book to tell you who you are but is a guide to help you to discover who you are and to go on discovering in the future.

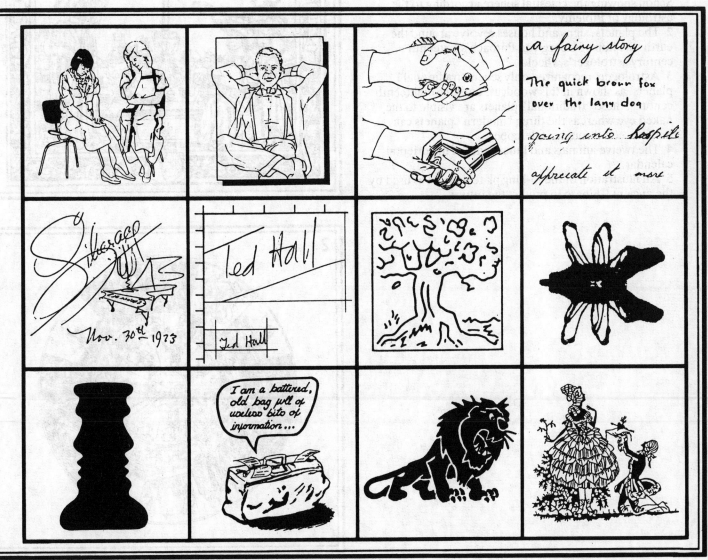

Chapter 1

YOUR PREDESTINED SELF

To be born into a body is to be born in time. This idea of predestination has existed for thousands of years. Many religions maintain that we are born for a purpose and live many lives...in different bodies, each timed so that we can fulfill the purposes assigned to us. Astrology links your time of birth with the positions of the planets, each planet and its position having symbolic meaning. In modern astrology, the link is made with your personality which would appear to match with the symbolic meaning of the positions of the planets at the time of birth.

1 A sixteenth century German woodcut by Erhard Schon showing the celestial sphere according to the astrology of Ptolemy.
2 The planets, signs and houses revolve around the earth, the hub of Georg von Purbach's sixteenth century astrologer's wheel.
3 Astrologers recognized only seven "traditional" planets, as shown in this woodcut, until the eighteenth century; these "traditional" planets are visible to the naked eye whereas the three "modern" planets can only be seen through a telescope.
4 The twelve animals and lunar years of the oriental calendar.
5 An illustration of the lo-king plate which was used by the ancient Chinese to predict the future.

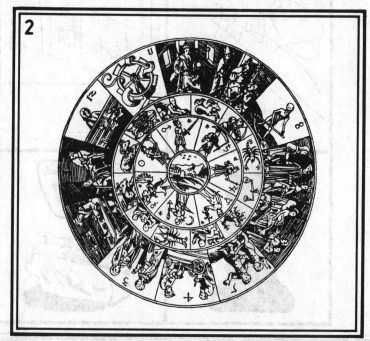

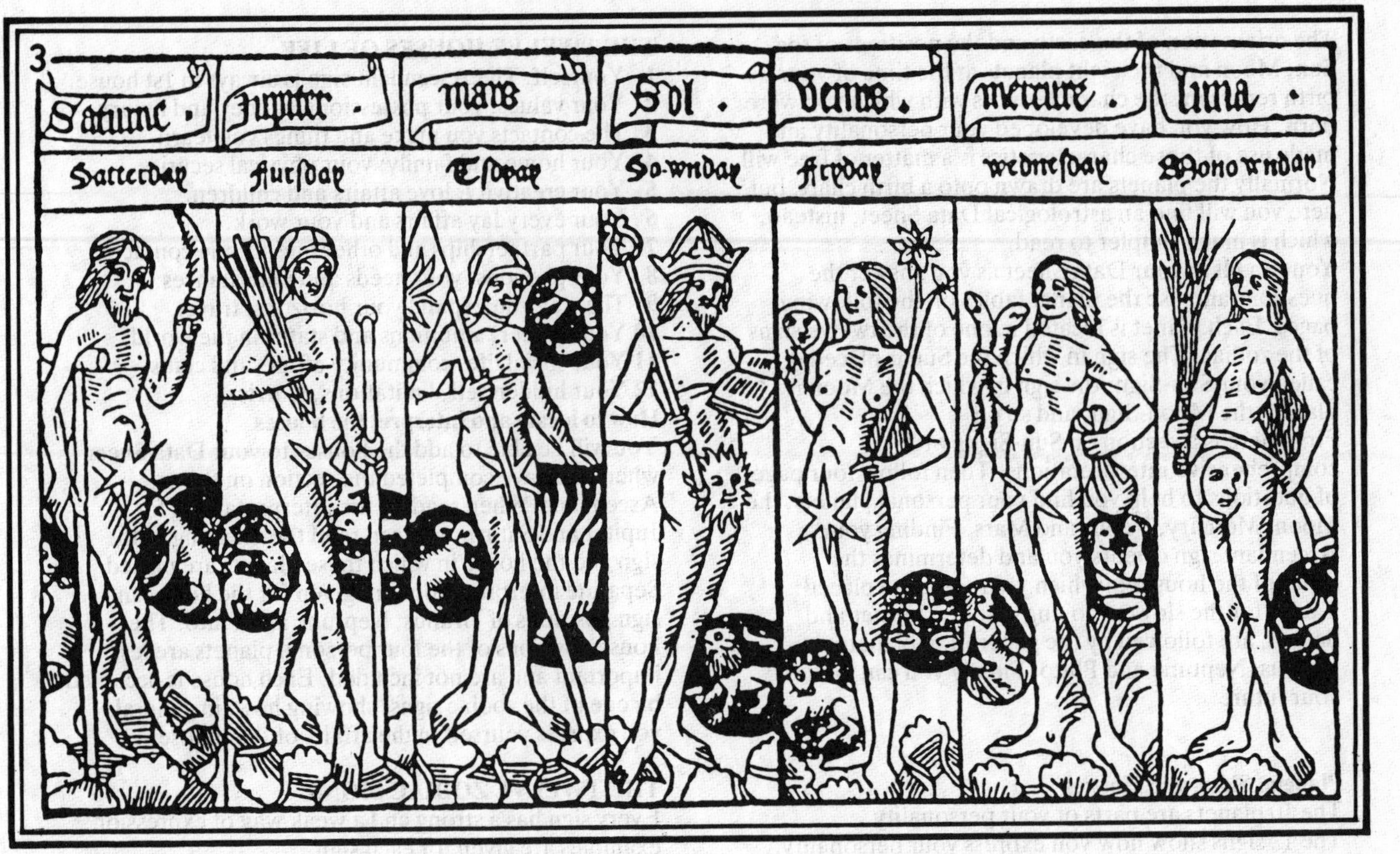

3

Saturne ·	Jupiter ·	Mars	Sol ·	Venus ·	Mercure ·	Luna ·
Saterday	Thursday	Tewsday	Sownday	Fryday	Wednesday	Monownday

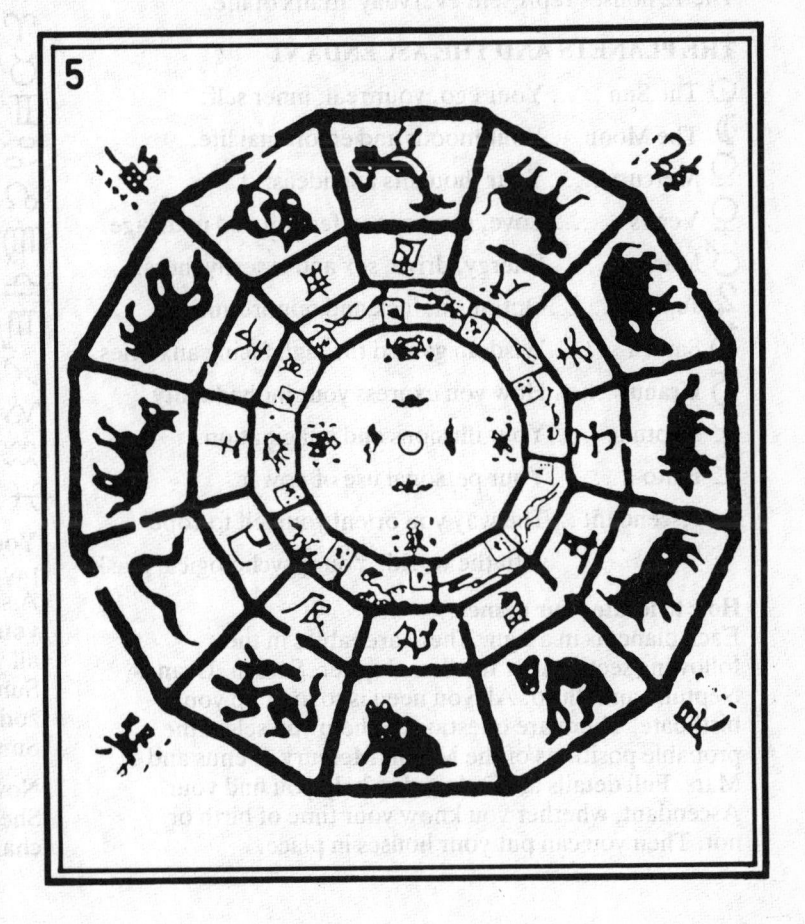

Your astrological character

The orientation of the earth and the positions of the Sun, Moon and the eight planets at the time of your birth represent the characteristics with which you were born. How you have developed your personality and made use of those characteristics is a matter of free will. Normally the planets are drawn onto a birth chart, but here you will find an astrological Data Sheet, instead, which is much simpler to read.

You can fill in your Data Sheet as you answer the questions and use the planet tables on the following pages. Each planet is located in one of the twelve signs of the zodiac. The sign in which the Sun is placed is called your Sun-Sign; the sign in which the Moon is placed, the Moon-Sign, and so on.

First there is a section on Sun-Signs with comprehensive interpretations. Then follow four pages of questions to help you find your personal planets, the Moon, Mercury, Venus and Mars. Finding your Ascendant sign orients you and determines the order of the houses in which your signs are placed. Tables for the slower moving planets, Jupiter and Saturn, are followed by the generation planets, Uranus, Neptune and Pluto. Finally you can look to your future.

Planets, Signs and Houses

The 10 planets are parts of your personality.
The 12 signs show how you express your personality.
The 12 houses represent everyday affairs of life.

THE PLANETS AND THE ASCENDANT

☉ The Sun ...... Your ego, your real, inner self.

☽ The Moon ... Your moods and emotional life.

☿ Mercury ...... Your thoughts and ideas.

♀ Venus .... Love, romance, affection and marriage.

♂ Mars .... Energy, drive, sex and assertiveness.

♃ Jupiter .... Optimism, luck and opportunities.

♄ Saturn .... Wisdom gained through facing anxieties.

♅ Uranus .... How you express your individuality.

♆ Neptune ...... Your illusions and imagination.

♇ Pluto .... Your personal use of power.

Ascendant ... The way you orient yourself to cope with the world. Your psychological mask.

How to locate your planets

Each planet is in a sign. There are tables in the following sections for the Sun, Jupiter, Saturn, Uranus, Neptune and Pluto. All you need is to look up your birthdate. There are questions to help you select the probable positions of the Moon, Mercury, Venus and Mars. Full details are included to help you find your Ascendant, whether you know your time of birth or not. Then you can put your houses in place.

THE TWELVE HOUSES OF LIFE

1 Yourself. The Ascendant sign is always in 1st house.
2 Your values, your possessions, money and luxury.
3 The contacts you make and things you learn.
4 Your home and family; your physical security.
5 Your creativity, love affairs and children.
6 Your everyday affairs and your work.
7 Your partnerships and other one-to-one contacts.
8 Your passions, your needs and inheritances.
9 The way you expand your horizons; travel.
10 Your career, ambitions and status in the world.
11 Your social life, community affairs and clubs.
12 Your hidden self, limitations, worries.

How to locate and interpret the houses

You will be able to add the houses to your Data Sheet when you have completed the section on the Ascendant. When reading the interpretations for Jupiter and Saturn, you can read the meaning of the sign and the house in which these planets are placed. Separate interpretations are given for the house and sign positions of Uranus, Neptune and Pluto. The house positions of the four personal planets are less important and are not included. Each house is occupied by one of the zodiac signs, showing how, in general, you express yourself in the affairs of that house.

THE TWELVE ZODIAC SIGNS

Every sign has a strong and a weak way of expression; examples are given for each sign.

♈ **Aries**, the ram, can initiate or aggressively dominate.

♉ **Taurus**, the bull, can build or waste resources.

♊ **Gemini**, the twins, can think or resort to scheming.

♋ **Cancer**, the crab, can protect or smother.

♌ **Leo**, the lion, can create or merely pretend.

♍ **Virgo,** the virgin, can analyze or worry.

♎ **Libra**, the scales, can cooperate or argue on principle.

♏ **Scorpio**, the scorpion, can discover or suspect.

♐ **Sagittarius**, the archer, can understand or exaggerate.

♑ **Capricorn,** the seagoat, can organize or restrict.

♒ **Aquarius**, the watercarrier, can explore or escape.

♓ **Pisces,** the fishes, can sympathize or confuse.

You have a little of every sign in your character, but the predominant ones are those in which you have planets. A sign with two or more planets may be as important as your Sun-Sign. As you learn to express yourself fully, all your characteristics are channelled through your Sun-Sign and your Ascendant mask begins to drop. The zodiac signs are described more fully in the sections on Sun-Signs.

Now you are ready to begin completing your Data Sheet as you discover your fascinating astrological character.

YOUR DATA SHEET – please use the information compiled from pages 12–35 to enable you to complete this sheet.

THE POSITIONS OF YOUR PLANETS AND ASCENDANT	HOUSES	ZODIAC SIGNS	QUALITY	ELEMENT
		♈ Aries	Cardinal	Fire
		♉ Taurus	Fixed	Earth
		♊ Gemini	Mutable	Air
		♋ Cancer	Cardinal	Water
		♌ Leo	Fixed	Fire
		♍ Virgo	Mutable	Earth
		♎ Libra	Cardinal	Air
		♏ Scorpio	Fixed	Water
		♐ Sagittarius	Mutable	Fire
		♑ Capricorn	Cardinal	Earth
		♒ Aquarius	Fixed	Air
		♓ Pisces	Mutable	Water

Do you have a predominant quality or element?
You have 10 planets and the Ascendant marked in your Data Sheet. Count how many are in each quality and element and write the numbers (*below*). A score of 5 or more is a strong emphasis. Do you have any missing that need developing? You are balanced if you have one or more of each. Interpretations of the qualities and elements are given on page 12.

Qualities

Cardinal _____

Fixed _____

Mutable _____

Elements

Fire _____

Earth _____

Air _____

Water _____

How are your 10 planets arranged?
Ignore the Ascendant in looking at the arrangement. (Note that Aries and Pisces count as adjacent.)
Two or more planets in one sign: a special talent.
All planets in four adjacent signs: a one-track mind.
All planets in six adjacent signs: a contained person.
A planet in each of nine or ten signs: broad-minded.
Planets in two distinct groups of four or five: two-sided.
All planets in six adjacent signs with one (or a pair) that is isolated: something unique to offer, or to develop, as indicated by the isolated planet or pair of planets.

©DIAGRAM

11

What is your sun-sign?

On this page you can find your zodiac Sun-Sign and on the next seven pages you will find descriptions of all the twelve ego-types known as Sun-Signs. You will have some of the characteristics of several signs, but they are all channelled through your personal Sun-Sign.

INTERPRETATIONS OF THE QUALITIES AND ELEMENTS
Every sign is associated with a quality and an element. You can look up your signs on the table (*opposite*).

THE QUALITIES
Cardinal Signs are rather passionate about getting things moving. They **use** abilities and don't like delay.
Fixed Signs can be relied upon to build with dogged persistence. They **stabilize** assets and never give up.
Mutable Signs are versatile and flexible in every new situation. They **adapt** to conditions and like variety.

THE ELEMENTS
Fire Signs are generally active, enthusiastic and warm, unless they need re-lighting. They burn lots of fuel.
Air Signs are usually chatty, stimulating and bright, unless the air gets stuffy. They need lots of space.
Earth Signs are practical, realistic, busy and usually stable, unless there's a landslide. They need time.
Water Signs are imaginative, emotional and refreshing, unless they evaporate. They need to be contained.

HOW TO READ THE SUN-SIGN TABLES
1 Find the appropriate year and look along the line.
2 Choose the column headed by the correct month.
3 Note the number where the line and the column meet.
4 If your birthdate was earlier than the number, then your Sun-Sign is at the head of the previous column.

5 If your birthdate was later than the number, then your Sun-Sign is at the head of that same column.
6 If your birthdate is the same as the number, then read the sign above and the previous sign and decide which feels more appropriate; you will have some of both.
For example, on May 19th, 1931, the Sun was in Taurus, and on May 29th, 1931, the Sun-Sign was Gemini.

Sun-Sign Table for 1916 to 1935

	JA	FE	MR	AP	MY	JN	JL	AU	SE	OC	NO	DE
	Aq	Pi	Ar	Ta	Ge	Cn	Le	Vi	Li	Sc	Sg	Cp
1916	21	19	20	20	21	21	23	23	23	23	21	22
1917	20	19	21	20	21	22	23	23	23	23	22	21
1918	20	19	21	20	21	22	23	23	23	24	23	22
1919	21	19	21	21	22	22	23	24	24	24	23	22
1920	21	19	20	20	21	21	23	23	23	23	22	22
1921	20	19	21	20	21	21	23	23	23	23	22	22
1922	20	19	21	20	21	22	23	23	23	24	23	22
1923	21	19	21	21	22	22	23	24	24	24	23	22
1924	21	19	20	20	21	21	23	23	23	23	22	22
1925	20	19	21	20	21	21	23	23	23	23	22	22
1926	20	19	21	20	21	22	23	23	23	24	23	22
1927	21	19	21	21	22	22	23	24	24	24	23	22
1928	21	19	20	20	21	21	23	23	23	23	22	22
1929	20	19	21	20	21	21	23	23	23	23	22	22
1930	20	19	21	20	21	22	23	23	23	24	23	22
1931	21	19	21	21	22	22	23	24	24	24	23	22
1932	21	19	20	20	21	21	23	23	23	23	22	22
1933	20	19	21	20	21	21	23	23	23	23	22	22
1934	20	19	21	20	21	22	23	23	23	24	23	22
1935	20	19	21	21	22	22	23	24	23	24	23	22

Sun-Sign Table for 1936 to 1955

	JA	FE	MR	AP	MY	JN	JL	AU	SE	OC	NO	DE
	Aq	Pi	Ar	Ta	Ge	Cn	Le	Vi	Li	Sc	Sg	Cp
1936	21	19	20	20	21	21	23	23	23	23	22	22
1937	20	19	21	20	21	21	23	23	23	23	22	22
1938	20	19	21	20	21	22	23	23	23	24	22	22
1939	20	19	21	20	21	22	23	24	23	24	23	22
1940	21	19	20	20	21	21	23	23	23	23	22	21
1941	20	19	21	20	21	21	23	23	23	23	22	22
1942	20	19	21	20	21	22	23	23	23	24	22	22
1943	20	19	21	20	21	22	23	23	23	24	23	22
1944	21	19	21	20	21	21	22	23	23	23	22	21
1945	20	19	20	20	22	21	23	23	23	23	22	22
1946	20	19	21	20	21	22	23	23	23	24	22	22
1947	20	19	21	21	21	22	23	24	23	24	23	22
1948	21	19	20	20	21	21	22	23	23	23	22	21
1949	20	18	21	20	21	21	23	23	23	23	22	22
1950	20	19	21	20	21	21	23	23	23	23	22	22
1951	20	19	21	20	21	22	23	23	23	23	22	22
1952	21	19	20	20	21	21	23	23	23	23	22	21
1953	20	18	20	20	21	21	23	23	23	23	22	22
1954	20	19	21	20	21	21	23	23	23	23	22	22
1955	20	19	21	20	21	22	23	23	23	23	23	22

	CARDINAL SIGNS	FIXED SIGNS	MUTABLE SIGNS
FIRE SIGNS	Aries — Uses energy to make things happen.	Leo — Stabilizes energy to create things.	Sagittarius — Adapts energy to explore life.
AIR SIGNS	Libra — Uses ideas to make judgments.	Aquarius — Stabilizes ideas to reform the world.	Gemini — Adapts ideas to communicate them.
EARTH SIGNS	Capricorn — Uses resources to accomplish goals.	Taurus — Stabilizes resources to build permanence.	Virgo — Adapts resources to improve conditions.
WATER SIGNS	Cancer — Uses emotions to act with compassion.	Scorpio — Stabilizes emotions before trusting.	Pisces — Adapts emotions to be able to sympathize.
WHICH ARE YOU?	A Passionate Cardinal Sign?	A Reliable Fixed Sign?	A Flexible Mutable Sign?

Key to abbreviations for months

JA January	MY May	SE September
FE February	JN June	OC October
MR March	JL July	NO November
AP April	AU August	DE December

Key to abbreviations for signs

Ar Aries	Le Leo	Sg Sagittarius
Ta Taurus	Vi Virgo	Cp Capricorn
Ge Gemini	Li Libra	Aq Aquarius
Cn Cancer	Sc Scorpio	Pi Pisces

Sun-Sign Table for 1956 to 1975

	Aq	Pi	Ar	Ta	Ge	Cn	Le	Vi	Li	Sc	Sg	Cp
	JA	FE	MR	AP	MY	JN	JL	AU	SE	OC	NO	DE
1956	21	19	20	20	21	21	22	23	23	23	22	21
1957	20	18	20	20	21	21	23	23	23	23	22	22
1958	20	19	21	20	21	21	23	23	23	23	22	22
1959	20	19	21	20	21	22	23	23	23	24	23	22
1960	21	19	20	20	21	21	22	23	23	23	22	21
1961	20	18	20	20	21	21	23	23	23	23	22	22
1962	20	19	21	20	21	21	23	23	23	23	22	22
1963	20	19	21	20	21	22	23	23	23	24	23	22
1964	20	19	20	20	21	21	22	23	23	23	22	21
1965	20	18	20	20	21	21	23	23	23	23	22	22
1966	20	19	21	20	21	21	23	23	23	23	22	22
1967	20	19	21	20	21	22	23	23	23	24	23	22
1968	20	19	20	20	21	21	22	23	23	23	22	21
1969	20	18	20	20	21	21	23	23	23	23	22	22
1970	20	19	21	20	21	21	23	23	23	23	22	22
1971	20	19	21	20	21	22	23	23	23	23	22	22
1972	20	19	20	19	20	21	22	23	23	23	22	21
1973	20	18	20	20	21	21	22	23	23	23	22	22
1974	20	19	21	20	21	21	23	23	23	23	22	22
1975	20	19	21	20	21	22	23	23	23	24	22	22

Sun-Sign Table for 1976 to 1995

	Aq	Pi	Ar	Ta	Ge	Cn	Le	Vi	Li	Sc	Sg	Cp
	JA	FE	MR	AP	MY	JN	JL	AU	SE	OC	NO	DE
1976	20	19	20	19	20	21	22	23	22	23	22	21
1977	20	18	20	20	21	21	22	23	23	23	22	21
1978	20	19	20	20	21	21	23	23	23	23	22	22
1979	20	19	21	20	21	21	23	23	23	24	22	22
1980	20	19	20	19	20	21	22	22	22	23	22	21
1981	20	18	20	20	21	21	22	23	23	23	22	21
1982	20	18	20	20	21	21	23	23	23	23	22	22
1983	20	19	21	20	21	21	23	23	23	23	22	22
1984	20	19	20	19	20	21	22	23	22	23	22	21
1985	20	18	20	20	21	21	22	23	23	23	22	21
1986	20	18	20	20	21	21	23	23	23	23	22	22
1987	20	19	21	20	21	21	23	23	23	23	22	22
1988	20	19	20	19	20	21	22	22	22	23	22	21
1989	20	18	20	20	21	21	22	23	23	23	22	21
1990	20	18	20	20	21	21	23	23	23	23	22	22
1991	20	19	21	20	21	21	23	23	23	23	22	22
1992	20	19	20	19	20	21	22	22	22	23	22	21
1993	20	18	20	20	21	21	22	23	23	23	22	21
1994	20	18	20	20	21	21	23	23	23	23	22	22
1995	20	19	21	20	21	21	23	23	23	23	22	22

©DIAGRAM

Are you passionately bossy?

Aries
The Ram

Cardinal
Fire

SUN IN ARIES

Like the ram, you go head first into everything. You may not always be aware of the effect you can have on other people, nor take responsibility for it. If you did you would have to grow up. Assertive, adventurous and noble, you will give up your time, your money and even your life for those you love. A great rescuer, like Robin Hood, you don't like to stay at home and fix the fuses, whether you are male or female. Impossible challenges excite you and your life is lived like an open book . Impulsive and rather self-centered you always want to believe the best of everyone, but you are not always the best judge of character.

Ruled by energetic Mars, you have an attitude that says "I can-do-it-by-myself" and that sometimes frightens off other people. You need a good friend to tell you when you are making a mess of things, as you tend to ignore warning clues until yet another mini-disaster strikes.

If you are typical of Aries, you can't stand being number two in anything, but you can take the initiative. Your secret fear is that you won't be liked or valued. Aries is a healthy sign; with all your natural warmth and enthusiasm you can stimulate others to take up new interests and give them leadership.

Arien Positives	Arien Negatives
enthusiastic	intolerant
eager	hasty
lives in present	lacks follow-through
independent	dominating
executive	quick-tempered
daring	tactless
original	uncompromising

Libra is your opposite sign
From Libra you can learn to cooperate, share and bring people together in harmony, express your ideas actively but tactfully, and therefore find balance.

Libra
The Scales

Cardinal
Air

SUN IN LIBRA

Like the scales of justice, you weigh the pros and cons of everything and you seem to have a mission to bring people and ideas together. However, if you are pushed in one direction, you tend to push back in the opposite way. You are frequently of two minds about things, so you may have initial difficulty in speaking up for yourself. Once your mind is made up, you then make your decisions known fairly forcibly.

Ruled by refined Venus, you are attractive, love harmony, music and wearing exactly the right clothes. You are romantic about love and usually find it quite unthinkable to be alone for long. A partner is essential to you.

You dislike abrasive, crude things and like to keep up appearances, so a good mirror is essential. Your forte is diplomacy; your secret power is the ability to contain a situation, using charm, persuasion, flattery, coercion, negotiation or straightforward manipulation. You have an expert mind and often are sure you are right.

If you are typical of Libra, you can adapt to almost any situation. Your secret fear is of being alone with yourself: Libra is a loving sign and you will find a way around any impasse to bring peace and harmony into your life and the lives of others; whatever you do you mean it from the bottom of your heart.

Libran Positives	Libran Negatives
cooperative	apathetic
companionable	loves intrigue
suave	peace at any price
refined	pouting
artistic	indecisive
compromising	fearful
concerned for others	craves admiration

Aries is your opposite sign
From Aries you can learn to take the initiative on your own and sometimes stand up for your beliefs without manipulation. This is the way to find identity.

Capricorn
The Seagoat

Cardinal
Earth

SUN IN CAPRICORN

Like the goat, you will sure-footedly find your way to the top, even if it takes you a hundred years. You plan ahead and can move mountains and steamroll anything that gets in your way. You may have had it hard at the beginning of life and carried many responsibilities. You may have seemed old as a child, but things get easier with age and hard work, and you usually get younger as you grow older. You may appear rather inhibited to some people, but inside you there is a little nanny-goat itching to get out and play. Ruled by wise old Saturn, you use adversity to spur yourself on to greater achievements. You can work harder than anyone to get what you want, and what you want is only the very best. Often dogged by anxiety and very aware of your own flaws you take up the challenge and improve yourself. A career, and the high status that accompanies it, is usually essential to you.

If you are typical of Capricorn, you will use anything and anyone to succeed. Your secret fear is of being weak or of failing to reach the very high standards of excellence you have set yourself. Capricorn is a sign of wisdom and you have a depth of loyalty and a feeling for beauty that leaves most people breathless.

Capricorn Positives	Capricorn Negatives
cautiously realistic	egotistical
scrupulous	unforgiving
conventional	fatalistic
hard-working	slave-driving
perfectionist	status-seeking
good organizer	stubbornly "right"
excellent standards	depressive

Cancer is your opposite sign
From Cancer you can learn to express emotions and use your own feelings to understand the needs of others. This is the way to find complete satisfaction.

Cancer
The Crab

Cardinal
Water

SUN IN CANCER

Like the crab, you are well protected on the outside but soft and pink on the inside. You are very good at sustaining people and seem to have a mission to take care of not only people themselves, but also their means of making a living. You are likely to have good business talents. Ruled by the moody Moon, you have a vivid emotional life and are careful to avoid hurting people, being sensitive to hurt yourself. Yes, you can have rather crabby moods too. You can extract the greatest degree of comfort from any set of circumstances and have an ability to hold on to almost anything. You accumulate things, collect bargains and love anything that is old, which includes your friends when they are old and tired. Home is where you excel, loading the table with goodies to welcome every visitor. You may turn to food yourself when feeling upset. Your mothering talents are many, whether you are man or woman, but you may tend to be a little smothering or possessive of loved ones.

If you are typical of Cancer, you may not always feel sure of yourself, but you are sure about how to nurture individuals or whole groups of people. Your secret fear is of being hurt and having no one to care for. You are emotional and perhaps shy, but you can teach people the secrets of human compassion.

Cancerian Positives	Cancerian Negatives
tenacious	moody
intuitive	too easily hurt
domestic	matriarchal at home
retentive memory	holds on to insults
helpful	lazily luxurious
sensitive to need	unrealistic
protective	overpowering

Capricorn is your opposite sign
From Capricorn you can learn to get things into a proper perspective and take a realistic view of life. In this way you can learn to make good judgments.

©DIAGRAM

Are you reliably stubborn?

Leo
The Lion

Fixed
Fire

SUN IN LEO

Like the lion, you are proud and enjoy being king or queen of your particular jungle. Leo people tend to toss their hair around, just like a lion's mane. You will always tend to look beautiful even covered with grease from the car or dust from the kitchen. Not that you really enjoy work, you do it because under no circumstances can you bear not being on top of your particular pile. You love to show off, in the nicest possible way and although proud and caring of your children, you will show them off too.

Ruled by the life-giving Sun, you are warm, friendly and a very generous host or hostess. Even if you are shy, you like the world to orbit around you and enjoy being appreciated. Even a little flattery boosts your rather shaky ego.

You tend to trust everyone, almost unwittingly. Often you get hurt as a consequence. If this happens, or a current project seems likely to fail, you prowl about like a sulky lion and retire to lick your wounds.

If you are typical of Leo, you can turn your hand to anything creative, including love and romance, but if crossed, you can leap out with a growl unexpectedly. Your secret fear is of not being seen to be important. Leo is an affectionate sign; you are lively and sunny and will bring joy and life to any dull day.

Leo Positives	Leo Negatives
dramatic	vain
proudly honest	childishly naive
dignified	mildly cruel
generous	pretentious
optimistic	autocratic
helpful	benevolently superior
energetic	won't share power

Aquarius is your opposite sign
From Aquarius you can learn to share in a caring way and leave the center of the stage to others occasionally, therefore learning to stand alone and value yourself.

Aquarius
The Watercarrier

Fixed
Air

SUN IN AQUARIUS

Like the watercarrier, you like to bring the waters of life to people through your new and often radical ideas. You like to know and keep in touch with all new developments, yet remain detached from any deep emotional involvement. Sometimes you have a look in your eye of faraway places; perhaps you just dropped in from outer space. Friendly and sociable to a point, you want the greatest good for the greatest number of people and are likely to put across your ideas in the most unexpected ways. Freedom of thought is vital to you and freedom of movement too. You like to see justice done, so long as it is your version of justice. You are likely to run a mile from emotions. Ruled by eccentric Uranus, you are often a little odd or you may feel at odds with yourself, unsure of who you really are, which is why you may sometimes be accused of being vague. Perhaps you feel guilty about being different from other people, but don't you know that everyone is different?

If you are typical of Aquarius, you ask endless, quite searching questions, all in a drive to understand. Your secret fear is of intimacy and romance as you aren't sure who you are. Aquarius is a pleasant sign; you are good to have around and care greatly about your friends, bringing new ideas and new values.

Aquarian Positives	Aquarian Negatives
independent	unpredictable
inventive	bored by detail
logical	fixed opinions
humane and caring	won't let go of an idea
altruistic	rebellious
persistent	unreliable
radical	odd and eccentric

Leo is your opposite sign
From Leo you can learn how to put your magnetic and powerful personality to good use and make choices to please yourself, thus becoming sure of yourself.

Taurus
The Bull

Fixed
Earth

SUN IN TAURUS
Like the bull, you do not move unless there is something worth moving for. You like to keep a firm hand on your possessions and nothing makes you happier than a nice, secure material prosperity. The good things in life are what you crave, because you love to luxuriate in sensual delights.

Ruled by romantic Venus, you are deeply loving, you have strong values and are very slow to make up your mind. You work hard at anything you see of value and look for the same qualities in a partner. Calm, reliable and patient, you may sometimes be accused of being boring or at the very least stubborn beyond belief. Waiting for the best can be boring indeed, but you can also withstand burdens that would knock less stable folks off balance. Your way is slow but sure, which may be why you sometimes have a sense that something is missing from your life. Perhaps you should let someone persuade you to get up and go somewhere new occasionally. Things of value are often worth going after.

If you are typical of Taurus, you can wait for anything, even wait to get angry. When you do you can be devastating. Your secret fear is of being left wanting or of being disturbed. Taurus is the most reliable and faithful sign; you are one of the builders of this world and can bring long-term plans to successful fruition.

Taurean Positives	Taurean Negatives
conservative	self-indulgent
dependable	obstinate
artistically inclined	materialistic
thorough and resourceful	slowmoving
attentive	nothing much to say
values others' talents	wastes time pondering
deeply loving	easily embarrassed

Scorpio is your opposite sign
From Scorpio you can learn to recognize the needs of other people. This way you will gain insight not only into the motives of others but into your own.

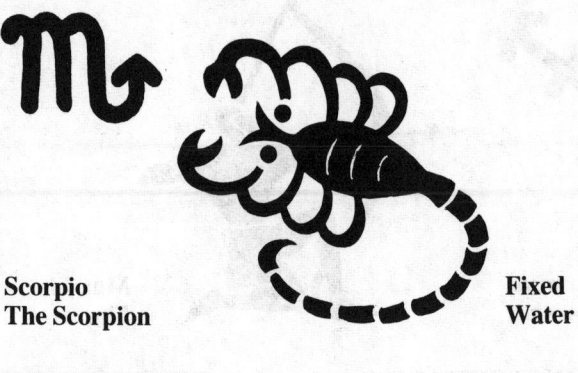

Scorpio
The Scorpion

Fixed
Water

SUN IN SCORPIO
Like the scorpion, you like to know what is going on just underneath the surface of things. You can keep your own and anyone else's secrets since you do not trust easily. You are reputed to be sexy, but a smoldering passion for anything you do or believe in would be a more accurate description. You have the longest memory on earth for anything done to harm people you love and rarely forgive such hurts. The secrets of the darker sides of human nature are no surprise to you, but your famous "sting in the tail" is more often used against yourself than against others. Ruled by searching Pluto, you usually know what people want before they know it themselves. Your instincts are accurate, which is why great detectives and great criminals are often Scorpios. You know too about suffering and do not suffer fools gladly. Self-respect is high on your list of priorities. Power is all to you, so you operate best in an executive position.

If you are typical of Scorpio, you can transform yourself and devote yourself to a few chosen projects and chosen people. Your secret fear is of someone finding out what you really want, in case it should be taken away from you. Scorpio is a gentle sign; like its other symbol the dove, you have compassion.

Scorpionic Positives	Scorpionic Negatives
motivated	vengeful
penetrating	overbearing
investigative	suspicious
probing	jealous
aware of motives	intolerant of mistakes
self-critical	demands the impossible
protective	possessive

Taurus is your opposite sign
From Taurus you can learn to appreciate the variety of other people's talents and value them as they truly deserve, thus becoming gentler with yourself.

Are you flexibly committed?

**Sagittarius
The Archer**

**Mutable
Fire**

SUN IN SAGITTARIUS

Like the archer, you aim for the stars but are tied to the earth. You have high principles but are often so bluntly honest, that you can end up making a mess, or leaving someone feeling bruised. You don't carry a grudge, so you soon forget. Being a bright, intelligent opportunist you always try to make up for your blunders with your delightful Pollyanna attitude "Oops! Well it will be all right tomorrow."

Ruled by expansive Jupiter, you hate to be fenced in on any subject, and generally enjoy traveling too. You are a generous, lucky philosopher, so long as the philosophy is the one you invented. You are often a little surprised to find that other people don't seem to live by the same rules as you do. But you see the broader view and tend to miss the details. You love dashing about, so often bump into things in your haste or trip over small things you didn't notice.

If you are typical of Sagittarius, you can inspire others but may be very reluctant to make commitments or take full responsibilities. Your secret fear is of the limitation of your freedom. Sagittarius is a very lively and breezy sign; you hide your sadnesses and laugh instead. You can see the whole world in a seed.

Sagittarian Positives	Sagittarian Negatives
straightforward	argumentative
optimistic	impatient
just and honest	a gambler at heart
religious	somewhat fanatical
enthusiastic	hot-headed
stimulating	given to preaching
disarmingly happy	denies sadness

Gemini is your opposite sign
From Gemini you can learn to notice the smaller things in life and think your way through problems about responsibility. This is the way to make choices.

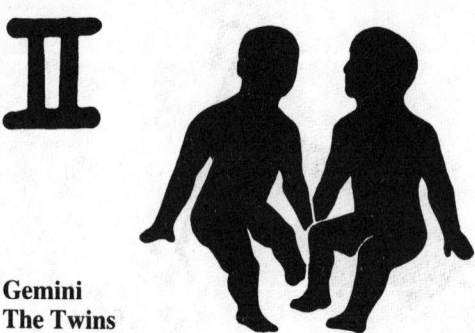

**Gemini
The Twins**

**Mutable
Air**

SUN IN GEMINI

Like the twins you can never seem to stick to being just one person. Sometimes bright, breezy and ecstatic like a glorious summer butterfly and at other times low, confused and in the depths of despair , you find it difficult to control the constant changes which toss you hither and thither. However, at all times, variety is the very spice of life to you. Caged up you shrivel, but roaming around you stimulate yourself and others with your endless curiosity and your interest in people and places.

Ruled by quicksilver Mercury, you have a brilliant mind and can do six things at once, though sometimes you scatter your talents. You get edgy when there is nothing to do. Bright and sociable, you notice every detail. Deeply intuitive, you sense every new message and when hurt your delicate, sensitive nerves stick out all over like an eccentric hedgehog.

If you are typical of Gemini, you can perceive with clarity and understand with a flash of insight. Your secret fear is of never finding your soul-mate for life. Gemini is a sensitive sign; you know the depths and heights of human experience and are the great communicator of this world, sharing your insights around generously.

Geminian Positives	Geminian Negatives
curious and searching	scatterbrained
expressive	restless
quick-witted	lacks concentration
dextrous	cunning
literary	gossipy
attentive to detail	blinkered
adventurous	gets distracted easily

Saggittarius is your opposite sign
From Sagittarius you can learn to take in a broader view of life, and give structure to the mass of information you collect. This way you can discover the truth.

**Virgo
The Virgin**

**Mutable
Earth**

SUN IN VIRGO

Like the original meaning of virgin, you are a very self-perfecting person. You may often live alone, feeling that nobody could live with someone who is not yet perfect enough.

Ruled by nervous Mercury, you can always sense quickly when something is wrong and there is no rest for anyone until order has been restored. You often nag a bit, but that only shows how much you care for a person. You may be truly shy and modest, hiding your deep sensuality behind a rather cool and critical exterior. Virgo is the sign of abundance, but you have always to work hard to get it. You are a good organizer and like to keep lists, collect meticulous details and are often faddy about food and worry about health.

Superbly adaptable, you don't talk about it but just get on with things. You can turn your hand to almost anything and are skilled to masterly levels.

If you are typical of Virgo, you often work incognito and have a discriminating, analytical mind. Your secret fear is of being found wanting, or indeed of it being discovered that you need someone. Virgo is an unassuming sign; you are a hard worker who can serve unflinchingly and give your heart too.

Virgoan Positives	Virgoan Negatives
studious	petty
humane and helpful	skeptical to a fault
scientific and logical	melancholic and lost
meticulously clean	sloppy and untidy
physically sensual	prudish
emotionally generous	emotionally insecure
painstaking	eccentric

Pisces is your opposite sign

From Pisces you can learn to let go and swim with the current, using your fertile imagination freely. This way you can accept human imperfections.

**Pisces
The Fishes**

**Mutable
Water**

SUN IN PISCES

Like the fish, you can swim in any direction, but may sometimes feel at the mercy of the currents of life. You are often confused about which direction to take. The result is either sacrifice, faith and love on the one hand or disorientation, self-pity and doubt on the other. Kind and gentle to anyone in trouble you also stir sympathy in others by your helpless attitude when confusion is the uppermost state of mind. You can learn a lot through flashes of insight that you can't explain and you are adept at picking up moods through your skin. When things go wrong you tend to take the blame on yourself. Ruled by imaginative Neptune, you have rich fantasy dreams for which you seek an outlet. You are one of the best listeners in the world and have to guard against taking the problems of the world on your shoulder. You are so romantic you can see beauty in everything, even in rubbish. Gentle and very understanding, you care for all suffering creatures.

If you are typical of Pisces, you have a lingering sense of guilt for not being good enough. Your secret fear is of really asserting yourself and standing alone on your own two feet. Pisces is an emotional sign; you believe in fate, but can achieve success in anything.

Your potential is enormous.

Piscean Positives	Piscean Negatives
intuitive	a brain-scrambler
charitable	pessimistic
compassionate	feels misunderstood
introspective	indolent
kind	timid
idealistic	procrastinating
well intentioned	flighty

Virgo is your opposite sign

From Virgo you can learn to apply yourself and improve your mastery of the many skills of which you are capable, therefore building your own self worth.

How moody and thoughtful are you?

The positions of the Moon and Mercury at your birth will tell how moody and thoughtful you are. However, all the four personal planets, Moon, Mercury, Venus and Mars move very quickly through the signs, so it is impossible to give here the tables for their many positions. Instead, here are four pages of questions to help you decide in which signs each of these planets were placed at your birth. Then you can add them to your Data Sheet.

HOW TO FIND YOUR MOON-SIGN

The Moon represents your emotional life, so all these questions relate to your emotions. First there are some general questions to help you make your first selection. The Moon could be in any of the 12 signs.

Choose which is most like you, A, B, or C.

A Your emotions drive you to get things done to influence people and events.

B You store up emotions and try to remain undisturbed no matter what happens.

C Your emotions change rapidly and you feel tossed about by them, sometimes up and sometimes down.

Now select which of the next four is most like you.

When you are feeling very emotional do you:

1 Feel a need to move around, do something, have sex?

2 Need time to think and understand what is happening?

3 Look for physical security or want to eat?

4 Feel confused, very insecure and want a drink?

Put a circle round the letter and number pair you have selected. The sign by them is your first selection for your Moon-Sign.

A1	Aries	**B1**	Leo	**C1**	Sagittarius
A2	Libra	**B2**	Aquarius	**C2**	Gemini
A3	Capricorn	**B3**	Taurus	**C3**	Virgo
A4	Cancer	**B4**	Scorpio	**C4**	Pisces

Now you can check out further by reading the questions describing each sign (*below*), selecting the set of questions to which you have answered YES most often and most emphatically. Is it the same sign as in your first selection? If not, perhaps you need to ask a friend to tell you how they see you emotionally!

YES NO

Moon in Aries
Do you tend to blow hot and cold?
Do you excel at making quick decisions?
Do you calm down when **you** are in charge?
Is it hard for you to ask for help?

Moon in Taurus
Do you ponder long on emotional issues?
Are you faithful and forbearing?
Does physical contact calm you down?
Is it hard for you to change your ways?

Moon in Gemini
Are you an emotional voyeur?
Are you sensitive to emotional nuances?
Does emotional distance calm you?
Do you have to think about feelings?

Moon in Cancer
Are you emotionally moody?
Are you devoted to other people?
Do you withdraw to calm down?
Do you tend to cling emotionally?

Moon in Leo
Do you have strong emotional needs?
Are you loyal, self-reliant and sexy?
Does winning calm you emotionally?
Do you tend to lack objectivity?

Moon in Virgo
Do you identify with others' emotions?
Are you intuitive and imaginative?
Does being needed calm you down?
In reality are you sad, lonely and lost?

Moon in Libra
Is emotion a difficult area for you?
Are you refined, charming, romantic?
Does music or thinking calm you?
Do you ever admit to feeling hysterical?

Moon in Scorpio
Are you sexually magnetic?
Do you make sacrifices for loved ones?
Does self-control calm you down?
Are you emotionally very possessive?

Moon in Sagittarius
Do you dislike emotional clutter?
Do you have acute judgment of mood?
Does helping others calm you down?
Do you feel everyone is just like you?

Moon in Capricorn
Are you emotionally shy and uncertain?
Do you persist with what makes you feel good?
Does work or aggression calm you down?
Are you really very soft and anxious?

Moon in Aquarius
Do you channel emotions into causes?
Are you quick to sense atmospheres?
Does emotional detachment calm you down?
Are you terrified of emotional contact?

Moon in Pisces
Are you emotionally impressionable?
Are you sympathetic and understanding?
Do you need love to calm you down?
Do emotions often toss you around?

The Moon and your age

Around about the ages of 20, 40, 60 and 80 the Moon is very important as these are times when emotional outlook undergoes some upheavals. The character of your Moon-Sign often describes the kind of person you feel sympathetic towards, especially women.

HOW TO FIND YOUR MERCURY-SIGN

The planet Mercury is most likely to be in the same sign as your Sun or in the first sign immediately before or after your Sun-Sign, so you have only to choose from three signs. Mercury represents the way you think, your view of reality and the way your mind works in general. Speech and communication are associated with Mercury. All the questions are related to these areas. There are some general questions to see if you are typical of your Mercury-Sign, then a set of questions for each sign.

First write down the three most likely signs in the boxes (*below*), placing your Sun-Sign in the middle box. Then add which quality and which element they each are. Choose the one to which you reply YES most often and most emphatically.

The twelve signs are listed for reference.

WHICH IS YOUR MERCURY-SIGN?

Your Sun-Sign	

Aries	Cardinal Fire
Taurus	Fixed Earth
Gemini	Mutable Air
Cancer	Cardinal Water
Leo	Fixed Fire
Virgo	Mutable Earth
Libra	Cardinal Air
Scorpio	Fixed Water
Sagittarius	Mutable Fire
Capricorn	Cardinal Earth
Aquarius	Fixed Air
Pisces	Mutable Water

As you work through the questions, put a mark in the box of the sign you select each time. The one with the most marks will be your Mercury-Sign. You should be aware that your Sun-Sign characteristics may influence your choice. You may like to note in the boxes any choices that are not characteristic of the signs and re-assess those later.

What is the quality of your Mercury-Sign?

If you had to give a speech, which of these three is most typical of the way you would set about it?

A Concentrate on putting across an idea you think is very important and doing it with authority?

B Concentrate on constructing a good speech with a proper introduction, middle and ending?

C Have several ideas and find difficulty in choosing which one to talk about, so you may ad lib a lot?

A is typical of cardinal signs. **B** is typical of fixed signs. **C** is typical of mutable signs. Put a mark in the appropriate box for the one you choose.

Which element is your Mercury-Sign?

Choose the most typical for you and score as before.

When you get an idea, does it most often:

A slowly emerge and need mulling over?

B develop from another idea and grow?

C have to feel right no matter how it occurred?

D come in a flash and appear complete?

A is typical of Earth. **B** is typical of air.

C is typical of water. **D** is typical of fire.

To learn about a car, would you:

A Want to take it apart yourself and learn that way?

B Learn from watching someone else work on it?

C Read or talk about it until you understand?

D Ask someone to show you how to do it yourself?

A is Fire. **B** is Water. **C** is Air. **D** is Earth.

Read the questions (*below*) corresponding to the three signs entered in the boxes (*left*) and choose one.

Mercury in Aries

Can you think quickly, get ideas rolling easily? Does your viewpoint begin from yourself?

Mercury in Taurus

Do you weigh evidence carefully for years before coming to a conclusion? Are your thoughts of value?

Mercury in Gemini

Are you bright, logical and perceptive with an insatiable curiosity about anything and everything?

Mercury in Cancer

Do you have a good memory and are you possessive with ideas? Are you adamant in your views?

Mercury in Leo

Are you a quick thinker who likes to speak with some authority and not be challenged?

Mercury in Virgo

Are you systematic, paying attention to details? Do you love words and put them to good, practical use?

Mercury in Libra

Can you see opposite points of view and are you persuasive and diplomatic? Do you hate to lose?

Mercury in Scorpio

Do you want to know everything? Are you shrewd in thought and forceful with words?

Mercury in Sagittarius

Are you a free-ranging thinker, open-minded or even scatter-brained? Are you often blunt with words?

Mercury in Capricorn

Do you control situations with words and collect a mass of information? Have you a satirical wit?

Mercury in Aquarius

Are you inventive, resourceful and likely to be thinking of unmentionable subjects?

Mercury in Pisces

Can you send messages without words? Are you vague or just brilliantly creative?

How loving and energetic are you?

Venus is the planet of love, romance, affection and marriage, while Mars is the planet of action, energy, assertion, sex and general drive. In matters of love, sex and marriage, Venus is the "feminine" side and Mars the "masculine" side of each of us.

WHICH IS YOUR VENUS-SIGN?

Write in the space below your Sun-Sign and the two signs either side of it. Your Venus will be in one of these five signs.

	Your Sun-Sign

Aries	Cardinal Fire
Taurus	Fixed Earth
Gemini	Mutable Air
Cancer	Cardinal Water
Leo	Fixed Fire
Virgo	Mutable Earth
Libra	Cardinal Air
Scorpio	Fixed Water
Sagittarius	Mutable Fire
Capricorn	Cardinal Earth
Aquarius	Fixed Air
Pisces	Mutable Water

Read the descriptions of the five signs you have chosen and select from these five which is most typical of your experience. Since your Sun or your Mercury may be in one of these signs, take this into account when making your selection.

Venus in Aries
You show affection impulsively and can be quite overwhelming and ardent. You often love more than one person at once and find it hard to be totally faithful. Very kind to people who have less than you, you are keen to demonstrate your beliefs. You like to be spoilt. You fall in love at first sight.

Venus in Taurus
Once you love, it is forever. You have a very strong, loving nature and your feelings influence all your decisions. You are likely to gain through marriage, but take care whom you choose as you often have only one real love. You like to touch and be touched; sensuality is essential to your well-being.

Venus in Gemini
You may have a string of admirers and like to have variety in your love experiences. Often you become strongly attached to two people and find it hard to balance the two! In some way relatives are likely to influence the course of your marriage and you may want to make a change.

Venus in Cancer
You are rather particular about whom you love, but once decided you will try to make yours into an ideal love. You may marry someone of a different age or social standing, whom you may meet while traveling. You are very influenced by the feelings of others to whom you become devoted. Marriage or children may be delayed for some reason.

Venus in Leo
You love to love and love to be noticed. You exude magnetism and are very demanding in love. Loyal in your affections you are likely to gain from a happy marriage, especially socially. You love children, pleasures and romance and may sometimes feel jealousy. You need love, so choose carefully.

Venus in Virgo
You tend to look for the ideal mate, so you may stay single or have a more platonic friendship or go in for clandestine affairs. Freedom is important to you in love and you may have more than one marriage. You are attracted to people younger than you or those in less fortunate circumstances. Delay is likely.

Venus in Libra
You are sensitive and affectionate. Without a loving partner you are lost. You also love company and have a wide social circle of friends and acquaintances. Gracious and appreciative, you value marriage more than a live-in relationship. You are attracted to people you think are in good positions socially.

Venus in Scorpio
Passion is your middle name and you love luxury, pleasure and sensuality. You may sometimes be hasty and choose unlikely mates who make huge demands on you or pervert the course of love. So proceed with caution and you will not be disappointed, as once attached you don't let go. Marriage may bring money.

Venus in Sagittarius
Sympathetic, kind and generous to a fault, you may have some odd love affairs and may get involved with a relative or be attracted to someone from abroad. You may marry more than once and to someone who has also been married before, but marriage will be good for you and bring advancements. You may meet traveling.

Venus in Capricorn
You may be slow to feel love deeply, but when you do it is often for life and you become very attached to your partner. You regard marriage as necessary to the improvement of your circumstances and often take status into account.

Venus in Aquarius
Friendship is everything to you, so you also need a partner who will be a good friend. Passion, emotion and loving demands are not for you, but you are looking for a soul-mate. You follow your heart and may have some very unusual affairs or an unusual marriage.

Venus in Pisces
You are loving and gentle but you may lack a clear view of who people really are. So guard against secret affairs. You feel tender and loving toward mankind, which may lead you into problems looking after lost souls or by becoming a lost soul yourself who needs looking after! You may marry more than once.

WHICH IS YOUR MARS-SIGN?

Your Mars could be in any of the 12 signs, so making a selection is more difficult. Each of the four boxes on this page has a set of twelve answers to the question at the top of the box. Choose two of the statements from each box and circle their numbers. Choose the two that are nearest the way you behave, not the way you would like to see yourself! Family and close friends may help.

In which of these situations is self-assertion easiest?

1 In competition.
2 Entertaining.
3 Unrestricted.
4 In comfort.
5 While aloof.
6 In authority.
7 While talking.
8 When dressed well.
9 When rebelling.
10 At home.
11 When in control.
12 Playing a role.

What kind of temper?

1 Sudden, volcanic and demanding; you feel crazy.
2 Grand and dramatic; you feel deeply insulted.
3 Quick, blunt but soon over; you feel restricted.
4 Rare but like a bulldozer; you feel disturbed.
5 Cantankerous, picky and naggy; you feel ill.
6 Quiet and devastating; you feel worthless.
7 Quick and volatile; you feel jumpy and frantic.
8 Provocative and bossy; you feel unbalanced.
9 Erratic and peppery; you feel lonely and lost.
10 Smoldering and hard to contain; you feel hurt.
11 Oozes out before exploding; you feel churned up.
12 Overwhelming and chaotic; you feel threatened.

Which are your strongest sexual assets?

1 You are spontaneous, adventurous and sexy.
2 You are creative, loving and very warm.
3 You are philosophical, rollicking and happy.
4 You are slow, sensuous and always ready.
5 You are healthy, devout and well informed.
6 You are slow, in charge, devoted and a knockout.
7 You are adaptable, sensitive and talkative.
8 You are romantic, sophisticated and popular.
9 You are intelligent, friendly and accomplished.
10 You are emotional, protective and giving.
11 You are magnetic, passionate and controlled.
12 You are subtle, graceful and affectionate.

How do you react when sexually uncertain?

1 You become swashbuckling but feel paranoid.
2 You put on a performance but feel ashamed.
3 You pretend to be an animal but feel guilty.
4 You become snobbish and feel cheated.
5 You are fussy and cool but feel imperfect.
6 You become gloomy and dominating but feel bad.
7 You become rather kinky but feel trapped.
8 You flirt madly but feel very rejected.
9 You do weird things but feel like running away.
10 You become coy but feel very insecure.
11 You become obsessive but feel let down.
12 You act the martyr but feel unworthy.

Find the number you have circled most frequently; it will probably be your Mars-Sign, but check if you have also chosen the number of your Sun-Sign, as the Sun also affects your general energy.

1 Aries	5 Virgo	9 Aquarius
2 Leo	6 Capricorn	10 Cancer
3 Sagittarius	7 Gemini	11 Scorpio
4 Taurus	8 Libra	12 Pisces

Now enter your Venus and Mars on your Data Sheet.

Mars in the four elements.

Since Mars is energy, you can think of your energy as similar to the element of your Mars-Sign. Fire signs burn brightly but need lighting-up. Air signs are only seen by the effect they produce. Earth signs get their energy moving slowly. Water signs are most powerful when flowing.

What is your ascendant sign?

Your Ascendant is the sign that was rising over the eastern horizon at the time you were born. It represents your psychological mask, the way you learned to orient yourself in life in order to cope with the world when you were a child. It is not your real, inner self; that is your Sun-Sign. Even if your Sun-Sign is the same as your Ascendant, you will tend to show only one side of your character. The Ascendant, or mask, is something we put up when we feel vulnerable, or when we want to impress people! Often we are not aware we are using our masks.

TWO WAYS TO FIND YOUR ASCENDANT SIGN

1 If you don't know your time of birth, answer the questions (below) and select which sign is most like the way you present yourself.
Questions to discover your Ascendant
Mark the number of the question to which you would reply with the **most** emphatic YES. Ask your friends, they will probably know how you are most likely to react. When you are feeling anxious, threatened or frightened, do you:
1 run around and drop things?
2 do something to dominate the situation?
3 feel upset but remain charming?
4 turn white or become cuttingly critical?
5 toss your head and put on an act?
6 feel disturbed and look threatening?
7 say nothing but try to look important?
8 feel confused, lost and want to cry?
9 feel very hurt and withdraw?
10 space out and try to do the right thing?
11 bear it but become implacably immobile?
12 feel intensely jittery and want to run?
Which number did you choose?
1 Sagittarius, 2 Aries, 3 Libra, 4 Virgo, 5 Leo, 6 Scorpio, 7 Capricorn, 8 Pisces, 9 Cancer, 10 Aquarius, 11 Taurus, 12 Gemini.
Now you have estimated which may be your Ascendant. Turn to the descriptions that follow the calculations (pages 28–29) and make a further selection if necessary.

2 If you know your time of birth, you can do the simple calculation shown on this page.
To do the calculation, you need to know which of the following is the nearest latitude to the place you were born. You can check in an atlas or use this list,
53° Canada, British Isles, N. Europe, N. Russia.
43° N. USA, S. Europe, S. Russia, N. China, New Zealand.
33° S. USA, N. Africa, Israel, S. Japan, S. Australia.
23° S. Africa, N. India, N. Australia, S. Brazil.
13° Near the Equator, N. Brazil, Mexico.

How to calculate your Ascendant
It is a very simple calculation. First complete the personal information table below. For the last three items you will need to look at the Tables on this page and pages 25, 26 and 27.

PERSONAL INFORMATION TABLE
Your date of birth:
Your time of birth (24-hour notation):
Your place of birth:
Choose the nearest latitude: 53° 43° 33° 23° 13°
Daylight saving time correction (Table 1):
Your birthplace correction (Table 2):
The key time for your birthdate (Table 3):

Now you are ready to use this information in the step by step calculation below.

ASCENDANT CALCULATION: Use 24-hour notation.	
Enter your time of birth here:	
1 Deduct daylight saving time:	
RESULT	
2 Add or subtract birthplace correction:	
RESULT	
3 Add your personal key time:	
If result is more than 24.00, subtract 24.00:	
RESULT	
If born south of the equator add 12.00:	
RESULT is your Ascendant Time:	
4 Look up your Ascendant on Table 4 (page 27).	

TABLE 1

DAYLIGHT SAVING TIME CORRECTION
USA and Canada Daylight Saving Times

In most states, daylight saving time runs from 2 am on the last Sunday in April until 2 am on the last Sunday in October. In general, if you were born between these dates you should subtract one hour (1.00) from your birth time. However, enquiries should be made locally as there are some variations. All time changes are listed in *Time Changes in the USA* and *Time Changes in Canada and Mexico* by Doris Chase Doane, published by The American Federation of Astrologers, Inc, PO Box 22040, Tempe, Arizona, 85282.

Netherlands Daylight Saving Time

If your year of birth appears below, check to see if your birthday is between the dates given. If so, you should subtract one hour (1.00) from your birth time. Daylight saving time began at 2 am on the first date and ended at 3 am on the second date, except where indicated. No adjustment is needed if your year of birth does not appear in this list.

1916	1 May to 1 Oct	1924	30 Mar to 5 Oct
1917	16 Apr to 17 Sept	1925	5 Jun to 4 Oct
1918	1 Apr to 30 Sept	1926	15 May to 3 Oct
1919	7 Apr to 29 Sept	1927	15 May to 2 Oct
1920	5 Apr to 27 Sept	1928	15 May to 7 Oct
1921	4 Apr to 26 Sept	1929	15 May to 6 Oct
1922	26 Mar to 10 Oct	1930	15 May to 5 Oct
1923	1 Jun to 7 Oct	1931	15 May to 4 Oct

1932	22 May to 2 Oct	**Sas van Gent**
1933	15 May to 8 Oct	to 9 am on 19 Sept 1945
1934	15 May to 7 Oct	**Eindhoven**
1935	15 May to 6 Oct	to 2 pm on 20 Sept 1945
1936	15 May to 4 Oct	**Heerlen**
1937	22 May to 3 Oct	to 3 am on 21 Sept 1945
1938	15 May to 2 Oct	**Sittard Weert**
1939	15 May to 8 Oct	to 3 am on 22 Sept 1945
1940	16 May through to	**Helmond**
1942	2 Nov	to 8 am on 26 Sept 1945
1943	29 Mar to 4 Oct	**Zalt-Bommel**
1944	3 Apr to 2 Oct	to 8 am on 6 May 1945
1945	2 Apr to 16 Sept*	

* except the following:
Maastricht
to 3 am on 9 Sept 1945

1977	3 Apr to 25 Sept
1978	2 Apr to 30 Sept
1979	1 Apr to 29 Sept
1980	6 Apr to 27 Sept

British Summer Time

If you were born in the British Isles, find your year of birth below. If you were born between 2 am on the first date and 2 am on the second date, subtract one hour (1.00) from your birth time.

1916	21 May to 1 Oct	1933	9 Apr to 8 Oct
1917	8 Apr to 17 Sept	1934	22 Apr to 7 Oct
1918	24 Mar to 30 Sept	1935	14 Apr to 6 Oct
1919	30 Mar to 29 Sept	1936	19 Apr to 4 Oct
1920	28 Mar to 25 Oct	1937	18 Apr to 3 Oct
1921	3 Apr to 3 Oct	1938	10 Apr to 2 Oct
1922	16 Mar to 8 Oct	1939	16 Apr to 19 Nov
1923	22 Apr to 16 Sept	1940	25 Feb to 31 Dec
1924	13 Apr to 21 Sept	*1941	1 Jan to 31 Dec
1925	19 Apr to 4 Oct	*1942	1 Jan to 31 Dec
1926	18 Apr to 3 Oct	*1943	1 Jan to 31 Dec
1927	10 Apr to 2 Oct	*1944	1 Jan to 31 Dec
1928	22 Apr to 7 Oct	*1945	1 Jan to 31 Dec
1929	21 Apr to 6 Oct	1946	14 Apr to 6 Oct
1930	13 Apr to 5 Oct	*1947	16 Mar to 2 Nov
1931	19 Apr to 4 Oct	1948	14 Mar to 31 Oct
1932	17 Apr to 2 Oct	1949	3 Apr to 30 Oct

1950	16 Apr to 22 Oct	1960	10 Apr to 2 Oct
1951	15 Apr to 21 Oct	1961	26 Mar to 29 Oct
1952	20 Apr to 26 Oct	1962	25 Mar to 28 Oct
1953	19 Apr to 4 Oct	1963	31 Mar to 27 Oct
1954	11 Apr to 3 Oct	1964	22 Mar to 25 Oct
1955	17 Apr to 2 Oct	1965	21 Mar to 24 Oct
1956	22 Apr to 7 Oct	1966	20 Mar to 23 Oct
1957	14 Apr to 6 Oct	1967	19 Mar to 29 Oct
1958	20 Apr to 5 Oct	1968	18 Feb through
1959	19 Apr to 4 Oct		to 31 Oct **1971**

From **1972** onwards British Summer Time has run from 2 am on the third Sunday in March to 2 am on the fourth Sunday in October.

* Double Summer Time

If you were born in a year marked * (*above*), you will already have subtracted one hour from your birth time. If you were born during any of the periods (*below*), you should subtract another hour.

*1941	4 May to 10 Aug	*1944	2 Apr to 17 Sept
*1942	5 Apr to 9 Aug	*1945	2 Apr to 15 July
*1943	4 Apr to 15 Aug	*1947	13 Apr to 10 Aug

All other parts of the world

In general, daylight saving time is during the summer months, and would require one hour to be subtracted from your birth time. Enquiries are best made locally.

All variations are listed in the standard reference book *Times Changes in the World* by Doris Chase Doane, available from the address in the section (*above*).

Are you in doubt about daylight saving time?

The only difference, if you are not sure, is between one Ascendant and the neighboring Ascendant, so go ahead with the calculations and you can make allowances later, as described in this Table and Tables 2–4 (pages 26–27).

©DIAGRAM

Ascendant tables

TABLE 2

BIRTHPLACE CORRECTIONS
Canada, USA, Central and South America
Choose the nearest city that is either in the same country or north or south of your birthplace. Subtract or add the number of minutes given. 0 means no correction necessary.

−04 Albuquerque	−24 Flagstaff	+04 Montreal
−38 Atlanta	−16 Halifax NS	+12 Nashville
+20 Augusta	−28 Havana	0 New Orleans
+12 Birmingham	−28 Helena	+04 New York
−44 Boise	−20 Houston	−04 Norfolk Vi
+16 Boston	−44 Idianapolis	−32 Oklahoma City
+16 Bowling Green	0 Jackson Mi	−24 Omaha
+04 Brazilia	−24 Jacksonville	−04 Ottawa
+08 Buenos Aires	−16 Kansas City	−16 Panama City
−36 Calgary	−04 Kingston Jam	−20 Pittsburgh
+02 Caracas	+20 Las Vegas	−12 Portland Or
+04 Carson City	−08 Lima	+16 Quebec
−04 Casper	−08 Little Rock	0 Regina
−20 Charleston SC	+08 Los Angeles	−08 Richmond Vi
−24 Charleston WV	+04 Madison	+08 Rio de Janeiro
+12 Chicago	+16 Managua	0 St. Louis
−24 Cleveland	−36 Mexico City	−28 Salt Lake City
+16 Concord NH	−20 Miami	−08 San Francisco
−12 Des Moines	+08 Milwaukee	−44 Santiago
−32 Detroit	−12 Minneapolis	−16 Toronto
−64 El Paso	+08 Mobile	−12 Vancouver
0 Falkland Isles	+12 Montpelier	−08 Washington DC

Europe, Africa and the Near East
Choose the nearest city to the north or south of your birthplace and subtract or add the number of minutes given. 0 by the city means no correction necessary.

+04 Abercorn	0 Cyprus	−40 Marseille
−16 Abidjan	−24 Dar es Salaam	−24 Milan
0 Accra	−28 Frankfurt	−14 Munich
−04 Addis Ababa	−07 Georgetown	−32 Nairobi
−48 Algiers	−20 Gibraltar	−16 Oslo
−40 Amsterdam	−20 Hamburg	−52 Paris
−28 Athens	−20 Helsinki	−32 Port Harcourt
−52 Barcelona	−04 Istanbul	−04 Prague
+20 Beirut	−08 Johannesburg	−12 Rome
−40 Benghazi	−52 Kampala	−04 Salisbury
−32 Berne	−08 Khartoum	−84 Seville
−60 Bordeaux	−48 Lagos	+16 Stockholm
−44 Brussels	−36 Lisbon	−06 Tehran
+04 Cairo	−08 Lobito	+20 Tel Aviv
−48 Cape Town	−08 Lusaka	−68 Tripoli
−28 Casablanca	−44 Lyon	−20 Tunis
−32 Cologne	−72 Madrid	+04 Vienna
−12 Copenhagen	−32 Marrakesh	−12 Yaounde

All locations in the Faeroe Islands deduct 24.
All locations in Iceland deduct 24.

For the British Isles in minutes
Choose the section of the map below in which you were born and deduct the number of minutes shown at the top of each section. If you were born in the right hand section, no correction is necessary.
If you were born on or very near to the edge of a section, you can split the difference for greater accuracy. For example, if you were born in Dundee, Blackpool or Liverpool, deduct 12 minutes.
For the Channel Islands deduct 10 minutes.
For the Orkney Islands deduct 14 minutes.
For the Shetland Islands deduct 8 minutes.

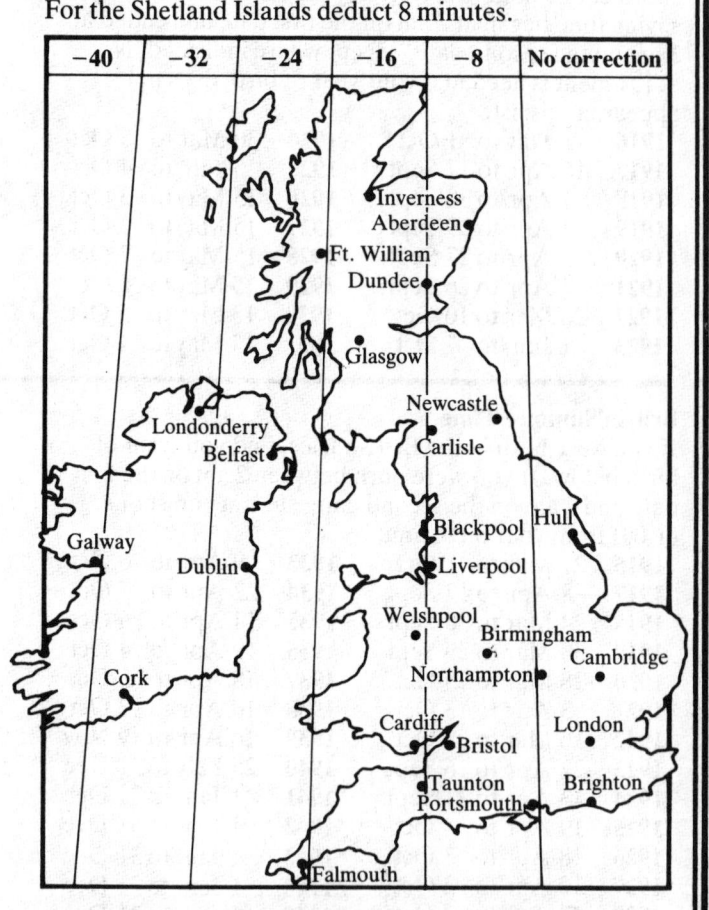

Australia, New Zealand, USSR, India and the Far East
Choose the nearest city within the same country that is north or south of your birthplace and subtract or add the number of minutes given. 0 means no correction necessary.

−14 Adelaide	−40 Dunedin	0 Pacific Islands
−24 Auckland	−12 Hobart	−16 Peking
−38 Bombay	−24 Hong Kong	−16 Perth
+12 Brisbane	−32 Karachi	+04 Sydney
0 Burma	−04 Lahore	−24 Shanghai
+22 Calcutta	−10 Madras	−34 Singapore
−32 Christchurch	+04 Manila	0 Sumatra
−12 Colombo	−20 Melbourne	0 Thailand
−50 Darwin	+28 Moscow	+20 Tokyo
−22 Delhi		

TABLE 3

KEY TIMES

Find your date of birth down the left-hand column and look along the line. Find your month of birth across the top and move down that column until you meet the line where you will find your Key Time in hours and minutes. Transfer this to your Ascendant Calculation Sheet.

Date	JA	FE	MR	AP	MY	JN	JL	AU	SE	OC	NO	DE	Date
1	6 38	8 41	10 35	12 37	14 35	16 38	18 36	20 38	22 40	0 39	2 41	4 39	1
2	6 42	8 45	10 39	12 41	14 39	16 42	18 40	20 42	22 41	0 43	2 45	4 43	2
3	6 46	8 49	10 43	12 45	14 43	16 46	18 44	20 46	22 48	0 47	2 49	4 47	3
4	6 50	8 52	10 47	12 49	14 47	16 50	18 48	20 50	22 52	0 51	2 53	4 51	4
5	6 54	8 56	10 51	12 53	14 51	16 53	18 52	20 54	22 56	0 54	2 57	4 55	5
6	6 58	9 00	10 55	12 57	14 55	16 57	18 56	20 58	23 00	0 58	3 01	4 59	6
7	7 02	9 04	10 59	13 01	14 59	17 01	19 00	21 02	23 04	1 02	3 05	5 03	7
8	7 06	9 08	11 03	13 05	15 03	17 05	19 04	21 06	23 08	1 06	3 08	5 07	8
9	7 10	9 12	11 07	13 09	15 07	17 09	19 08	21 10	23 12	1 10	3 12	5 11	9
10	7 14	9 16	11 10	13 13	15 11	17 13	19 11	21 14	23 16	1 14	3 16	5 15	10
11	7 18	9 20	11 14	13 17	15 15	17 17	19 15	21 18	23 20	1 18	3 20	5 19	11
12	7 22	9 24	11 18	13 21	15 19	17 21	19 19	21 22	23 24	1 22	3 24	5 23	12
13	7 26	9 28	11 22	13 24	15 23	17 25	19 23	21 25	23 28	1 26	3 28	5 26	13
14	7 29	9 32	11 26	13 28	15 27	17 29	19 27	21 29	23 32	1 30	3 32	5 30	14
15	7 34	9 36	11 30	13 32	15 31	17 33	19 31	21 33	23 36	1 34	3 36	5 34	15
16	7 38	9 40	11 34	13 36	15 35	17 37	19 35	21 37	23 40	1 38	3 40	5 38	16
17	7 41	9 44	11 38	13 40	15 39	17 41	19 39	21 41	23 43	1 42	3 44	5 42	17
18	7 45	9 48	11 42	13 44	15 42	17 45	19 43	21 45	23 47	1 46	3 48	5 46	18
19	7 49	9 52	11 46	13 48	15 46	17 49	19 47	21 49	23 51	1 50	3 52	5 50	19
20	7 53	9 56	11 50	13 52	15 50	17 53	19 51	21 53	23 55	1 54	3 56	5 54	20
21	7 57	9 59	11 54	13 56	15 54	17 57	19 55	21 57	23 59	1 58	4 00	5 58	21
22	8 01	10 03	11 58	14 00	15 58	18 00	19 59	22 01	0 03	2 01	4 04	6 02	22
23	8 05	10 07	12 02	14 04	16 02	18 04	20 03	22 05	0 07	2 05	4 08	6 06	23
24	8 09	10 11	12 06	14 08	16 06	18 08	20 07	22 09	0 11	2 09	4 12	6 10	24
25	8 13	10 15	12 10	14 12	16 10	18 12	20 11	22 13	0 15	2 13	4 16	6 14	25
26	8 17	10 19	12 14	14 16	16 14	18 16	20 15	22 17	0 19	2 17	4 19	6 18	26
27	8 21	10 23	12 17	14 20	16 18	18 20	20 18	22 21	0 23	2 21	4 23	6 22	27
28	8 25	10 27	12 21	14 24	16 22	18 24	20 22	22 25	0 27	2 25	4 27	6 26	28
29	8 29	10 31	12 25	14 28	16 26	18 28	20 26	22 29	0 31	2 29	4 31	6 30	29
30	8 33		12 29	14 32	16 30	18 32	20 30	22 33	0 35	2 33	4 35	6 31	30
31	8 37		12 33		16 34		20 34	22 36		2 37		6 37	31

TABLE 4

ASCENDANT TIMES

Find the latitude north or south which is nearest to your place of birth. Look down that column until you find where your Ascendant Time would be placed. Note that the times given are the beginning of the sign, and the Ascendant stays the same until the next time given. For example, for 53° at 18.45 the Ascendant would be Aries, but becomes Taurus at 18.52. Now you can read about your Ascendant on the next page.

* If you were born south of the equator, select the zodiac sign in this column.

	53°	43°	33°	23°	13°	*
Aries	18 00	18 00	18 00	18 00	18 00	Li
Taurus	18 52	19 09	19 22	19 35	19 44	Sc
Gemini	19 56	20 29	20 58	21 18	21 34	Sg
Cancer	21 37	22 24	22 57	23 20	23 38	Cp
Leo	0 11	0 48	1 14	1 36	1 52	Aq
Virgo	3 06	3 26	3 39	3 51	4 00	Pi
Libra	6 00	6 00	6 00	6 00	6 00	Ar
Scorpio	8 58	8 38	8 25	8 13	8 05	Ta
Sagittarius	11 53	11 14	10 50	10 27	10 12	Ge
Capricorn	14 26	13 40	13 06	12 44	12 26	Cn
Aquarius	16 08	15 35	15 06	14 46	14 30	Le
Pisces	17 12	16 55	16 42	16 29	16 21	Vi
Aries	18 00	18 00	18 00	18 00	18 00	Li

©DIAGRAM

Which mask do you use?

The Ascendant represents our mask; the way we have oriented ourselves to cope with the world. It is said by many astrologers that we have to become fully aware of our mask and use its characteristics positively. The mask can then be used by choice, instead of only unconsciously, leaving us free to develop our real, inner Sun-Sign personality. Often this is a difficult process of self-development, because we feel protected by our mask! You can make further assessments if you don't know your birthtime (see page 24) by answering the following questions. If you identify strongly with parts of other signs, check if you have other planets in those signs.

Ascendant Aries
1 Are you normally self-confident with high energy?
2 Do you sometimes tread on other people's toes?
3 Do you like traveling, exploring and challenges?
4 Do you prefer positions of leadership and authority?
5 Have you changed your occupation often?
6 Do you resent being pushed, restricted or dominated?
7 Are you sometimes irritable and restless?
8 Do you deplete your energy and need to rest?
9 Do you like to tell the best story at dinner?
10 In an emergency do you really shine?
11 Do you like to dominate and hate criticism?
12 Do you work better when you are given praise?
13 Are you hard-headed in controlling your money?

Ascendant Taurus
1 Does it take a lot to cause you disturbance?
2 Do you dislike change or even going out much?
3 Do you own your own house or other property?
4 Would you like even more comfort and luxury?
5 Can you work long, hard hours without tiring?
6 Can you sing or are you artistic in some way?
7 Do you enjoy making or building things?
8 Is a stable bank balance in credit important?
9 Have you been in the same job for a long time?
10 Would you stick by a friend even if they hurt you?
11 Do you like to grow things, especially food?
12 Do you stick by what you believe, regardless?
13 Do you study things slowly but thoroughly?

Ascendant Gemini
1 Have you moved house many times, or wanted to?
2 Do you move the furniture around frequently?
3 Can you talk almost non-stop for hours on end?
4 Do you usually have several projects on at once?
5 Do you read the end of a book first?
6 Are you nimble with your hands and very active?
7 Do you enjoy writing and using the telephone?
8 Are you especially interested in gadgets?
9 Do you have difficulty finishing things properly?
10 Can you tell a good joke or a story?
11 Are you single or divorced?
12 Do you best express emotions through actions?
13 Does money tend to slip through your fingers?

Ascendant Cancer
1 Do you prefer friends and family to strangers?
2 Can you be economical and cautious if necessary?
3 Are you rather shy, especially in company?
4 Is much of your attention given to family affairs?
5 Are you rather moody and sometimes nervous?
6 Do you get very upset if someone is hurt?
7 Are you interested in antiques and history?
8 Do you enjoy being noticed and thanked?
9 Do you make a fuss of people or spoil children?
10 Are you a romantic but also very tenacious?
11 Do you have good, sound business ideas?
12 Do you need a sense of security before relaxing?
13 Can you make money grow slowly but surely?

Ascendant Leo
1 Do you enjoy drama and entertaining people?
2 Do you get very upset if someone tells lies?
3 Do you have very high goals and want to get there?
4 Are you sympathetic to people who appeal to you?
5 Do you like to be admired and even flattered?
6 Do you like to feel you are in the limelight?
7 Are you romantic in a very creative way?
8 Do you have or would you like lots of love affairs?
9 Are you particularly fond of children?
10 Do you enjoy dressing-up for effect?
11 Is your hair very important to you?
12 Are you usually generous, lively and cheerful?
13 Do you love pleasures and holidays?

Ascendant Virgo
1 Do you make lists, keep notes and bits of paper?
2 Do you like to appear cool in all circumstances?
3 Are you able to analyze minute details?
4 Can you talk and write well and accurately?
5 Do you often feel you carry much responsibility?
6 Can you see several points of view in discussion?
7 Are you fanatically tidy or extremely untidy?
8 Would you say you are sometimes unsure?
9 Are you rather self-critical inwardly?
10 Do you try to get things perfect and make a mess?
11 Are you instinctively good at business?
12 Does the food value of meals interest you?
13 Are you retiring but really very sensual?

Ascendant Libra?
1 Do you try to keep the peace at all costs?
2 Are you soothed by music and do you need it often?
3 Can you listen to others without interrupting?
4 Do you love clothes and feel lost without a mirror?
5 Do you prefer company and dislike being alone?
6 Do you feel you have obligations towards others?
7 Have other people been influential in your life?
8 Do you feel you have to pass judgment on issues?
9 Are you keen to have your point of view heard?
10 Do you think you would make a good politician?
11 Do you dislike menial tasks or dirty work?
12 Do you procrastinate and delay decisions?
13 Are you often careless with your belongings?

Ascendant Scorpio

1 Are you good at keeping secrets?
2 Do you feel things passionately and deeply?
3 Are you liable to be scathingly critical?
4 Do you take time to trust other people?
5 Have you ever inherited money or goods?
6 Do you hate hospitals and fear being ill?
7 Are you good at doing things with your hands?
8 Do you think you have ever been deceived?
9 Are you aware, more than most, of others' motives?
10 Do you set very high standards and expect respect?
11 Would you admit to ever feeling very jealous?
12 Do you often become angry and threatening?
13 Are you a subtle and very astute thinker?

Ascendant Sagittarius

1 Do you move a lot and like walking and sports?
2 Do you ever think you are outspoken or rather blunt?
3 Do you get itchy feet when you feel restricted?
4 Do you dream about future events often?
5 Are you worried if something is left unfinished?
6 Are you interested that justice be done?
7 Are you prone to dashing around and dropping things?
8 Do you love horses or other animals?
9 Can you write well and give a good speech?
10 Are you amoral but very interested in morality?
11 Do you tend to expect a great deal of others?
12 Do you, or would you, enjoy world travel?
13 Do you prefer money to come from others?

Ascendant Capricorn

1 Do you feel responsible for a lot of things?
2 Are you slow to respond and cautious with people?
3 Do you admire people of high standing?
4 Are you determined to fulfill your plans?
5 Do you make long-term plans for your career?
6 Have you spent more time with older people?
7 Do you sometimes get an urge to do silly things?
8 On the whole would you call yourself careful?
9 Is it difficult for you to make friends?
10 Do you find it hard to accept affection?
11 Are you careful on what you spend your money?
12 Are you faithful to one person mostly?
13 Does world opinion matter to you?

Ascendant Aquarius

1 Are you likely to do unexpected things?
2 Are you rather wary of close emotional involvement?
3 Are you a kind and very friendly person mostly?
4 Do you have a lot of bright, new ideas?
5 Have you ever been told that you are a mystery?
6 Are you very trusting but sometimes feel let down?
7 Do you lose opportunities for lack of effort?
8 Do you enjoy having many friends and acquaintances?
9 Are you especially kind to animals?
10 Do you forget good advice given by others?
11 Are you inclined to disappear frequently?
12 Are you attracted to unusual people and events?
13 Does money just seem to come and go?

Ascendant Pisces

1 Do you know a lot about many subjects?
2 Are you rather indifferent to personal comfort?
3 Do you feel sympathy for helpless people?
4 Are you good at working in poor conditions?
5 Are you somewhat shy and retiring?
6 Is standing up for your rights very difficult?
7 Do you think many people are better than you?
8 Do you get rather depressed or sad sometimes?
9 Do you have trouble with your feet sometimes?
10 Are you a bit of a dreamer on the whole?
11 Are you a kind and considerate listener?
12 Can you do detailed work and keep a secret?
13 Do you know how to use persuasion to advantage?

© DIAGRAM

Signs	Houses
Aries	
Taurus	
Gemini	
Cancer	
Leo	
Virgo	
Libra	
Scorpio	
Sagittarius	
Capricorn	
Aquarius	
Pisces	

YOUR HOUSE NUMBERS

Having found your Ascendant, locate it on the list (*left*). Put number 1 in the box by it. Then continue numbering in order 2 to 12, down the column of signs, returning to the top when necessary. The finished list shows the houses in which each of your signs is placed. Transfer this to your Data Sheet (page 11) as you will need the house numbers when reading pages 30–35.

How optimistic and wise are you?

Tables for the slower moving planets, Jupiter and Saturn, are given on this page and the opposite page; those for the generation planets, Uranus, Neptune and Pluto, are given on pages 32–33.
When reading the interpretations for Jupiter and Saturn, you can read the meaning of the sign together with the house in which the planets are placed. Separate interpretations are given for the house and sign positions of Uranus, Neptune and Pluto.

First of all, find your birthdate in the table (*below*). The sign next to it is the position of your Jupiter. Enter this on your Data Sheet (p. 11), where you will also find the house position. Then read the interpretation for your sign and house position of Jupiter. Repeat this exercise for Saturn (p. 31); Uranus, Neptune and Pluto (pp. 32–33).

2

JUPITER IN THE SIGNS AND HOUSES

Jupiter in Aries or in the 1st house
Breezy, optimistic and humorous, you are the impulsive executive type who takes every opportunity to sell yourself with great zest and you also love compliments.

Jupiter in Taurus or in the 2nd house
Extravagant, prosperous and likeable, you enjoy money and like to improve on its value. Even if you are poor you will get by. Generous in every way possible, you may get stuck into business and forget to enjoy life.

Jupiter in Gemini or in the 3rd house
Original, alert and temperamental, you are the happy-go-lucky type, always on the move. You enjoy gossip, new ideas, having fun and learning languages.

Jupiter in Cancer or in the 4th house
Sentimental, out-going and "motherly," you love food. Lucky in property affairs, you like to stay in control. You are the wheeler-dealer in business affairs.

Jupiter in Leo or in the 5th house
Romantic, playful and exuberant, you like to make those romantic dreams come true. Children love you; you are a kid at heart yourself. You play at gambling too.

Jupiter in Virgo or in the 6th house
Cheerful, willing and high-principled, you love hard work and can reduce mountains to molehills. You like to improve standards and generally work hard at it.

Jupiter in Libra or in the 7th house
A happy, hospitable match-maker, you love the social life and would wither away on your own. You can be good for other people and they will love you for it.

Jupiter in Scorpio or in the 8th house
Very positive, resourceful and discerning, you like to do things on the grand scale. Often you may be rather uncompromising and excesses are usual, one way or another. You like to bring good things to others.

Jupiter in Sagittarius or in the 9th house
Popular, caring and honorable, you are invariably optimistic and can get along with most people. You should take care as sometimes you can be a soft touch.

Jupiter in Capricorn or in the 10th house
Proud, self-reliant and orthodox, you are the leader type who may well become a martyr to work. You love a powerful position and will make sacrifices for it.

Jupiter in Aquarius or in the 11th house
Sociable and benevolent, you love people and are good at organizing things, earning money and you like weird ideas. You may even invent new things.

Jupiter in Pisces or in the 12th house
Kind, helpful and unassuming, you never turn away anyone who is in trouble. You have the gift of intuition and often know exactly what someone needs, but beware of collecting waifs and strays.

TABLE FOR JUPITER
Jupiter moved into the zodiac signs given on these dates and stayed in the same sign until the next date shown.

Year	Date	Sign	Year	Date	Sign	Year	Date	Sign	Year	Date	Sign	Year	Date	Sign	Year	Date	Sign
1916	12 Feb	Ari	1934	11 Oct	Scp		15 Sep	Aqu		12 Aug	Cap		11 Sep	Sag	1986	20 Feb	Pic
	26 Jun	Tau	1935	9 Nov	Sag		1 Dec	Pic		4 Nov	Aqu	1972	6 Feb	Cap	1987	2 Mar	Ari
	26 Oct	Ari	1936	2 Dec	Cap	1951	21 Apr	Ari	1962	25 Mar	Pic		24 Jul	Sag	1988	8 Mar	Tau
1917	12 Feb	Tau	1937	20 Dec	Aqu	1952	28 Apr	Tau	1963	4 Apr	Ari		25 Sep	Cap		22 Jul	Gem
	30 Jun	Gem	1938	14 May	Pic	1953	9 May	Gem	1964	12 Apr	Tau	1973	23 Feb	Aqu		30 Nov	Tau
1918	13 Jul	Can		30 Jul	Aqu	1954	24 May	Can	1965	22 Apr	Gem	1974	8 Mar	Pic	1989	11 Mar	Gem
1919	2 Aug	Leo		29 Dec	Pic	1955	13 Jun	Leo		21 Sep	Can	1975	18 Mar	Ari		30 Jul	Can
1920	27 Aug	Vir	1939	11 May	Ari		17 Nov	Vir		17 Nov	Gem	1976	26 Mar	Tau	1990	18 Aug	Leo
1921	26 Sep	Lib		30 Oct	Pic	1956	18 Jan	Leo	1966	5 May	Can		23 Aug	Gem	1991	12 Sep	Vir
1922	26 Oct	Scp		20 Dec	Ari		7 Jul	Vir		27 Sep	Leo		16 Oct	Tau	1992	10 Oct	Lib
1923	24 Nov	Sag	1940	16 May	Tau		13 Dec	Vir	1967	16 Jan	Can	1977	3 Apr	Gem	1993	10 Nov	Scp
1924	18 Dec	Cap	1941	26 May	Gem	1957	19 Feb	Vir		23 May	Leo		20 Aug	Can	1994	9 Dec	Sag
1926	6 Jan	Aqu	1942	10 Jun	Can		7 Aug	Lib		19 Oct	Vir		31 Dec	Gem	1996	3 Jan	Cap
1927	18 Jan	Pic	1943	30 Jun	Leo	1958	13 Jan	Scp	1968	27 Feb	Leo	1978	12 Apr	Can	1997	21 Jan	Aqu
	6 Jun	Ari	1944	26 Jul	Vir		20 Mar	Lib		15 Jun	Vir		5 Sep	Leo	1998	4 Feb	Pic
	11 Sep	Pic	1945	25 Aug	Lib		7 Sep	Scp		15 Nov	Lib	1979	1 Mar	Can	1999	13 Feb	Ari
1928	23 Jan	Ari	1946	25 Sep	Scp	1959	10 Feb	Sag	1969	30 Mar	Vir		20 Apr	Leo		28 Jun	Tau
	4 Jun	Tau	1947	24 Oct	Sag		24 Apr	Scp		15 Jul	Lib		29 Sep	Vir		23 Oct	Ari
1929	12 Jun	Gem	1948	15 Nov	Cap		5 Oct	Sag		16 Dec	Scp	1980	27 Oct	Lib	2000	14 Feb	Tau
1930	27 Jun	Can	1949	12 Apr	Aqu	1960	1 Mar	Cap	1970	30 Apr	Lib	1981	27 Nov	Scp		30 Jun	Gem
1931	17 Jul	Leo		27 Jun	Cap		10 Jun	Sag		15 Aug	Scp	1982	26 Dec	Sag			
1932	11 Aug	Vir		30 Nov	Aqu		26 Oct	Cap	1971	14 Jan	Sag	1984	19 Jan	Cap			
1933	10 Sep	Lib	1950	15 Apr	Pic	1961	15 Mar	Aqu		5 Jun	Scp	1985	6 Feb	Aqu			

SATURN IN THE SIGNS AND HOUSES

Saturn in Aries or in the 1st house
You may have anxieties about self-assertion or more physical problems. You have wit, staying power and ingenuity, enabling you to turn any apparent disadvantage into an asset. Wisdom grows as you learn to please and appreciate yourself with gentleness.

Saturn in Taurus or in the 2nd house
You may have anxieties about security, money, self-worth or your possessions. You are patient, kind and trustworthy. You have nothing to be ashamed of; wisdom grows as you recognize how best to apply your qualities of persistence with generosity.

Saturn in Gemini or in the 3rd house
You may have anxieties about confiding in others, for fear of being thought stupid. You are highly intelligent, loyal and know how to keep a secret. Wisdom grows from the discovery that close contact and sharing is the way to make a friend for life.

Saturn in Cancer or in the 4th house
You may have anxieties about aging, about your family or home base or about being alone. You have integrity, sensitivity and the skills to build roots and care for yourself. Wisdom grows as you realize you deserve a place of your own.

Saturn in Leo or in the 5th house
You may have anxieties about pleasure, playing, love, children or expressing yourself creatively. You are warm, generous and have a wealth of undiscovered talents. Wisdom grows as you learn to let go, laugh and do things for personal satisfaction.

Saturn in Virgo or in the 6th house
You may have anxieties about work, health, chaos or having to live up to standards of perfection. You have energy, intuition and an ability to work hard, giving attention to details. Wisdom grows as you drop guilt, sort your priorities and love yourself.

Saturn in Libra or in the 7th house
You may have anxieties about relationships, needing others, being alone or being equal. You have a sense of justice, intelligence and a love of peace and harmony. Wisdom grows as you apply these and discover you can be free yet merge with another.

Saturn in Scorpio or in the 8th house
You may have anxieties about success or about your own passions. You have integrity, drive and an ability to stand on your own two feet. Wisdom grows as you learn to share your secrets with discrimination and trust yourself to love.

Saturn in Sagittarius or in the 9th house
You may have anxieties about commitment, restrictions or settling down. You have optimism, an open mind and can see the broader view with a sense of humor. The urge to travel can be unsettling. Wisdom grows as you realize that decisions do not tie you down forever.

Saturn in Capricorn or in the 10th house
You may have anxieties about people in authority, or about your own status, power or career. You may also be anxious about trusting yourself to love. You are already a wise and responsible person with much of value to give the world; do it with love.

Saturn in Aquarius or in the 11th house
You may be anxious about any kind of emotional involvement; you may even question your own worth or normalcy. You are friendly, inventive, caring and independent. Wisdom grows as you accept love and set your own goals; then you belong to yourself.

Saturn in Pisces or in the 12th house
You may be anxious about real intimacy or about sickness and uncontrollable events. You have insight, compassion and imagination. Wisdom grows as you learn to help others help themselves, rather than by taking the problems of the world on yourself.

TABLE FOR SATURN
Saturn moved into the zodiac signs given on these dates and stayed in the same sign until the next date shown. If a year is not shown it is because there was no movement, so look where Saturn was the previous year.

Year	Date	Sign	Year	Date	Sign	Year	Date	Sign	Year	Date	Sign	Year	Date	Sign
1916	17 Oct	Leo	1937	25 Apr	Ari	1956	12 Jan	Sag	1975	17 Sep	Leo		30 Jun	Aqu
	7 Dec	Can		18 Oct	Pic		14 May	Scp	1976	14 Jan	Can	1994	29 Jan	Pic
1917	24 Jun	Leo	1938	14 Jan	Ari		10 Oct	Sag		5 Jun	Leo	1996	7 Apr	Ari
1919	12 Aug	Vir	1939	6 Jul	Tau	1959	5 Jan	Cap	1977	17 Nov	Vir	1998	9 Jun	Tau
1921	7 Oct	Lib	1939	22 Sep	Ari	1962	3 Jan	Aqu	1978	5 Jan	Leo		25 Oct	Ari
1923	20 Dec	Scp	1940	20 Mar	Tau	1964	24 Mar	Pic		26 Jul	Vir	1999	1 Mar	Tau
1924	6 Apr	Lib	1942	8 May	Gem		16 Sep	Aqu	1980	21 Sep	Lib	2000	10 Aug	Gem
	13 Sep	Scp	1944	20 Jun	Can		16 Dec	Pic	1982	29 Nov	Scp		16 Oct	Tau
1926	2 Dec	Sag	1946	2 Aug	Leo	1967	3 Mar	Ari	1983	6 May	Lib			
1929	15 Mar	Cap	1948	19 Sep	Vir	1969	29 Apr	Tau		24 Aug	Scp			
1929	5 May	Sag	1949	3 Apr	Leo	1971	18 Jun	Gem	1985	17 Nov	Sag			
	30 Nov	Cap		29 May	Vir	1972	10 Jan	Tau	1988	14 Feb	Cap			
1932	24 Feb	Aqu	1950	20 Nov	Lib		21 Feb	Gem	1988	10 Jun	Cap			
	13 Aug	Cap	1951	7 Mar	Vir	1973	2 Aug	Can		12 Nov	Cap			
	20 Nov	Aqu	1951	13 Aug	Lib	1974	7 Jan	Gem	1991	6 Feb	Aqu			
1935	14 Feb	Pic	1953	22 Oct	Scp		19 Apr	Can	1993	21 May	Pic			

If you were born on date given also read previous sign.

Are you typical of your generation?

URANUS IN THE SIGNS AND HOUSES
URANUS IN THE SIGNS Expressing individuality.

In Aries You are very bright, rebellious, though very generous and you just don't like being told what to do.

In Taurus You are great at coping with instability and like to make money freelance or part-time.

In Gemini You are brilliant and love TV, radio, fast cars and any kind of rushing about, variety or change.

In Cancer You are prone to ecstasy and depression as you want to get away from conventional ties.

In Leo You are unusually creative, especially in affairs of the heart, so you may suffer from guilt.

In Virgo You find it hard to stick to schedules, so may prefer self-employment. You care about animals.

In Libra You want a partner and total freedom and that makes you jumpy. Things improve later in life.

In Scorpio You like to experiment with everything life has to offer, so stick to imagination.

In Sagittarius You love travel, space and any kind of new religion, even the one you invented.

In Capricorn You simply have to be in charge at something and you are going to change the world.

In Aquarius You will be there when there is work to be done and you'll get everyone helping a common cause.

In Pisces You have an eccentric personal radar system and can walk where angels fear to tread.

URANUS IN THE HOUSES Focussing individuality.

In the 1st house The focus is on yourself. You will probably have unusual talents or an unusual background.

In the 2nd house The focus is on money, possessions or ways to improve your material comfort.

In the 3rd house The focus is on the intellect, on learning and making contact with your intuition.

In the 4th house The focus is on physical security, home, family or your historical roots.

In the 5th house The focus is on love, romance, children and finding your identity.

In the 6th house The focus is on work, health and the way you run your everyday affairs.

In the 7th house The focus is on partnerships and trying to find the perfect match in love or work.

In the 8th house The focus is on getting whatever it is you think you most need in life.

In the 9th house The focus is on trying to make decisions without losing out on freedom of action.

In the 10th house The focus is on career, status and the use of authority and power.

In the 11th house The focus is on friendship and social activities; also on non-conformist ideas.

In the 12th house The focus is on secret inner drives and hidden motives; also on imaginative projects.

TABLES FOR THE GENERATION PLANETS
The dates given in these three tables are when the three planets, Uranus, Neptune and Pluto moved into a new sign. If your year of birth is not given, look where the planet was in the next earlier year. These planets often move in and out of a sign before settling down for a lengthy period. If your birthdate is near a change, take the adjacent sign into account.

Table for Uranus

Year	Date	Sign		Year	Date	Sign
1912	12 Nov	Aqu		1968	28 Sep	Lib
1919	1 Apr	Pic		1969	20 May	Vir
	17 Aug	Aqu			24 Jun	Lib
1920	22 Jan	Pic		1974	21 Nov	Scp
1927	31 Mar	Ari		1975	1 May	Lib
	4 Nov	Pic			8 Sep	Scp
1928	13 Jan	Ari		1981	17 Feb	Sag
1934	6 Jun	Tau			20 Mar	Scp
	10 Oct	Ari			16 Nov	Sag
1935	28 Mar	Tau		1988	15 Feb	Cap
1941	7 Aug	Gem			27 May	Sag
	5 Oct	Tau			2 Dec	Cap
1942	15 May	Gem		1995	1 Apr	Aqu
1948	30 Aug	Can			9 Jun	Cap
	12 Nov	Gem		1996	12 Jan	Aqu
1949	10 Jun	Can				
1955	24 Aug	Leo				
1956	28 Jan	Can				
	10 Jun	Leo				
1961	1 Nov	Vir				
1962	10 Jan	Leo				
	10 Aug	Vir				

Table for Neptune

1916	19 Mar	Can
	2 May	Leo
1928	21 Sep	Vir
1929	19 Feb	Leo
	24 Jul	Vir
1942	3 Oct	Lib
1943	17 Apr	Vir
	2 Aug	Lib
1955	24 Dec	Scp
1956	12 Mar	Lib
	19 Oct	Scp
1957	15 Jun	Lib
	6 Aug	Scp
1970	4 Jan	Sag
	3 May	Scp
	6 Nov	Sag
1984	19 Jan	Cap
	23 Jun	Sag
	21 Nov	Cap
1998	29 Jan	Aqu
	23 Aug	Cap
	27 Nov	Aqu

Table for Pluto

Year	Date	Sign
1914	27 May	Can
1937	7 Oct	Leo
	25 Nov	Can
1938	3 Aug	Leo
1939	7 Feb	Can
	14 Jun	Leo
1956	20 Oct	Vir
1957	15 Jan	Leo
	19 Aug	Vir
1958	11 Apr	Leo
	10 Jun	Vir
1971	5 Oct	Lib
1972	17 Apr	Vir
	30 Jul	Lib
1983	5 Nov	Scp
1984	18 May	Lib
	28 Aug	Scp
1995	16 Jan	Sag
	21 Apr	Scp
	10 Nov	Sag

Uranus will remain in Aquarius until the 21st century.

Neptune and Pluto stay in last sign given until 2000

NEPTUNE IN THE SIGNS AND HOUSES

NEPTUNE IN THE SIGNS Your imagination.

In Aries You tend to be radical, charismatic and have a very strong imagination and illusions about yourself.

In Taurus You tend to be intuitive, sentimental and artistic and may be financially impractical.

In Gemini You tend to be restless, idealistic and try to plan a utopia with your head in the clouds.

In Cancer You tend to be emotionally loyal to your home and imagine the perfect family organization.

In Leo You tend to be powerful, speculative and have a flair for new developments, and romantic illusions.

In Virgo You tend to fight battles between reason and emotion. You are poetic, lonely and often lost.

In Libra You tend to love peace and harmony and have illusions about other people. You are impractical.

In Scorpio You tend to have a passionate interest in finding the truth but have illusions about what is truth.

In Sagittarius You tend to be tolerant and intellectual but have illusions about achieving ideals socially.

In Capricorn You tend to be conscientious and practical but have illusions about the value of status.

In Aquarius You tend to be philosophical and intuitive and have illusions about achieving perfect peace.

In Pisces You tend to be wise and aware and are always looking for those elusive ideals for the future.

NEPTUNE IN THE HOUSES Using your imagination?

In the 1st house Your imagination is best used to improve yourself and develop your own maturity.

In the 2nd house Your imagination is best used to acquire material things and express your sensuality.

In the 3rd house Your imagination is best used to learn, to think and to communicate.

In the 4th house Your imagination is best used to build a family feeling and a secure home.

In the 5th house Your imagination is best used for creative activities including bringing up children.

In the 6th house Your imagination is best used for organizing good work and health activities.

In the 7th house Your imagination is best used to improve relationships and mediate in disputes.

In the 8th house Your imagination is best used to understand and resolve your deeper needs.

In the 9th house Your imagination is best used to expand your horizons and understand morality.

In the 10th house Your imagination is best used to further your public career or work in public affairs.

In the 11th house Your imagination is best used to help others express themselves more fully.

In the 12th house Your imagination is best used to resolve your own unconscious fears and anxieties.

PLUTO IN THE SIGNS AND HOUSES

PLUTO IN THE SIGNS Pluto shows the characteristics of the generation into which you were born and how that generation applied their personal power collectively. Pluto's movement is said to mark major periods of changing attitudes.

Pluto in Cancer A period of sentimentality, family loyalty and patriotism. People experienced instability and developed feeling and maturity.

Pluto in Leo A period of self-centeredness, family disruption and new energy. People experienced new desires and developed the permissive society.

Pluto in Virgo A period of perfectionism, analysis and improved conditions. People gave attention to health, conditions and women. Computers emerged.

Pluto in Libra A period of new social reforms, a new attitude to marriage and awareness of inequalities and sexual and racial differences. China emerged.

Pluto in Scorpio A period of great changes when the most complex problems will be transformed radically. A new realization of passion, love and sex.

Pluto in Sagittarius A period of fundamental reforms in religion, the law and the meaning of freedom. A major interest in expansion of resources and space.

PLUTO IN THE HOUSES The house position shows the area of life where your personal urge for power may best be used to transform your life, bringing pleasure and satisfaction.

Pluto in the 1st house Concentrate on how to express your understanding of the world unambiguously.

Pluto in the 2nd house Concentrate on building a set of positive values and applying them realistically.

Pluto in the 3rd house Concentrate on communicating and helping others to adapt to rapid changes.

Pluto in the 4th house Concentrate on identifying the need for emotional security and sharing it with others.

Pluto in the 5th house Concentrate on taking creative risks and demonstrating the meaning of love.

Pluto in the 6th house Concentrate on finding a real purpose in life and applying yourself to it.

Pluto in the 7th house Concentrate on building honest, reliable relationships with a sense of equality.

Pluto in the 8th house Concentrate on understanding hidden drives and directing them creatively.

Pluto in the 9th house Concentrate on making those dreams for the future a reality in the present.

Pluto in the 10th house Concentrate on making a success of your gift to the world, compassionately.

Pluto in the 11th house Concentrate on building stable foundations, accepting what others have to give you.

Pluto in the 12th house Concentrate on accepting yourself as you are and helping others do the same.

©DIAGRAM

What of your future?

As the planets, Jupiter, Saturn, Uranus, Neptune and Pluto continue to move around the Sun, they can stimulate you in several ways. Their general effect upon the planets and the signs is described in the section (*immediately right*). These descriptions apply when any of these five planets returns to the sign it was in when you were born, although Neptune and Pluto won't return to your birth position during your lifetime. Uranus only returns if you live to be 84.

The most profound effects are usually when Jupiter, Saturn, Uranus, Neptune or Pluto pass into your Sun-Sign or your Ascendant-Sign. You can find out when this may happen by consulting the Tables given on the previous four pages.

It is interesting that the "mid-life" crisis period around the age of 40 to 44 coincides with Saturn returning to your birth position and Uranus being in the sign opposite to where it was at your birth. Take both these planets into account around this age.

Finally, look up where these five planets are now. Write down their positions and today's date (*below*). Look at the sign they are in and find which of your houses those signs are in and write that down too. Now you can read the interpretation of the possible effect of each of these planets due to them being in your houses. The interpretations are on the opposite page, listed with the house numbers.

THE CURRENT POSITIONS OF THE FIVE PLANETS

Zodiac Signs	My Houses	Date: Positions of J, S, U, N, P.
Aries		
Taurus		
Gemini		
Cancer		
Leo		
Virgo		
Libra		
Scorpio		
Sagittarius		
Capricorn		
Aquarius		
Pisces		

JUPITER brings openings and a chance to make the very best of yourself. Luck, foresight, opportunities and forward planning all grow and thrive with Jupiter. This is the opulent planet that will give you a push and inspire you to start something new, learn a new skill or make money. Even if life has recently handed you a lemon, you'll soon be making lemonade! However, Jupiter can be too much of a good thing, so take care not to exaggerate or show-off when he is around.

SATURN brings shape and form to your life, helping you to lay firm foundations. Maturity comes from facing your limitations and anxieties when Saturn is around. This is the planet of increasing wisdom that will oblige you to learn from experience and give you a tremendous sense of achievement and satisfaction when you have done it. Saturn's presence indicates that it's time for hard work. If you don't do it he will make you miserable, gloomy and depressed.

URANUS brings upheavals and changes in the most unexpected ways, offering you bright ideas, sudden insights or very itchy feet! Magnetism, weird ventures, changes of direction and bouts of eccentric desires simply pour out of your brilliant mind under the influence of Uranus. This is the planet of thunder, lightning and clouds with silver linings. Use him creatively, otherwise you will experience a crisis and end up in chaos and unhappy.

NEPTUNE brings mystery and imagination helping you to realize your dreams or turn what you thought was a reality into nothing more than a formless illusion! You never know with Neptune which direction to take next, unless you have a well-developed intuition. No amount of logic will help when Neptune is around. So sort out your pet neurosis soon, for you may be tossed on the beach of a desert island or lost at sea; the victim of a glamorous deception.

PLUTO brings situations you can't avoid and long hidden skeletons out of your cupboard. Psychological garbage, deep, dark desires and all the clutter of your life will be brought to the surface when Pluto is around. It's a good time to clear out all kinds of encumbrances and a chance to undergo the most amazing metamorphosis. Pluto can produce a Phoenix from the ashes; transform your life or make you into a power-crazed tyrant. The choice is truly yours.

The possible effect of Jupiter when it moves through your houses, as numbered.

1 Renewed vitality and a desire to enjoy yourself.
2 More money available and life becomes comfortable.
3 Good for interviews, letters and trips.
4 A good time to redecorate the house or even move.

5 Children are good to be with. Romance blossoms.
6 Confidence and health improving daily.
7 Relationships should be excellent now. Have fun.
8 Something good turns up out of the blue beyond!

9 Good for travel or foreign contacts.
10 Time to start those new projects.
11 New friends and social activities abound.
12 Take a rest, write a poem; lie low now.

The possible effect of Saturn when it moves through your houses, as numbered.

1 Extra responsibility or work so take care.
2 Check your finances and save for a rainy day.
3 You must concentrate on correspondence.
4 Family affairs need some careful attention.

5 No, this isn't the best time for romance.
6 Work needs organization and may be difficult.
7 Relationship problems must be discussed.
8 Some gains and some losses are likely.

9 Future plans can now be successfully laid.
10 Handle authority or your career with great care.
11 Attend to friendships and social affairs.
12 A period for productive reflection and thought.

The possible effect of Uranus when it moves through your houses, as numbered.

1 Personal changes, tension and amazing insights.
2 Unusual transactions and material gains or crises.
3 Your thoughts are free; travel and learning?
4 What's cooking on the home front; more change?

5 Creative activities and odd love affairs.
6 Employment changes and your nerves prickle.
7 Your relationships are definitely changing.
8 Unexpected benefits or losses. New energy.

9 Your imagination and dreams are wildly free.
10 Unexpected developments in your career or job.
11 New, unusual social interests and friends.
12 Expect anything: flashes of insight; ups and downs.

The possible effect of Neptune when it moves through your houses, as numbered.

1 Confusion, glamor, and artistic productions.
2 Pie-in-the-sky ideas for making money abound.
3 Musical and psychic interests are developed.
4 Family affairs are rather confusing, take care.

5 Cupid has a rather deceptive arrow now.
6 You have illusions about your working conditions.
7 Illusions over contacts or partnerships.
8 A tendency to be rather wasteful.

9 You tend to get "high" but keep feet grounded.
10 Be more realistic about your working prospects.
11 Great interest in those creative types.
12 You may have some very mystical experiences.

The possible effect of Pluto when it moves through your houses, as numbered.

1 Your personal power is at a peak. Use it well.
2 Hidden resources come to light; marvellous!
3 You have great interest in psychology and life.
4 Home and family are the root of your power.

5 Check new enterprises well; love is power now.
6 Power comes from hard work and good health.
7 Use the power of your partnerships wisely.
8 Sexual drives are on the rise. Stay in control.

9 A great desire to study life at deeper levels.
10 You have a desire for power in the world.
11 Friends can become your most powerful allies.
12 Your hidden power must be put to good use.

What's your animal nature?

"The animal that hides in your heart" is the oriental way of describing the animal that rules the year of your birth – and whose characteristics are reputed to influence your personality, your behavior, and the course of your life. There are 12 animal signs in oriental astrology, each ruling a year in turn. Because the years of this 12-year cycle are lunar years (based on the phases of the Moon), they do not coincide with the solar years of the western calendar. Each lunar year begins on a different date in January or February: the exact dates are shown in the table (below).
Each animal in the cycle has its own symbolic significance – but remember that these animals are animals of the Far East, and that the oriental conception of their characters and qualities is very different from western thinking. For example, in the east it is a sincere compliment to call someone a snake, as it suggests that the person is both wise and beautiful. Remember, too, that individual animals lead very different lives: a dog may be a lapdog or a member of a hunting pack, a horse may be a thoroughbred or a carthorse, a rat may live in a drain or be someone's favorite pet…
So are you a hardworking Buffalo, or a colorful Rooster, or a fascinating Dragon? Find out by checking your birthdate in the table and then reading about the good – and bad – sides of your animal sign.

THE LUNAR YEARS AND RULING ANIMALS

1925 BUFFALO (January 25, 1925–February 13, 1926)
1926 TIGER (February 14, 1926–February 2, 1927)
1927 RABBIT (February 3, 1927–January 22, 1928)
1928 DRAGON (January 23, 1928–February 10, 1929)
1929 SNAKE (February 11, 1929–January 30, 1930)
1930 HORSE (January 31, 1930–February 17, 1931)
1931 GOAT (February 18, 1931–February 6, 1932)
1932 MONKEY (February 7, 1932–January 25, 1933)
1933 ROOSTER (January 26, 1933–February 13, 1934)
1934 DOG (February 14, 1934–February 4, 1935)
1935 PIG (February 5, 1935–January 23, 1936)
1936 RAT (January 24, 1936–February 11, 1937)
1937 BUFFALO (February 12, 1937–January 31, 1938)
1938 TIGER (February 1, 1938–February 18, 1939)
1939 RABBIT (February 19, 1939–February 7, 1940)
1940 DRAGON (February 8, 1940–January 27, 1941)
1941 SNAKE (January 28, 1941–February 15, 1942)
1942 HORSE (February 16, 1942–February 4, 1943)
1943 GOAT (February 5, 1943–January 25, 1944)
1944 MONKEY (January 26, 1944–February 12, 1945)
1945 ROOSTER (February 13, 1945–February 1, 1946)
1946 DOG (February 2, 1946–January 21, 1947)
1947 PIG (January 22, 1947–February 9, 1948)
1948 RAT (February 10, 1948–January 29, 1949)
1949 BUFFALO (January 30, 1949–February 17, 1950)
1950 TIGER (February 18, 1950–February 6, 1951)
1951 RABBIT (February 7, 1951–January 26, 1952)
1952 DRAGON (January 27, 1952–February 14, 1953)
1953 SNAKE (February 15, 1953–February 3, 1954)
1954 HORSE (February 4, 1954–January 23, 1955)
1955 GOAT (January 24, 1955–February 11, 1956)
1956 MONKEY (February 12, 1956–January 30, 1957)
1957 ROOSTER (January 31, 1957–February 18, 1958)
1958 DOG (February 19, 1958–February 7, 1959)
1959 PIG (February 8, 1959–January 27, 1960)
1960 RAT (January 28, 1960–February 15, 1961)

1961 BUFFALO (February 16, 1961–February 4, 1962)
1962 TIGER (February 5, 1962–January 25, 1963)
1963 RABBIT (January 26, 1963–February 13, 1964)
1964 DRAGON (February 14, 1964–February 2, 1965)
1965 SNAKE (February 3, 1965–January 21, 1966)
1966 HORSE (January 22, 1966–February 8, 1967)
1967 GOAT (February 9, 1967–January 29, 1968)
1968 MONKEY (January 30, 1968–February 16, 1969)
1969 ROOSTER (February 17, 1969–February 5, 1970)
1970 DOG (February 6, 1970–January 26, 1971)
1971 PIG (January 27, 1971–February 18, 1972)
1972 RAT (February 19, 1972–February 2, 1973)
1973 BUFFALO (February 3, 1973–January 23, 1974)
1974 TIGER (January 24, 1974–February 10, 1975)
1975 RABBIT (February 11, 1975–January 30, 1976)
1976 DRAGON (January 31, 1976–February 17, 1977)
1977 SNAKE (February 18, 1977–February 7, 1978)
1978 HORSE (February 8, 1978–January 27, 1979)
1979 GOAT (January 28, 1979–February 15, 1980)
1980 MONKEY (February 16, 1980–February 4, 1981)
1981 ROOSTER (February 5, 1981–January 24, 1982)
1982 DOG (January 25, 1982–February 12, 1983)
1983 PIG (February 13, 1983–February 1, 1984)
1984 RAT (February 2, 1984–February 19, 1985)
1985 BUFFALO (February 20, 1985–February 8, 1986)
1986 TIGER (February 9, 1986–January 28, 1987)
1987 RABBIT (January 29, 1987–February 16, 1988)
1988 DRAGON (February 17, 1988–February 5, 1989)
1989 SNAKE (February 6, 1989–January 26, 1990)
1990 HORSE (January 27, 1990–February 14, 1991)
1991 GOAT (February 15, 1991–February 3, 1992)
1992 MONKEY (February 4, 1992–January 22, 1993)
1993 ROOSTER (January 23, 1993–February 9, 1994)
1994 DOG (February 10, 1994–January 30, 1995)
1995 PIG (January 31, 1995–February 18, 1996)

If you're a Rat...
you're charming and imaginative, cautious and highly strung, honest and thrifty, clever and intellectual, independent and highly individual, very romantic and passionate, generous to your friends, and always aiming to please those around you...
But you're also...
aggressive and self-willed, avaricious and acquisitive, inquisitive and suspicious, calculating and opportunistic, always looking for a profit and capable of exploiting anyone, continually having to live by your wits and conceal your anxious, introverted nature under your confident exterior, and incapable of passing up a bargain at the sales!

If you're a Buffalo...
you're loyal and trustworthy, honest and thrifty, patient and persevering, hardworking and responsible, logical and efficient, independent and self-reliant, methodical and well balanced, down-to-earth and difficult to provoke, an original and intelligent thinker, and a natural leader who brings order out of chaos and inspires confidence...
But you're also...
stubborn and slow-moving, proud and choleric, terribly conventional and conformist, authoritarian and outspoken to the point of rudeness, given to explosive rages and impossible to stop when provoked, homely and unromantic, and frequently misunderstood!

If you're a Tiger...
you're impulsive and enthusiastic, humorous and generous, vivacious and magnetic, honorable and sincere, intense and passionate, optimistic and unmaterialistic, powerful and daring, romantic and affectionate, a natural leader who always gives 100%...
But you're also...
rash and hotheaded, disobedient and contentious, restless and reckless, volatile and egoistic, rebellious and demanding, stubborn and suspicious, indecisive and quick-tempered, always demanding to be the center of attention, and difficult to live with!

If you're a Rabbit...
you're attentive and hospitable, adaptable and diplomatic, discreet and prudent, elegant and sophisticated, serious and intellectual, happy and sociable, intuitive and circumspect, tolerant and gracious, honest and thorough, suave and debonair, a sympathetic listener who likes company...
But you're also...
hesitant and faint-hearted, superficial and sentimental, unpredictable and easily offended, pedantic and snobbish, subjective and moody, egoistic and hedonistic, cunning in business, and a very sharp negotiator!

Your animal nature

If you're a Dragon...
you're energetic and athletic, fascinating and full of vitality, enthusiastic and impetuous, lucky and successful, scrupulous and straight, intelligent and generous, eager and extroverted, self-assured and self-sufficient, a doer who is always on the go...

But you're also...
demanding and overpowering, intolerant and intimidating, brash and overconfident, stubborn and proud, irritable and short tempered, tactless and eccentric, unromantic and deeply discontented, and a chatterbox who is easily bored!

If you're a Snake...
you're wise and intuitive, charismatic and attractive, calm and reflective, gentle and romantic, elegant and cultured, helpful and charming, well bred and distinguished, quiet and reserved, decisive and self-critical, with a taste for the finer things in life...

But you're also...
suffocating and clinging, jealous and possessive, cold and hostile, lazy and dishonest, paranoid and stingy, and a philanderer who likes extra-marital affairs!

If you're a Horse...
you're cheerful and popular, earthy and sexy, quick witted and sociable, vivacious and energetic, enterprising and gregarious, agile and athletic, loyal and persuasive, practical and realistic, independent and capable of creating your own security, and always the center of attention...

But you're also...
hot-blooded and hot-headed, inconsiderate and absentminded, inconsistent and self-centered, impatient and selfish, intolerant and prone to childish fits of rage, stubborn and immodest, demanding and unpredictable, lacking in staying power and frightened of failure, and always jumping to conclusions!

If you're a Goat...
you're mild-mannered and gentle, compassionate and understanding, kind hearted and sincere, peaceful and adaptable, lucky and generous, graceful and romantic, creative and elegant, a survivor who has great passive endurance, and a follower who will always find someone to keep you in style...

But you're also...
indisciplined and irresponsible, timid and weak-willed, withdrawn and pessimistic, wheedling and indecisive, supersensitive and self-pitying, self-indulgent and bad with money, sulky and always late, irresponsible and generous with other people's property, capricious and lacking in self-control, and always in need of a bossy person to keep you up to the mark!

If you're a Monkey...
you're intelligent and clear sighted, chivalrous and sociable, responsible and decisive, light-hearted and gregarious, confident and versatile, amusing and shrewd, observant and ironic, warm and full of *joie de vivre*, original and inventive, objective and rational, efficient and independent, talkative and entertaining, with an unquenchable thirst for knowledge...

But you're also...
cunning and guileful, jealous and critical, sly and manipulative, superior and vengeful, vain and mischevious, impatient and ambitious, unscrupulous and forceful, sharp and tricky, a charlatan and a con artist, self-preoccupied with an elastic conscience, and suspected by the people around you!

If you're a Rooster...
you're bold and self-reliant, entertaining and stimulating company, good looking and popular, efficient and good with money, precise and organized, loyal and sincere, hardworking and energetic, colorful and creative, logical and knowledgeable, brave and generous, positive and helpful, with a lot of stamina and a good memory...

But you're also...
blunt and undiplomatic, boastful and opinionated, conservative and puritanical, abrasive and full of bravado, a daydreamer and teller of tall stories, perfectionist and always giving advice, easily impressed by awards and titles, incapable of admitting you could be in the wrong, and insistent that you should always come first!

If you're a Dog...
you're devoted and dependable, faithful and reliable, tough and resourceful, persevering and responsible, generous and attentive, dignified and discreet, helpful and hardworking, tolerant and matter-of-fact, noble and unpretentious, confidence-inspiring and a good listener, unselfish and straightforward, a champion of freedom with simple tastes and a passion for fair play...

But you're also...
pessimistic and introverted, stubborn and cynical, defensive and sharp-tongued, antisocial and cantankerous, impatient and bad tempered, pugnacious and discontented, a doom-laden worrier with a black sense of humor and a distrust of strangers!

If you're a Pig...
you're courteous and sincere, gallant and gentle, impartial and trustworthy, lively and impulsive, calm and peace-loving, obliging and chivalrous, confident and courageous, resilient and diligent, popular and gregarious, generous and unable to bear a grudge...

But you're also...
gullible and naive, thick-skinned and shallow, stubborn and sad, defenseless and easily duped, easily seduced and incapable of saying no, given to treating other people's property as if it were your own, materialistic and inclined to wallow in sensuality, simplistic and superficial, an uncompetitive do-gooder who never looks to the future!

Your companion in life

The cycle of the animals of the oriental horoscope applies to the hours of the day and the months of the year as well as to the years themselves, and the animals ruling the hour and month of your birth are held to play a part in determining your character. The natures of the animals do not change whether they are ruling a year, a month, or an hour, so once you have discovered the animals that are important in your horoscope you can read about their good and bad qualities on pages 37–39.

Your companion in life
The animal sign ruling the hour of your birth is known as your "companion in life": it is the eastern equivalent of the Ascendant in solar astrology (see pages 24–29). Your companion in life is regarded as your second self,

sometimes taking the role of guardian angel, sometimes playing devil's advocate. Your companion is thought to provide the stimulus in your life, sometimes acting in harmony with your year sign, sometimes in conflict. Because of this it is the combination of companion and year sign that is considered important – the companion is never interpreted alone.

Your Moon-Sign
The animal that rules the month of your birth is known as your Moon-Sign. The months ruled by the oriental animals match closely with the 12 zodiac signs of the solar horoscope, so if you know your Sun-Sign it is easy to find your Moon-Sign in the chart (*below right*).

FINDING YOUR COMPANION
The 24-hour cycle of the animals is shown in the table (*right*) and the diagrams (*below*). The hours given refer to local standard time. If you were born in a month when daylight saving or summer time were in use, you will need to deduct an hour (sometimes two) from your birth time before looking up the sign of your companion.

Time of birth	Sign of companion
11pm–1am	Rat
1am–3am	Buffalo
3am–5am	Tiger
5am–7am	Rabbit
7am–9am	Dragon
9am–11am	Snake
11am–1pm	Horse
1pm–3pm	Goat
3pm–5pm	Monkey
5pm–7pm	Rooster
7pm–9pm	Dog
9pm–11pm	Pig

Analyzing the animals

In your oriental horoscope, the most important factor is the animal ruling the year of your birth; next is your companion in life, and third is your Moon-Sign. Read about all three and discover how compatible they are with one another (see the charts on pp. 42–45), then consider how they will affect each other. For example, suppose you were born in the year of the Buffalo, that your companion in life was the Rat, and your Moon-Sign was the Snake. The Buffalo is compatible with both the Rat and the Snake, and the Rat and the Snake are not in conflict with each other. You could thus expect the Rat's charm and romanticism to lighten the Buffalo's more solid qualities, with the Snake making the combination even more attractive. Of course, the less good qualities of the three signs will also reinforce each other . . .

If the signs are incompatible, the result could be a more complicated and curious mixture. For example, a Rooster whose companion in life is a Rabbit could be very faint-hearted behind that colorful exterior. If this Rooster's Moon-Sign was the Tiger (who is antagonistic to the Rabbit, and cool at best with the Rooster), there could also be a layer of resentment – the type of people who are angry because their own weaknesses prevent them taking the leading place in the world that they feel is rightfully theirs. But such a Rooster could, with hard work, use the Tiger's commitment and the Rabbit's charm to overcome these difficulties and make some daydreams come true.

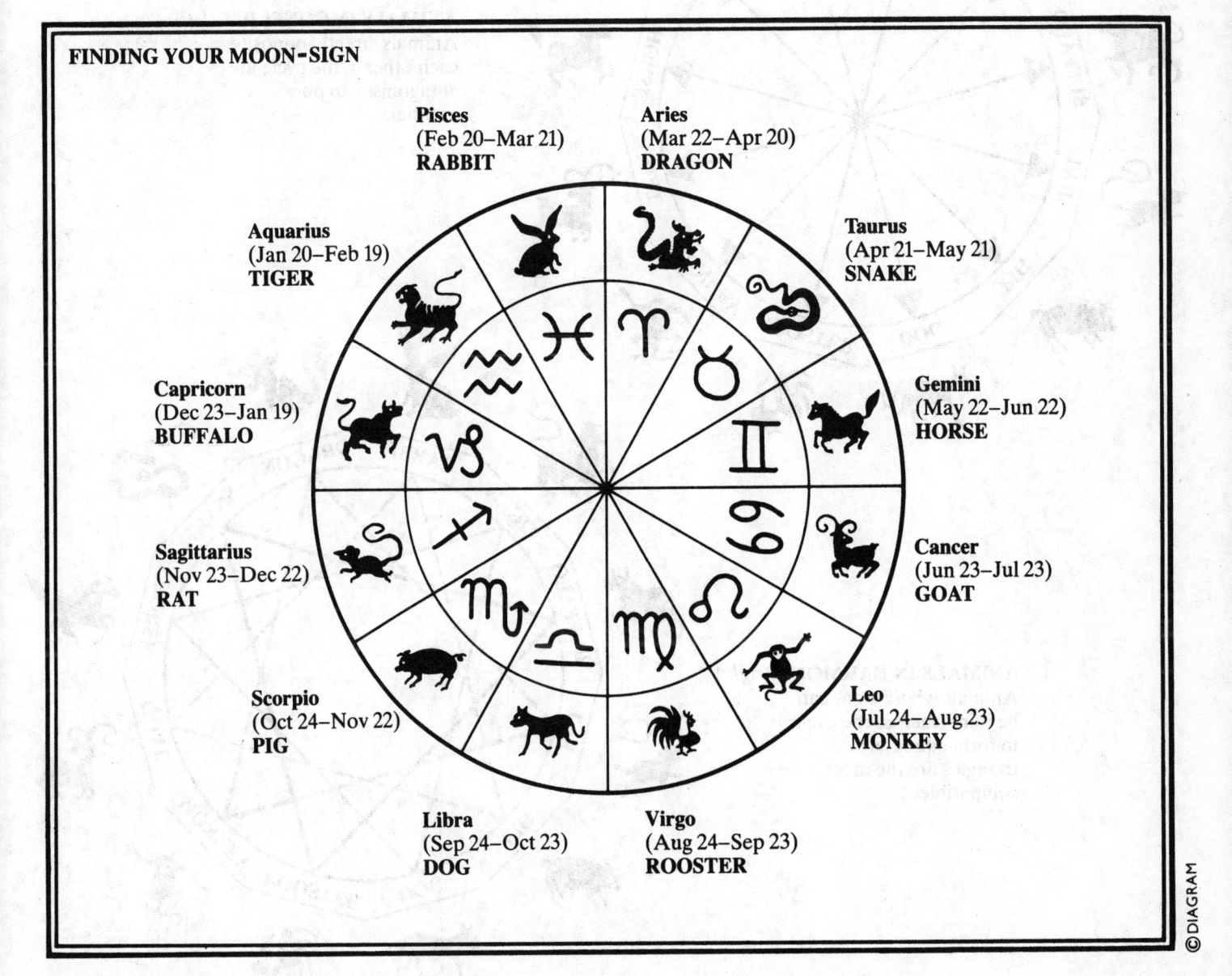

FINDING YOUR MOON-SIGN

Pisces (Feb 20–Mar 21) **RABBIT**

Aries (Mar 22–Apr 20) **DRAGON**

Aquarius (Jan 20–Feb 19) **TIGER**

Taurus (Apr 21–May 21) **SNAKE**

Capricorn (Dec 23–Jan 19) **BUFFALO**

Gemini (May 22–Jun 22) **HORSE**

Sagittarius (Nov 23–Dec 22) **RAT**

Cancer (Jun 23–Jul 23) **GOAT**

Scorpio (Oct 24–Nov 22) **PIG**

Leo (Jul 24–Aug 23) **MONKEY**

Libra (Sep 24–Oct 23) **DOG**

Virgo (Aug 24–Sep 23) **ROOSTER**

Compatibility of the animals

Opposites certainly do not attract in the oriental horoscope! The signs most likely to be in conflict are directly opposite each other in the cycle of the animals. It is the signs that can be joined together to form an equilateral triangle that are in the greatest harmony. Combinations of other signs are compatible to different extents. You can discover just how you relate to the other signs by looking at the diagram for your particular animal. For example, if you are a Rat you will be highly compatible with a Buffalo, have no conflict with a Tiger, have an amicable relationship with a Rabbit, and so on.

Remember to take the rest of your oriental horoscope into account when considering compatibility – you may well find yourself strongly attracted to someone whose year sign is the same as the sign of your companion in life...

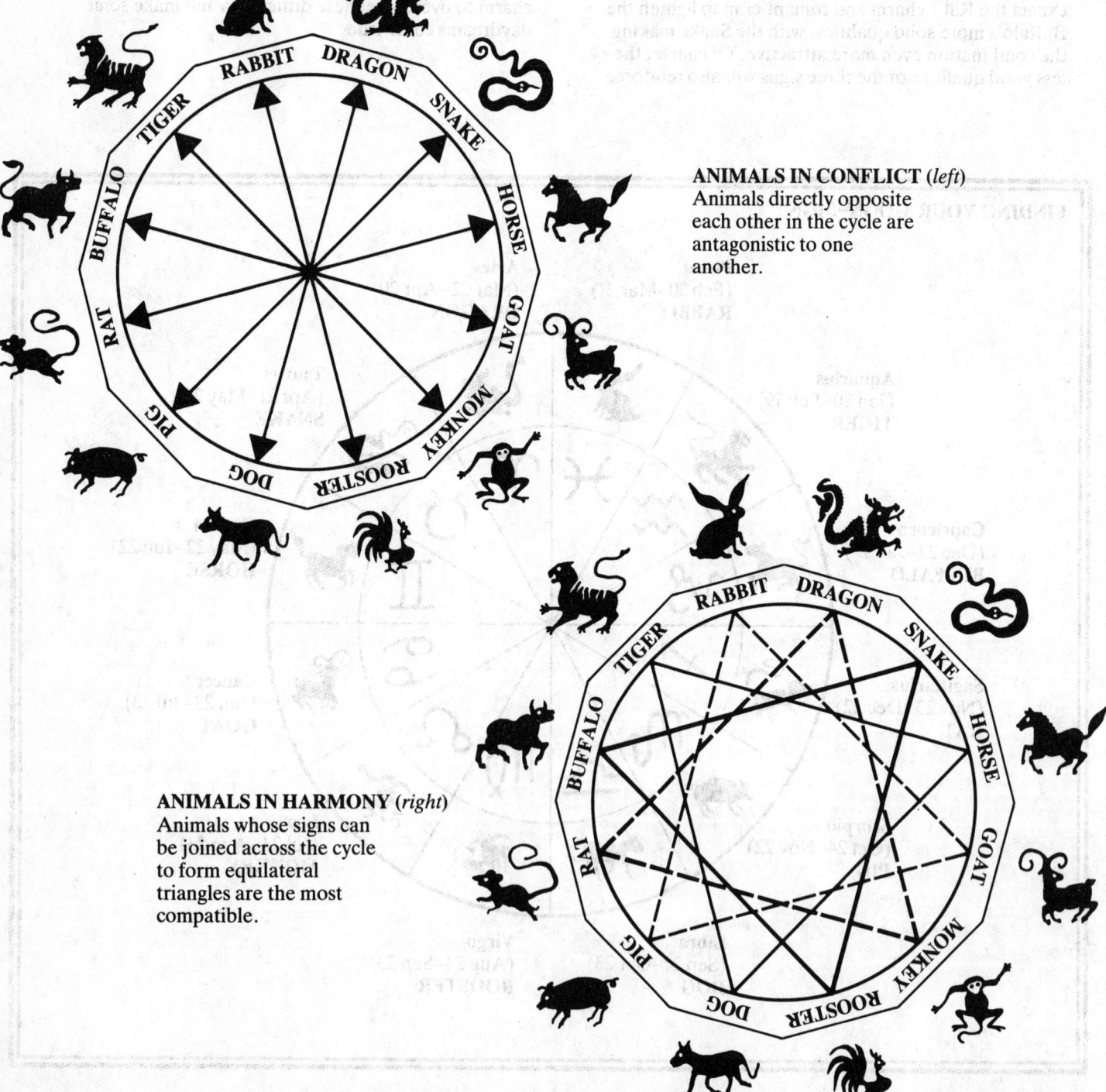

ANIMALS IN CONFLICT (*left*)
Animals directly opposite each other in the cycle are antagonistic to one another.

ANIMALS IN HARMONY (*right*)
Animals whose signs can be joined across the cycle to form equilateral triangles are the most compatible.

43

©DIAGRAM

Compatibility of the animals

KEY

Highly compatible	○ ○
Amicable	○
No conflict, but needs effort	◑
Lack of sympathy	●
Antagonistic	● ●

Compatibility of the animals

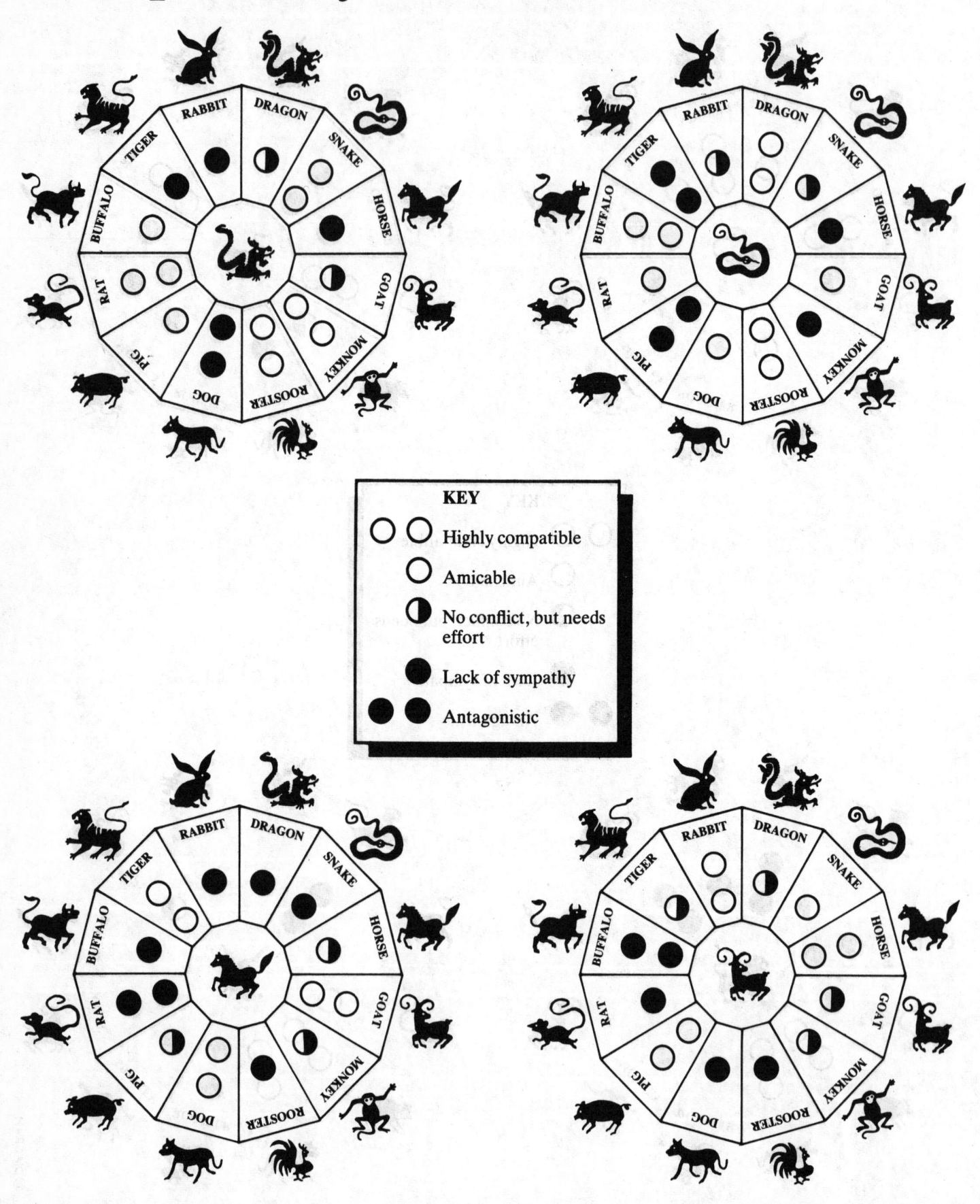

KEY

◯ ◯	Highly compatible	
◯	Amicable	
◑	No conflict, but needs effort	
●	Lack of sympathy	
● ●	Antagonistic	

KEY

○○ Highly compatible

○ Amicable

◐ No conflict, but needs effort

● Lack of sympathy

●● Antagonistic

45

©DIAGRAM

Your oriental element

The year of your birth is not only ruled by an animal, it is also influenced by an element. There are five elements in oriental astrology – wood, fire, earth, metal, and water. Each element influences two years in turn: the first year of the two is a *yang* year, and the second is a *yin* year (for more on *yin* and *yang*, see pages 68–69). You can discover the element of the year of your birth from the table (*below*). (The dates are lunar years, not solar years – for the exact dates see p. 36.) *Yang* years are marked (+), and *yin* years are marked (−).

As you can also see from the table, each of the 12 ruling animals is permanently associated with an element. In addition, six of the animals are *yin* and six are *yang*. If you were born in 1960, for example, you were born in a *yang* metal year, ruled by the Rat, which is a *yin* water animal. It is considered fortunate to have as many of the elements as possible represented in your horoscope. The element of the year of your birth is considered the most important, but you should also take into account the elements associated with your ruling animal, your companion in life, and your Moon-Sign. Very few of us are born with a perfect balance between the elements, and in most of us one element dominates while others may be missing altogether. In the East this lack of balance is easily corrected at birth by incorporating the names of any missing elements into the new baby's name. An alternative possibility is to associate as much as possible with people whose dominant elements are the elements missing from your own horoscope, as they will then be able to compensate for your deficiencies!

THE ELEMENTS, RULING ANIMALS AND LUNAR YEARS

ELEMENTS	WOOD	FIRE	EARTH	WATER	METAL
ANIMAL SIGNS	Tiger (+) Rabbit (−)	Snake (+) Horse (+)	Buffalo (−) Dragon (+) Goat (+) Dog (−)	Rat (−) Pig (−)	Monkey (−) Rooster (+)
LUNAR YEARS	1925 (−) 1934 (+) 1935 (−) 1944 (+) 1945 (−) 1954 (+) 1955 (−) 1964 (+) 1965 (−) 1974 (+) 1975 (−) 1984 (+) 1985 (−) 1994 (+) 1995 (−)	1926 (+) 1927 (−) 1936 (+) 1937 (−) 1946 (+) 1947 (−) 1956 (+) 1957 (−) 1966 (+) 1967 (−) 1976 (+) 1977 (−) 1986 (+) 1987 (−)	1928 (+) 1929 (−) 1938 (+) 1939 (−) 1948 (+) 1949 (−) 1958 (+) 1959 (−) 1968 (+) 1969 (−) 1978 (+) 1979 (−) 1988 (+) 1989 (−)	1932 (+) 1933 (−) 1942 (+) 1943 (−) 1952 (+) 1953 (−) 1962 (+) 1963 (−) 1972 (+) 1973 (−) 1982 (+) 1983 (−) 1992 (+) 1993 (−)	1930 (+) 1931 (−) 1940 (+) 1941 (−) 1950 (+) 1951 (−) 1960 (+) 1961 (−) 1970 (+) 1971 (−) 1980 (+) 1981 (−) 1990 (+) 1991 (−)

THE FIVE ELEMENTS

Wood
Wood represents self-confidence and dignity, generosity and expansiveness, temperance and harmony, beauty and elegance, compassion and concentration, and a strong moral sense. Wood subjects are creative but susceptible, and have a tendency to bite off more than they can chew. They need to concentrate their resources and control their tempers.

Fire
Fire represents decisiveness and lucidity, innovation and rapid change, adventure and creativity, joy and prosperity, warmth and brilliance, and a capacity for achievement. Fire subjects are wise but passionate, and carry within them a potential for destruction. They need to curb their tongues and channel their energies in positive directions.

Earth
Earth represents honesty and responsibility, prudence and forethought, fertility and abundance, intelligence and objectivity, self-discipline and hard work, and a strong sense of the practical. Earth subjects are enterprising but slow moving, and can spend almost too much time thinking before they act. They need to be more adventurous and to give more rein to their imaginations.

Metal
Metal represents firmness and integrity, clarity and purity, eloquence and ambition, energy and sustained effort, constancy and dependability, and an ability to make independent decisions. Metal subjects are tireless when they pursue an objective, but can be too rigid and inflexible. They need to learn to compromise and to relax and let go.

Water

Water represents communication and persuasion, diplomacy and flexibility, calm and intuition, self-restraint and quiet persistence, and an awareness of future trends and potentials. Water subjects are skilled at influencing others but can be too passive and conciliatory. They need to become more assertive and to be prepared to lead from the front.

Harmony and the elements
Just as some of the animal signs are compatible while others are hostile, so some of the elements are in harmony while others are antagonistic. The relationships between the elements are influenced by whether they are *yin* or *yang*, and, in turn, the elements influence and modify the relationships between the animal signs. For example, the Tiger and the Snake are usually at cross-purposes. But if the Tiger was born in 1950 (a *yang* metal year) and the Snake was born in 1953 (a *yin* water year), the elements of their birth years would be in such harmony that the pair would probably be able to live side by side without conflict, and with some effort could even develop mutual respect and affection.

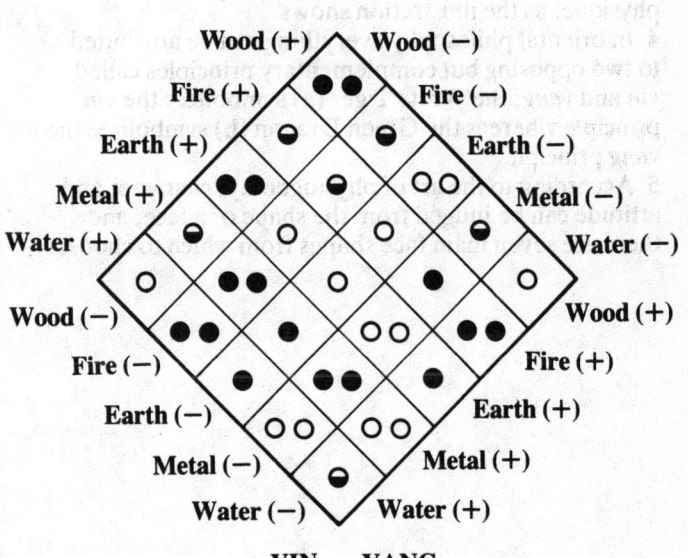

KEY

○○	Highly compatible
○	Amicable
◓	No conflict, but needs effort
●	Lack of sympathy
●●	Antagonistic

©DIAGRAM

47

Chapter 2

YOUR PHYSICAL SELF

The place and family into which you are born give you a physical identity. You are your body and, because your body is always changing, your personality also changes and develops. Your physical features and body balances show your character more clearly as the years pass.

1 With models from Charles Atlas to Arnold Schwartzenegger to follow, many body-building advertisements have long answered a perennial, masculine need.

2 The life and head lines on this right hand print of a physicist show both well developed intellectual abilities and physical capabilities.

3 Men come in all shapes and sizes and there is no ideal physique, as the illustration shows.

4 In oriental philosophy everything can be attributed to two opposing but complementary principles called *yin* and *yang*; the White Tiger (**a**) symbolizes the *yin* principle whereas the Green Dragon (**b**) symbolizes the *yang* principle.

5 According to the art of physiognomy, character and attitude can be judged from the shape of a face, and there are seven main face shapes from which to choose.

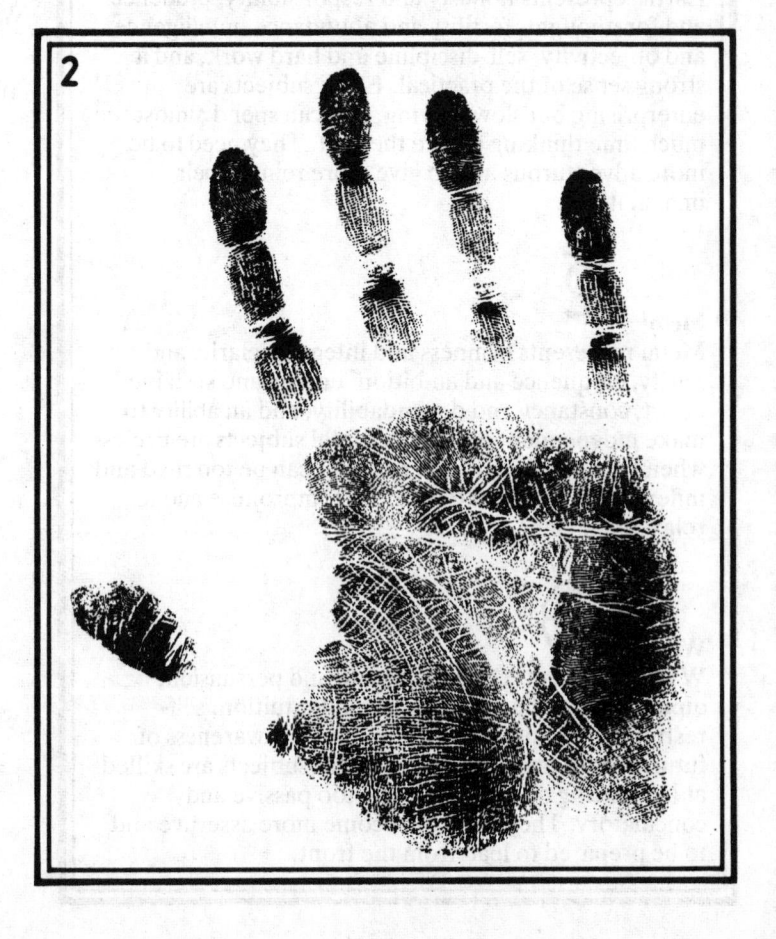

3

4

a

b

5

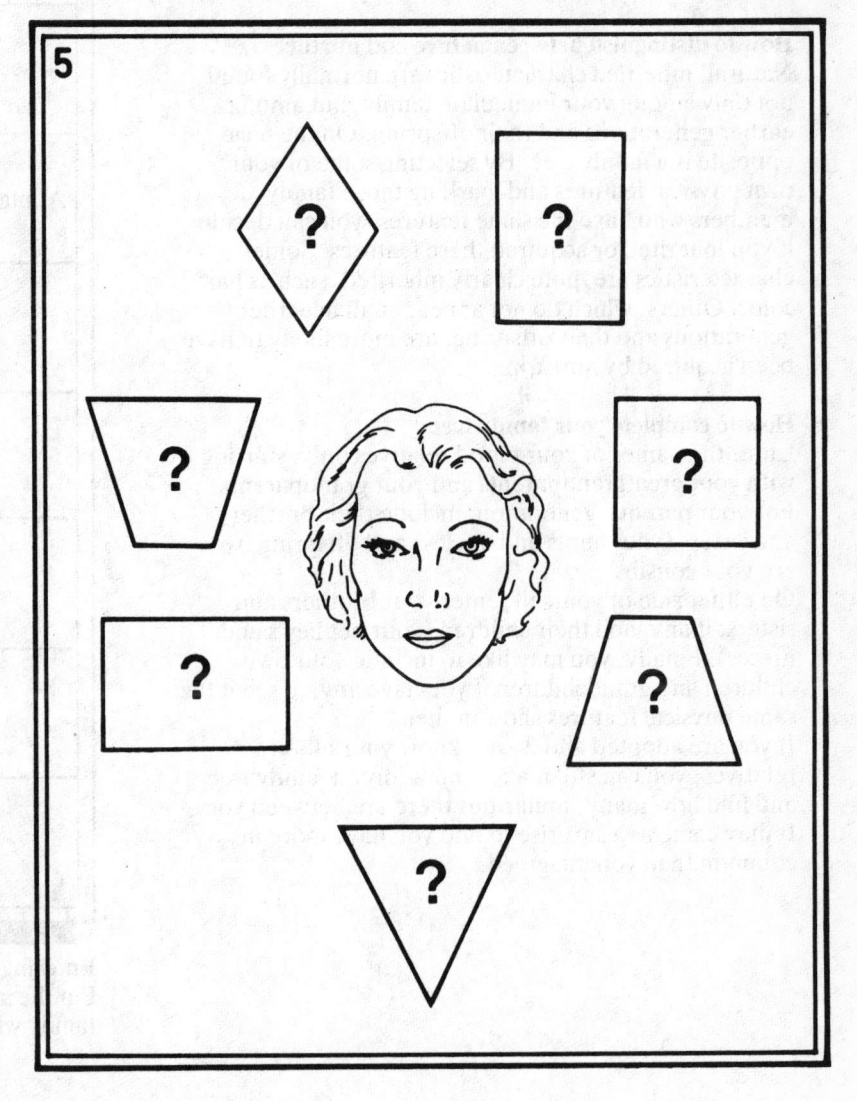

Where did you get that body?

Contained in every cell of your body is a genetic blueprint which determines hundreds of physical characteristics, for example, your hair and skin color, your sex and many of your potential skills.

Nature gave you this blueprint, half from your mother and half from your father, which they in turn inherited from their parents, and so on.

During the process of growing up, you were taught many things, for example, how to eat your food and how to behave in social situations. This process is called nurturing.

In adulthood a fascinating question arises: which parts did you inherit by nature and what did you acquire by nurture? It is not always an easy question to answer. If, for example, you were adopted there are no natural blood ties between you and the parents who nurtured you. Yet it is intriguing to discover many similarities among members of families who have been nurtured together. Indeed, even husbands and wives seem to grow like each other over a period of time and they normally do not have any blood ties between them either! Do people choose each other because there are potential similarities between them?

How to distinguish between nature and nurture

Natural, inherited characteristics are normally found not only among your immediate family, but among earlier generations and their offspring. On the page opposite is a family tree. By selecting some of your own physical features and marking those family members who have the same features, you can decide if you inherited or acquired these features. Some characteristics are quite clearly inherited, such as hair color. Others, which do not appear at all in earlier generations and their offspring, are more likely to have been acquired by nurturing.

How to complete your family tree

Enter the names of your blood relatives only, starting with your greatgrandparents and your grandparents. For your parents' generation, include their brothers and sisters (your aunts and uncles) and offspring, who are your cousins.

On either side of yourself, enter your brothers and sisters, if any, and their children (your nephews and nieces). Finally, you may like to include your own children and grandchildren if you have any, to see if the same physical features show in them.

If you are adopted and do not know your blood relatives, you can still make your adopted family tree and find how many similarities there are between you. It may come as a surprise to find you have more in common than you imagined.

Your physical characteristics

In the table (*below*), enter the physical features you would like to trace back in your family. The first three have been entered ready for you to complete.

In the box opposite each feature put a colored dot or a symbol. For example, hair colors are basically black, brown, red, blonde or white, so you could use a colored dot for your hair color. Adult heights can be separated into T for tall (over 6 feet or 183cm) M for medium (5–6 feet or 152–183cm) and S for short (less than 5 feet or 152cm). Noses come in all shapes and sizes, but you are only looking for noses that are like yours, so choose an appropriate symbol.

When choosing features, include any disabilities or oddities such as flat feet or eyes of different colors. Also include some skills such as "good at languages".

KEY TO MY PHYSICAL CHARACTERISTICS			
Hair color			
Nose shape			
Adult height			

Entering the characteristics on your family tree
Put the symbols in the boxes of all the people in your family who have the same characteristics as you.

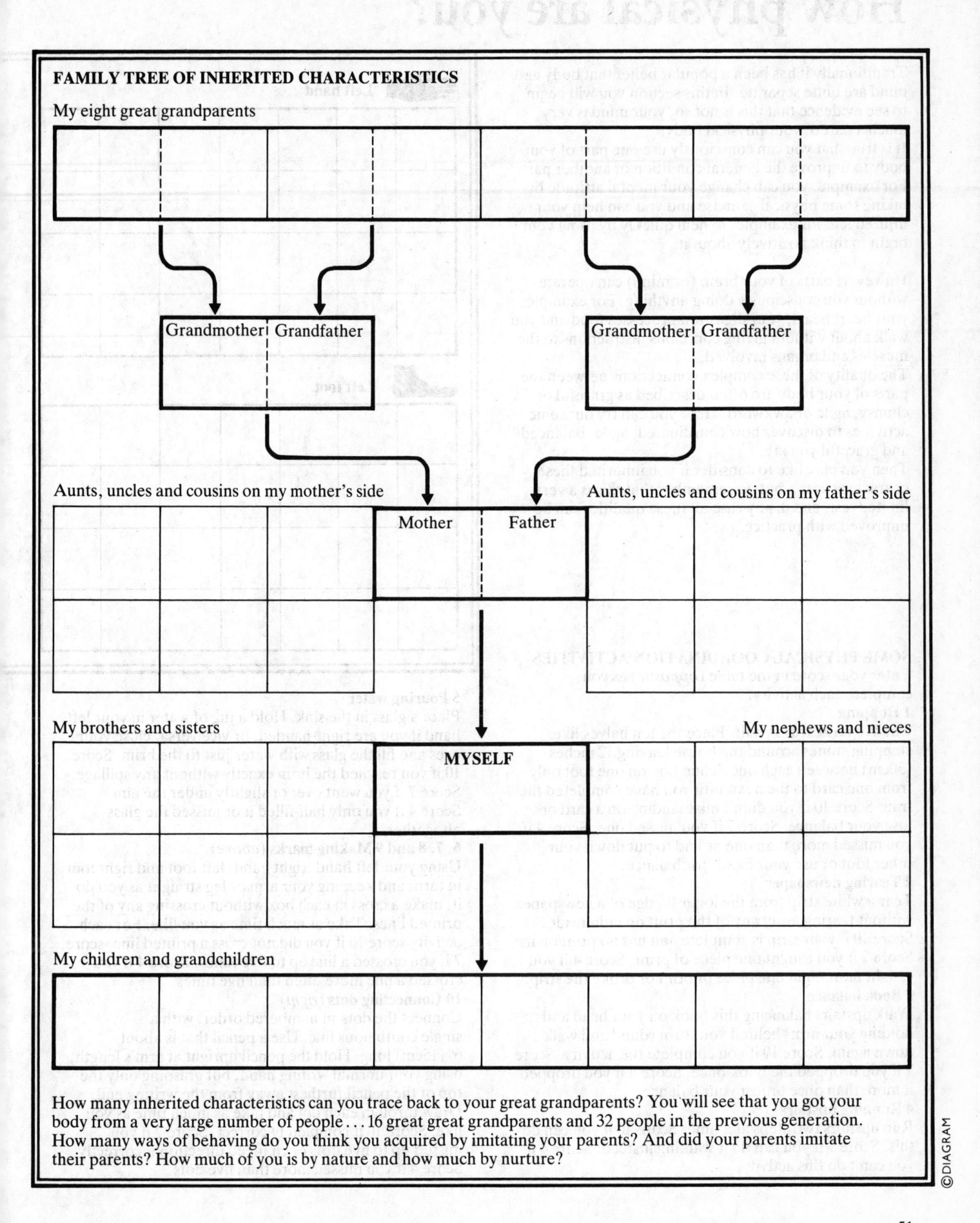

FAMILY TREE OF INHERITED CHARACTERISTICS

My eight great grandparents

Grandmother | Grandfather   Grandmother | Grandfather

Aunts, uncles and cousins on my mother's side   Aunts, uncles and cousins on my father's side

Mother | Father

My brothers and sisters   My nephews and nieces

MYSELF

My children and grandchildren

How many inherited characteristics can you trace back to your great grandparents? You will see that you got your body from a very large number of people . . . 16 great great grandparents and 32 people in the previous generation. How many ways of behaving do you think you acquired by imitating your parents? And did your parents imitate their parents? How much of you is by nature and how much by nurture?

How physical are you?

Traditionally it has been a popular belief that body and mind are quite separate. In this section you will begin to see evidence that this is not so; your mind is very much a part of your physical body.

It is true that you can consciously use one part of your body to improve the general condition of another part. For example, you can change your mental attitude by taking some physical exercise and you can help your injured leg, for example, to heal quickly by using your brain to think positively about it.

However, parts of your brain (or mind) can operate without you consciously doing anything. For example, your heart beats, your digestion processes food and you walk about without giving conscious instructions to the muscles and organs involved.

The quality of these complex connections between the parts of your body are often described as graceful or clumsy, agile or awkward. Here you can try out some activities to discover how coordinated, agile, balanced and graceful you are.

Then you may like to consider if you inherited these characteristics... but do remember that this is a very limited test, and in any case all these qualities can be improved with practice.

Left hand

Left foot

SOME PHYSICAL COORDINATION ACTIVITIES

Enter your score in the table (*opposite*) as you complete each activity.

1 Hopping
Cut five postcards in half. Place the ten halves like stepping stones around the house leaving 12 inches (30cm) between each one. Then hop on one foot only from one card to the next until you have completed the trail. Score 10 if you didn't miss landing on a card or lose your balance. Score 7 if you missed one. Score 4 if you missed more than one or had to put down your other foot or use your hands for balance.

2 Tearing newspaper
Tear a white strip from the longest edge of a newspaper without tearing away any of the print on either side. Score 10 if your strip is complete and has no print on it. Score 7 if you caught one piece of print. Score 4 if you caught more than one piece of print or broke the strip.

3 Book balance
Walk upstairs balancing this book on your head and holding your arms behind you, turn round and walk down again. Score 10 if you complete the activity. Score 7 if you dropped the book once. Score 4 if you dropped it more than once or lost your balance.

4 Running upstairs
Run upstairs two steps at a time. Score 10 if you can do this. Score 7 if you can do it walking instead. Score 4 if you can't do this activity.

5 Pouring water
Place a glass in the sink. Hold a jug of water in your left hand if you are right-handed, or vice versa, close your eyes and fill the glass with water just to the brim. Score 10 if you reached the brim exactly without any spillage. Score 7 if you went over or slightly under the aim. Score 4 if you only half-filled it or missed the glass altogether.

6, 7, 8 and 9 Making marks (*above*)
Using your left hand, right hand, left foot and right foot in turn, and keeping your arm or leg straight as you do it, make a cross in each box without crossing any of the printed lines. Take as much time as you like. For each activity score 10 if you did not cross a printed line, score 7 if you crossed a line up to five times. Score 4 if you crossed a line more often than five times.

10 Connecting dots (*right*)
Connect the dots in numbered order, with a single continuous line. Use a pencil that is about 6″ (15cm) long. Hold the pencil upright at arm's length, using your normal writing hand, but grasping only the top of the pencil furthest away from the writing end. Draw through each dot and take as much time as you like. Score 10 if completely correct. Score 7 if you missed up to five dots or changed direction incorrectly. Score 4 if you missed more than five dots.

Right hand

Right foot

PHYSICAL COORDINATION SCORES
Draw a circle round your score for each test.

1 Hopping	4	7	10
2 Tearing newspaper	4	7	10
3 Book balance	4	7	10
4 Running upstairs	4	7	10
5 Pouring water	4	7	10
6 Left hand marks	4	7	10
7 Right hand marks	4	7	10
8 Left foot marks	4	7	10
9 Right foot marks	4	7	10
10 Connecting dots	4	7	10

Add together the scores you have circled to find your grand total score. Enter it below.

A Less than 50	B 51 to 80	C 81 to 100

21	22	25	4	3
23	20	5	2	7
14	24	1	6	8
13	15	19	9	18
12	11	10	16	17

Interpreting your coordination score
A Not very well-coordinated. This result applies only to these particular tests. You may, for example, be well-coordinated at other kinds of activities such as playing darts or climbing ladders, so try out a few different activities. Do take into account age or physical disabilities.
B Good average coordination. Taking into account that age and physical disabilities will make a difference to your score, you should be pleased to find you are fairly well-coordinated, graceful, agile and balanced physically.
C Above average coordination. If you have scored more than 90 this means you are extremely well-balanced physically, so aim to keep at this level.

How did you grow your shape?

Earlier this century Dr. Wilhelm Reich, a psychiatrist, proposed that we build into the muscles of our bodies the "shape" of our beliefs and attitudes. He suggested that our bodies have minds of their own! He called the particular shape each of us grows a "character armor." Your character armor reflects your life experiences and shows the way you have come to terms with living in a world that is not always very kind to human vulnerabilities.

It is likely you have developed one part of yourself, i.e. one part of your body, more than other parts. You have grown a shape that is uniquely you. Consequently parts of your body may be disproportionate in size or shape to other parts.

The five main body divisions
First note, in the spaces provided on the page (*opposite*), any differences in proportion between each part of your body. The diagrams (*below*) show which parts to compare. You can best find out by looking at yourself in a long mirror, preferably naked. Do be kind to yourself and look objectively. You are who you are and there are **NO** right or wrong body-shapes. Age will change your shape and that, too, is natural. When you have completed your notes, read the meaning that has generally been found to be true of the different proportions between the parts of the body. Are you top-heavy or bottom-heavy? Are your limbs long compared with your torso? Have a close look.

THE FIVE MAIN BODY DIVISIONS

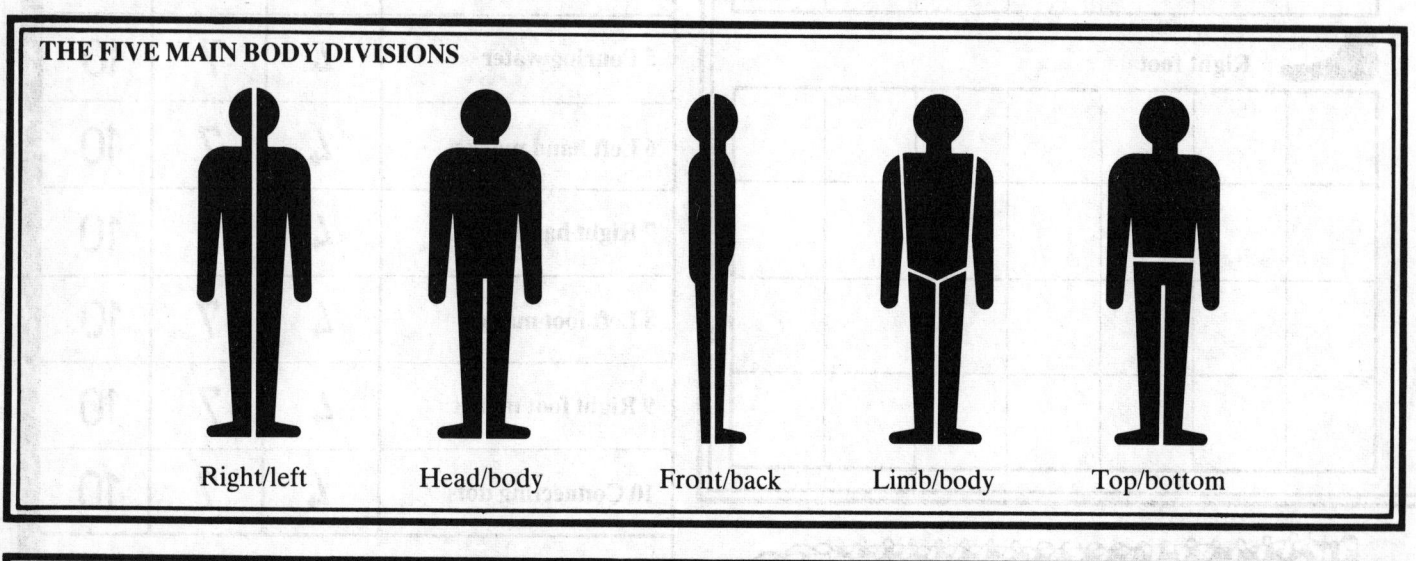

Right/left   Head/body   Front/back   Limb/body   Top/bottom

EXAMPLES OF THE TOP/BOTTOM PROPORTIONS

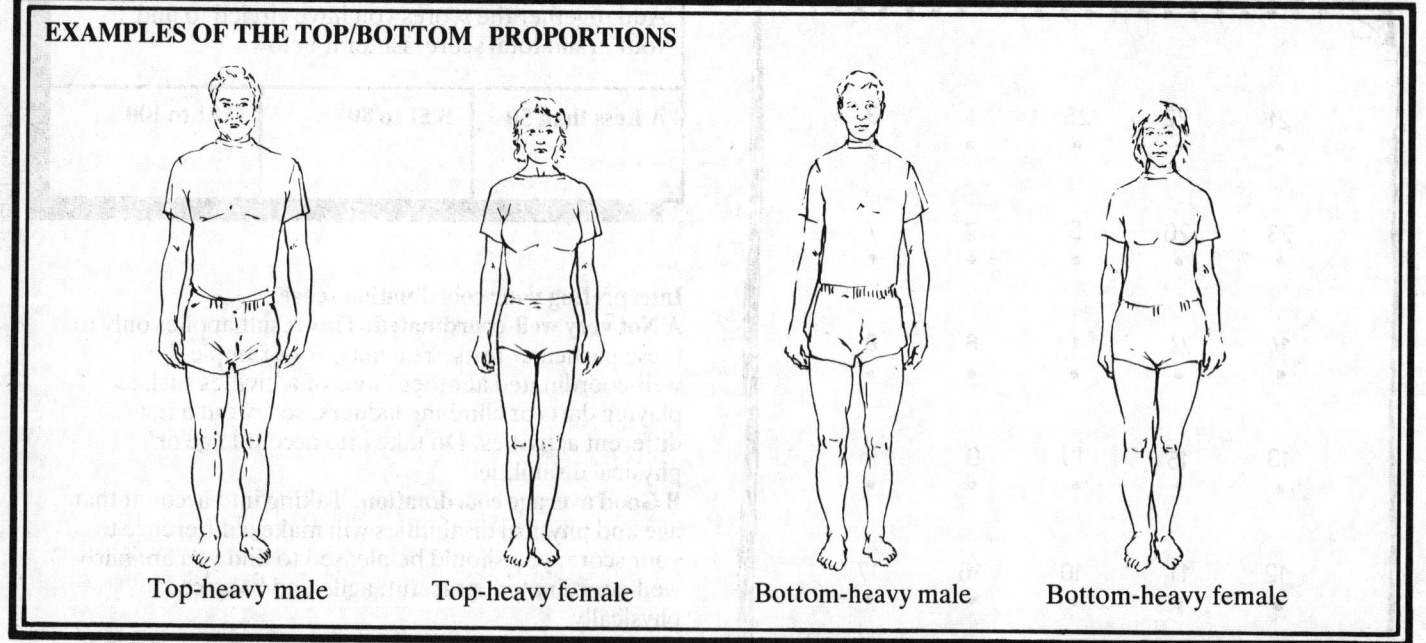

Top-heavy male   Top-heavy female   Bottom-heavy male   Bottom-heavy female

Whatever your height and weight, you will probably find you match one of these examples. Look carefully at your shoulder width and hip width, your chest or bust size compared with your hip size.

Right/left proportions

_____
_____
_____
_____

Interpretations

Regardless of right- or left-handedness, one side of your body may be stronger than the other. If it is the left side, then you have spent time protecting your more vulnerable self passively rather than developing your aggressive self. If the right is stronger, you have developed a more aggressive response to the world.

Head/body proportions

_____
_____
_____
_____

Interpretations

Is your head big _compared_ with your body or small? A larger head indicates a need to cope with the world intellectually, ignoring feelings. A larger body means a need to cope with the world emotionally and ignore thinking. Does your head tilt? A disconnection between thought and feeling is indicated.

Front/back proportions

_____
_____
_____
_____

Interpretations

The front is the more conscious side of you and the back the more unconscious part of yourself. Tight, flat backsides mean hidden aggression. Big, round backsides may be sexy, but they also mean private, inner power and a great deal of anger. Have you a kind, soft pleasant front and a tight hard aggressive back?

Limb/body proportions

_____
_____
_____
_____

Interpretations

Arms or legs that are much thinner or fatter, longer or shorter, in _comparison_ with the rest of the body show many characteristics, for example, extremely thin legs may mean you have problems taking a stand on important issues. Heavy or longer arms often mean a need to reach out to make contact with others, while short arms mean a fear of doing so.

My top/bottom proportions

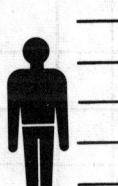

_____
_____
_____
_____
_____
_____

Interpretations

If the upper part of your body is larger or more well-developed than the lower half, you have spent more time on making contacts that help you to achieve power, success or to express your ideas in the world. Assertion, communication and action are easier than more passive, reflective ways of being.

If the lower half of your body is larger or more well-developed than the top half, you have given more time to securing an emotional basis of strength. You feel things strongly but may not give your true feelings assertive expression. This is the private part of you that is more stable than the upper, public part of you.

©DIAGRAM

NOTE

To analyze your character fully from your body-shape would need the assistance of an expert in Reichian character analysis. However, becoming more aware of your own shape can lead you to a greater understanding of yourself... and of your family inheritance. How much of your shape do you think is due to nature and how much due to your nurturing? Do any of your family members have similar body-shapes?

How do you feel?

Many people find it very difficult to answer this question, unless their feelings are roused to a very intense level. Feelings are processes that happen in both the brain and several other parts of the body at the same time. They occur when we are stimulated either by something happening outside ourselves or by something happening inside ourselves.

Emotions are our feelings when they move outwards, i.e. when we express our feelings. Anger, fear, love and grief are four of the most basic feelings that every human being has in common. All the other names we give to feelings of an emotional nature are variations of these four.

We also have other feelings we call hunger, thirst, pain, pleasure, cold, itchiness, loneliness, desire, and so on. Some people can connect feelings. For example "see" a tune, or "hear" a color. So how do *you* feel all these things?

Becoming more aware of how you feel

Throughout the next week try stopping every now and then to consider how you feel. Notice *where in your body you feel* any sensations, aches, movements or changes of temperature. Try describing exactly what you are feeling inside your body. You may discover that many different feelings give you the same sensations. Some feelings may never seem to quite get to the surface and leave you feeling aching or sick instead. These are usually blocked feelings. Going cold or shivery is another way in which feelings become blocked.

Do you have one kind of feeling more often than others? Do you tend to express an emotion that is opposite to what you really feel, such as getting angry when you feel like crying or vice versa? Do you avoid finding out what you feel? Are you repressing your feelings?

Completing your feeling diary

A list of feelings is shown (*opposite*), with space for you to add more of your own if you wish. Over a week make a note each day of which feelings you were aware of experiencing that day, by checking the names of the feelings on this list. Then mark the diagram on the page (*opposite*) to show *where* you felt these emotions in your body, adding any notes you wish, to make the description clear. THERE ARE NO RIGHT OR WRONG WAYS TO FEEL.

When you have completed your diary, you may like to consider whether or not one or other of your parents might have produced a similar feeling diary. Are your feelings natural or acquired?

MY PERSONAL FEELING DIARY FOR THE WEEK BEGINNING:

—/—/—	S	M	T	W	T	F	S
Anger							
Irritation							
Frustration							
Hostility							
Fear							
Nervousness							
Embarrassment							
Confusion							
Sadness							
Grief							
Hurt							
Loneliness							
Need							
Love							
Sexual desire							
Excitement							
Happiness							
Joy							
Pleasure							
Mischievousness							

**WHERE AND HOW I EXPERIENCED MY
FEELINGS**

©DIAGRAM

Is your life in your hands?

Palmists claim that our lives are marked by the lines on our hands. Certainly an experienced palmist can give an uncannily accurate character reading from a hand-print.

Regardless of whether you are right- or left-handed, your left hand is said to represent inherited talents, abilities, skills and natural desires and your right hand reveals how many of these characteristics you have developed so far in your life. Over the years the lines on the right hand change, sometimes quite radically, while those on the left develop but do not change. The greater the differences between your two hands, the more changes and adjustments you have made during your life.

It is not the intention here for you to analyze your hand-character in detail, but to compare your hands so that you can see what palmistry has to tell you about the difference nurturing has made to your given nature.

The three main lines of the hand

In the diagrams (*below*), lightly dotted lines show the average positions of the three most important and strongest lines on the hands. Conventionally they are called, in order from the fingers, the heart line, the head line and the life line. It is also a convention in palmistry to speak of the beginning and end of a line. In the diagrams the direction is shown by the positions of the arrowheads.

Marking the positions of your lines

Place your left hand next to the diagram of the left hand and note the positions of your heart, head and life lines compared with the average placings shown. Draw your lines onto the diagram lightly in pencil. It is very unlikely that they look like those in the diagram. Lines often bend, swing up or down and may be crossed or be placed nearer together or farther apart. Repeat the process for your right hand. You may have some little creases above or near the end of the heart line. Mark these in too. Finally color or mark your lines clearly.

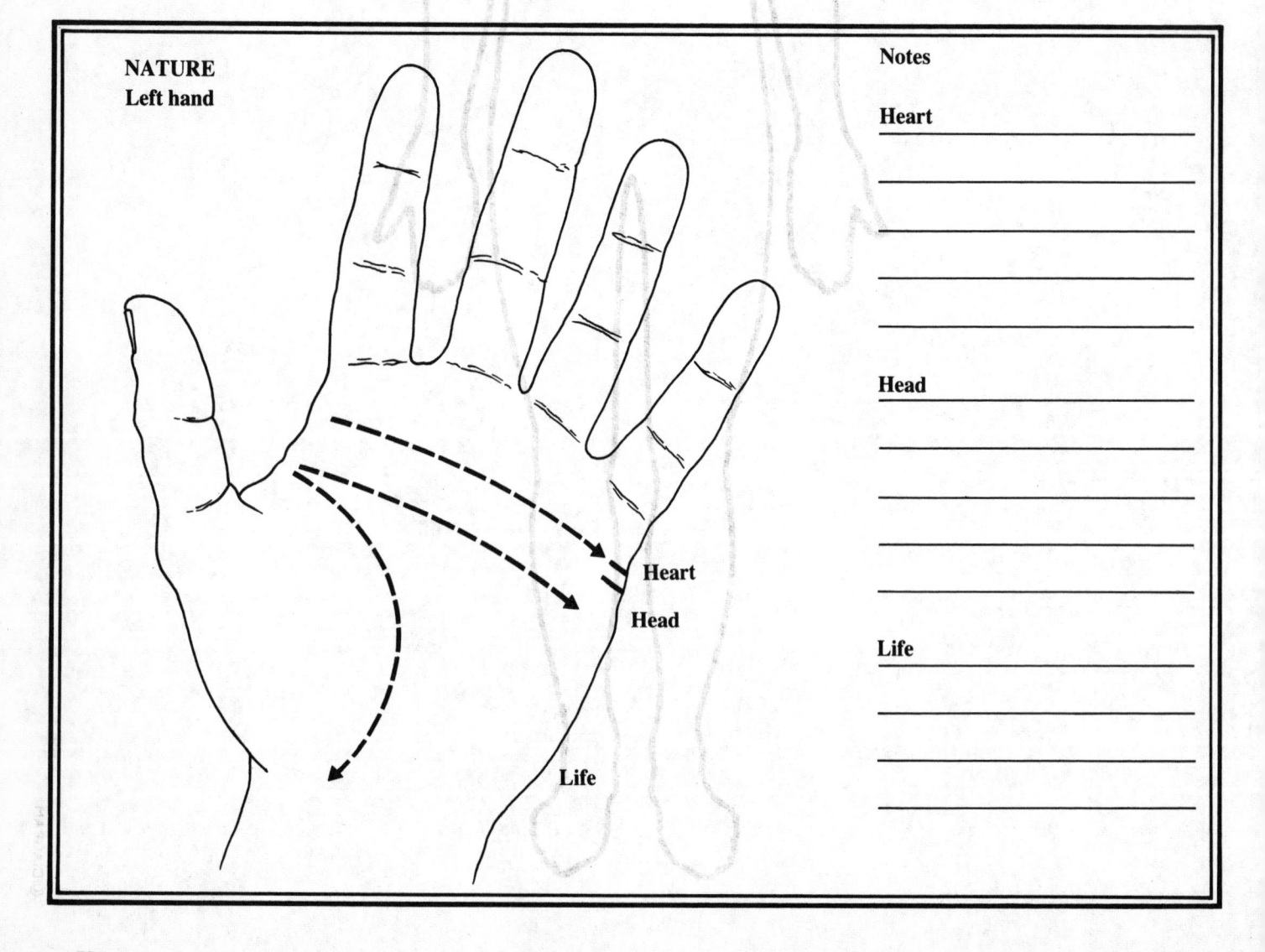

NATURE
Left hand

Heart

Head

Life

Notes

Heart
_____

_____

_____

_____

Head
_____

_____

_____

_____

Life
_____

_____

_____

The general meaning of the lines

Like cables carrying electricity, the more breaks, crosses and obstructions there are on your lines, the more problems it is likely you have encountered. Deep, continuous unbroken lines show a straightforward personality and life-style. To detect breaks a magnifying glass would be helpful.

Breaks show that something happened to interfere temporarily with the energy of that line. For example, illness, a change of career or a break away from an emotional attachment. If you have several loops, islands or fringes to your lines, these too indicate when you have had to adapt to changes of circumstances or when you have been unsure which direction to take. The little creases at the side of your hands are the number of important love affairs in your life; these may or may not be with people . . . they could be hobbies or interests. If you have creases on the left hand but none on the right, it would appear you have not yet become involved in the love of your life!

COMPARING YOUR HANDS

There is some space for you to make any notes you wish next to the diagrams.

1 Your heart lines Is the one on your right hand stronger, longer or clearer than the one on your left?
YES: You have developed your emotional strengths and are capable of getting your needs fulfilled.
NO: Your emotional life is under-developed as yet.

2 Your head lines Is the one on your right hand stronger, longer or clearer than the one on the left?
YES: You have made use of your intellectual abilities.
NO: You have not yet developed your intellect fully.

3 Your life lines Is the one on your right hand stronger, longer or clearer than the one on the left?
YES: You have taken advantage of your physical situation and built yourself a firm base.
NO: You have not yet found the right environment for yourself or developed your physical capacities.

4 Are your life and head lines tied together at their beginning on the left hand but separated on the right?
YES: You have overcome early family attachments.
NO: You have yet to emancipate yourself from your parental ties.

Notes

Heart
_____
_____
_____
_____
_____

Head
_____
_____
_____
_____

Life
_____
_____
_____
_____
_____

NURTURE
Right hand

Heart

Head

Life

©DIAGRAM

Do you care for yourself?

Caring is part of nurturing whatever you were given by nature. When you care for someone, you find out what they like and give them something they will enjoy. The same applies to caring for yourself. This section is not about what you ought or should do, but about discovering what gives you pleasure; how often do you give yourself pleasure and where did you learn or inherit these activities?

It may be that you deny yourself some simple caring activities because you were taught too many "oughts" and "shoulds." Perhaps you learned you weren't worthy of attention, or that giving yourself attention was selfish.

If it is good to be kind to other people, it is surely good to be kind to yourself?

Some simple caring activities

Not all of these will be your particular pleasures so some space has been left for you to add some personal caring activities of your own choosing. Go down the list and answer YES or NO to the question: *Do you enjoy doing this?* Then try to remember if your mother and your father enjoyed any of these things.

Caring by nature or nurture?

It is surprising how many kind, caring people are very hard on themselves and vice versa! When you have answered YES or NO in the first three columns, you may find it interesting to compare your attitude with the attitudes of your parents. In the column headed My notes..., write any comments that occur to you. *The following questions are worth exploring:*

1 Did either or both your parents teach you by example or by encouragement to enjoy the simple pleasures of caring for yourself?
2 Did either or both your parents make any of these activities into a duty or a chore?
3 Were you put under pressure to conform to a particular family standard in these things?
4 Were these kind of activities either ignored or done only in private in your family?
5 Do you feel bad about not caring for yourself?
6 Do you really know what you like and enjoy most?
7 Do you give yourself this kind of realistic caring, without being a "shouldnik?"
8 Do you know the difference, for you, between extreme self-neglect and extreme self-indulgence?
9 What else would you like to do to give yourself pleasure?
10 If it doesn't harm anyone else, are you going to improve caring for yourself?

Some simple caring activities
Having a bath or shower at leisure for relaxation.
Washing, combing or setting hair or having it done.
Shaving or grooming beard.
Using make-up or perfumes including after-shave.
Washing and massaging your feet and talking to them.
Giving yourself a massage in comfort with music.
Giving someone you love a gentle massage.
Playing at a sport rather than competing.
Singing, humming or whistling around the house.
Laughing for real, until you wobble all over.
Wearing clothes that feel nice on your skin.
Wearing casual, loose, colorful clothes.
Wearing formal, dressed-up clothes.
Being held close and relaxed without sex.
Sitting watching the world go by, quietly alone.
Going for a walk without a reason.
Letting the wind blow through your hair.
Inventing things, painting, writing, playing.
Cooking without using a cookbook.
Smelling new cloth, new paper, flowers.
Imagining things in the clouds or in a fire.
Listening to silences outside.

Do you enjoy doing this?	Did your mother enjoy doing this?	Did your father enjoy doing this?	My notes on caring for myself

©DIAGRAM

61

Are you eating comfortably?

Are you a happy eater, a sweet-tooth, a nibbler or one of the estimated 80% of the population who suffer from the symptoms of low blood-sugar, a condition that results from eating too many foods containing sugar? Here are two ways to find out. First you will need to keep records for a 10-day period, starting on a Friday. The eating inventory is on this page and the low blood-sugar indicator on the opposite page. After 10 days you can then complete your eating profile and assess if you are likely to suffer from low blood-sugar. There are also some guidelines to help you balance your blood-sugar.

How to complete your eating inventory
Each day put one mark in the columns for every helping of each kind of food you eat during that day. The foods are grouped in boxes **A** to **F**, so choose the correct box for foods that are not listed. For example, yogurt is a milk product and goes in box **A**. A ¼ pint of milk counts as one mark. In general, the milk in four cups of tea or coffee counts as one mark. For sandwiches, count the filling as one and two slices of bread as one mark.

What can your eating profile tell you?
Fill in your total marks from your eating inventory under the appropriate letters. The shaded areas show the average scores for a comfortable eater. If you have a fairly sedentary or a very active lifestyle, you can allow five marks either way; higher scores for the more active, lower ones for the less active. Now draw a line across each column for your scores. Columns **A, B** and **C** will show if you have a happy nutritional balance between the three main categories of food. Scores of more than five marks above or below the average will tell you if your nutrition is unbalanced. Columns **D** and **E** will tell you how much of a sweet tooth you have. Scores of more than five marks above these averages are a warning that your sugar intake is too high, so check your low blood-sugar ratings. Column **F** is for nibblers. Any score above this line is a warning, especially if you nibble sweet things, chips and packaged foods. If your scores for **C, D** or **E** shoot off the top of the profile you are probably overweight or skinny but frantically active and prone to stress-related diseases. In general, it is wise to eat a good breakfast, including items from columns **A** and **B.** Then you are less likely to need excesses of **C, D** and **E** later in the day.

YOUR EATING INVENTORY

	Fri	Sat	Sun	Mon	Tues	Wed	Thurs	Fri	Sat	Sun	Total
A Meat, poultry, offal, fish, seafood, cheese, nuts, lentils, seeds, eggs, milk.											
B Salads, fresh and dried fruit, juices, vegetables.											
C Potatoes, two slices bread, pasta, muesli, cereals, oats, baked beans, chips, sauces, batter, french fries.											
D Pastries, puddings, cake, biscuits, toffees(3), ice-cream, chocolate (small bar), tinned fruit, desserts, cream, custard, trifle, jelly.											
E Mark one for every time you add a teaspoon of sugar.											
F Mark one for every time you nibble between meals.											

YOUR EATING PROFILE

A		
B		
C		
D		
E		
F		

Your marks	5	10	15	20	25	30	35	40	45	50

Marks per helping for each kind of food

LOW BLOOD-SUGAR INDICATOR

Here are some of the symptoms associated with low blood-sugar. Each day, during the 10-day period, mark once for any of these that occur with a maximum 10 marks against each symptom. Only do this if you are in otherwise normal good health. Count up all the marks and add any of the applicable items at the bottom. Then read the section on low blood-sugar.

Symptoms	Number of symptoms during 10 day period	Total
Couldn't sleep properly.		
Slow start this morning.		
Felt shaky when hungry.		
Gums felt sore.		
Vision was blurred.		
Dropped something today.		
Bumped into something.		
Forgot something today.		
Had cramps or twitches.		
Hands or feet were cold.		
Couldn't concentrate.		
Couldn't make decisions.		
Had a headache.		
Had indigestion.		

Symptoms		
Was moody or irritable.		
Drowsy after lunch.		
Suddenly sweaty or hot.		
Heart sometimes raced.		
Felt stressed/depressed.		
Felt bored/hopeless.		
Craved sweet things.		
Couldn't wait to eat.		
Unhappy/sad/tearful.		
Drank 8+ teas/coffees.		
Drank alcohol.		
Add 10 marks if you have any kind of allergy.		
Add 10 marks if your sex drive is lower than usual.		

Total Marks:

Do you suffer from low blood-sugar symptoms?
0–5 marks
Your blood-sugar is balanced and you are probably a healthy, happy person.
5–40 marks
Any adjustment to your eating should be easy and the symptoms should vanish quickly.
40–80 marks
If these symptoms are regular, it may be useful to adjust your sugar intake and check again in a few weeks' time. If you are on a reducing diet, try slow-release carbohydrates from box **C** instead of quick-release sugars from box **D**. You are likely to suffer from blood-sugar imbalance.

80–100 marks
Consult your eating profile and adjust your nutrition balance. Check over two or three months and if symptoms don't diminish, see your doctor.
120+ marks
You probably have severe and frequent blood-sugar imbalances, especially if you are aware that you have had many of the symptoms over a long period of time. Consult your doctor and get your eating pattern properly balanced.

©DIAGRAM

How fit are you?

Fitness has three essential components: strength, suppleness, and stamina. Strength means that your muscles can exert force as and when it is needed, e.g. when you need to carry something heavy. Suppleness means that your body is flexible, that you can bend, twist, and stretch easily and without strain. Stamina means that you can keep going without becoming exhausted and breathless, i.e. that your heart and lungs are working effectively and efficiently. All these aspects of fitness are included in the tests on these pages: if you score "good" or better on each and every test, you can consider yourself fit. Remember that some of the tests are very strenuous. If you find yourself in any sort of physical distress (especially if you have any chest pain or extreme difficulty in breathing), stop immediately.

SUPPLENESS TESTS

1 Back pull
Stand upright or sit cross-legged on the floor. Place your right hand behind your back and take your left arm back over your shoulder to meet it. Try to clasp your hands together as shown. Reverse your arms and repeat.

2 Spinal curl
Kneel on all fours on the floor with your hands in line with your shoulders. Bend your head down and your left knee up, trying to touch your forehead to your knee, as shown. Repeat with your right leg.

3 Toe touch
Sit upright on the floor with your legs straight out in front of you, heels about 5in apart (a). Mark the line between your heels with a fixed piece of tape. Place a yardstick on the floor between your legs, with the 15in mark at the near edge of the tape, and the lower measurements towards you (b). Without jerking, reach forward with both hands as far as you can (c), touching your fingers to the yardstick. Note the measurement you touch. Repeat three times and take your best score.

4 Toe flex
Sit on a hard chair with your knees together. Keeping your heels on the floor, raise your big toes as high off the ground as you can. Measure the distance between the top of your toes and the floor.

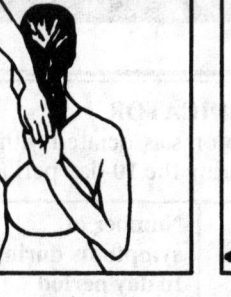
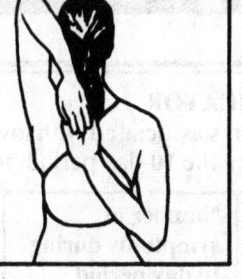
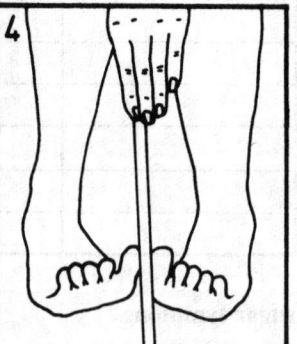
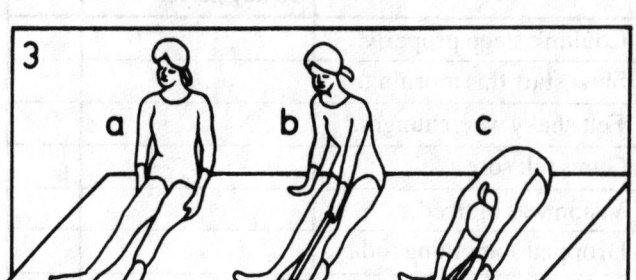

Scoring

1	
Poor	Fingers do not meet
Fair	Fingers just touch
Good	Able to clasp fingers together

3	Men	Women
Average	14–19in	16–20in
Good	20–21in	21–23in
Very good	22–23in	24–27in

2	
Poor	Forehead and knee are 4in or more apart
Fair	Forehead almost touches knee
Good	Forehead touches knee

4	
Poor	Less than 4in
Fair	4–5in
Good	5–6in

STRENGTH TESTS

1 Sit ups
Lie on your back with your legs together, knees slightly bent, hands clasped behind your neck (a). Tuck your feet under a heavy piece of furniture if you find it helpful. Keeping your feet flat on the floor, sit up and lean forward until your head touches your knees (b). Lower yourself to the starting position and repeat as many times as you can.

2 Push ups
Men
Lie face down on the floor with your legs straight and together, toes tucked under, hands palms down and under your shoulders (a). Keeping your body and legs straight, raise your body by straightening your arms (b). Lower your body to the ground and repeat as many times as possible.

Women
Women should test themselves with modified push ups at an angle of 45°, using a table wedged against a wall for support (c). Your hands should be shoulder width apart, and you should keep your body straight as you raise it by straightening your arms (d).

3 Knee bends
Stand with your feet together about 18in from a wall. Lean back so that your back is braced against the wall, hands by your sides (a). Keeping your feet flat on the floor, slide your back down the wall until your thighs are parallel with the ground (b). Push yourself back up the wall and repeat as many times as possible.

Scoring

1	Men	Women
Average	20	10
Good	30	15
Very good	50	25

2	Men	Women
Average	10	10
Good	20	15
Very good	30	20

3	Men	Women
Average	15	10
Good	25	20
Very good	35	30

STAMINA TEST

Step test
Stand facing an 8in high solid box or bench (a). Put your left foot on the bench (b), bring your right foot up alongside it (c), step down with your left foot (d), and step down with your right foot (e). This sequence counts as one step.

To complete the test, step on and off the bench for three minutes at a rate of 24 steps per minute. After you have completed the exercise, wait for exactly one minute and then take your pulse.

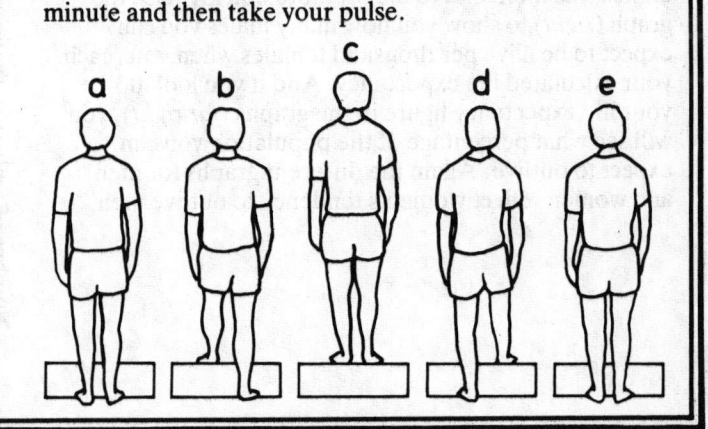

Scoring

	Pulse Rate	
	Men	**Women**
Average	80–89	86–94
Good	68–79	76–85
Very good	Below 68	Below 76

©DIAGRAM

65

How long could you live?

According to the statistics, the best recipe for a long life is to avoid such life-shortening activities as overeating and smoking while having been very careful in your choice of grandparents. Provided that you are over 20 and in reasonable health, this test will show you how long the actuaries and other life insurance experts expect you to live. Answer YES or NO to each question.

Scoring

Only YES answers score. Start with a life expectancy of 72 and then, for each question to which you answered YES, add or subtract the number of years allocated in the list (*below*). For example, if you answered YES to questions 1, 4, 8, 10, 15, 19, and 22, your life expectancy would be $72 - 3 + 3 - 2 - 3 - 3 + 1 + 3 = 68$ years.

1 Subtract 3 years	**19** Add 1 year
2 Add 4 years	**20** Subtract 2 years
3 Add 2 years	**21** Subtract 3 years
4 Add 3 years	**22** Add 3 years
5 Add 4 years	**23** Subtract 1 year
6 Add 5 years	**24** Subtract 8 years
7 Add 3 years	**25** Subtract 6 years
8 Subtract 2 years	**26** Subtract 3 years
9 Add 2 years	**27** Subtract 1 year
10 Subtract 3 years	**28** Subtract 8 years
11 Add 5 years	**29** Subtract 4 years
12 Add 1 year	**30** Subtract 2 years
13 Add 2 years	**31** Add 2 years
14 Subtract 2 years	**32** Add 2 years
15 Subtract 3 years	**33** Add 6 years
16 Add 3 years	**34** Subtract 4 years
17 Add 2 years	**35** Subtract 3 years
18 Subtract 4 years	

	YES	NO
1 Are you male?		
2 Are you female?		
3 Is your age between 30 and 40?		
4 Is your age between 40 and 50?		
5 Is your age between 50 and 70?		
6 Is your age over 70?		
7 If you are aged over 65, are you still working?		
8 Do you live in an urban area with a population of two million or more?		
9 Do you live in a town or rural area with a population of 10,000 or less?		
10 Do you live alone?		
11 Do you live with a partner or a close friend?		
12 Do you have a college or university degree?		
13 Do you have a postgraduate degree or similar professional qualification?		
14 Is your income greater than that of 95% of the population?		

MALE AND FEMALE LIFE EXPECTANCY

If you live to reach your calculated life expectancy, how many of your contemporaries can you expect to outlive, and what will be the ratio between the sexes? Although about 1050 male babies are born for every 1000 female babies, the men tend to die off more quickly. Use the graph (*right*) to show you how many males you can expect to be alive per thousand females when you reach your calculated life expectancy. And if you look up your life expectancy figure in the graphs (*far right*), you will see what percentage of the population you can expect to outlive. Again the different graphs for men and women reflect women's tendency to outlive men.

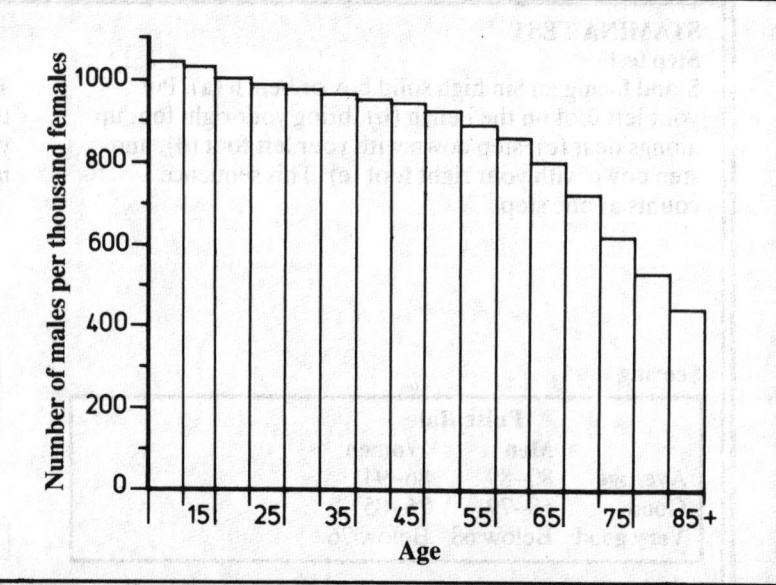

66

	YES	NO
15 Do you work in a mainly sedentary occupation?		
16 Does your work involve you in strenuous physical activity?		
17 Do you exercise strenuously for at least 20–30 minutes at least three times a week?		
18 On average, do you sleep for more than ten hours in any 24-hour period?		
19 Are you happy?		
20 Are you unhappy?		
21 Are you quick-tempered and aggressive?		
22 Are you relaxed and easy-tempered?		
23 Have you had any sort of traffic accident (major or minor) in the last twelve months?		
24 Do you smoke more than 40 cigarettes a day?		
25 Do you smoke 20–40 cigarettes a day?		
26 Do you smoke 1–10 cigarettes a day?		
27 Do you drink ¼ bottle of spirits a day or its equivalent in other types of alcohol?		

	YES	NO
28 Are you more than 50lb overweight?		
29 Are you 30–50lb overweight?		
30 Are you 10–30lb overweight?		
31 Do you have an annual medical checkup?		
32 Did any of your grandparents live to be 85 or older?		
33 Did all four of your grandparents live to be 80 or older?		
34 Did either of your parents die of a stroke or a heart attack before they reached 50?		
35 Did either of your parents or any of your brothers or sisters develop cancer or a heart condition before they were 50?		

Write here your life expectancy ....

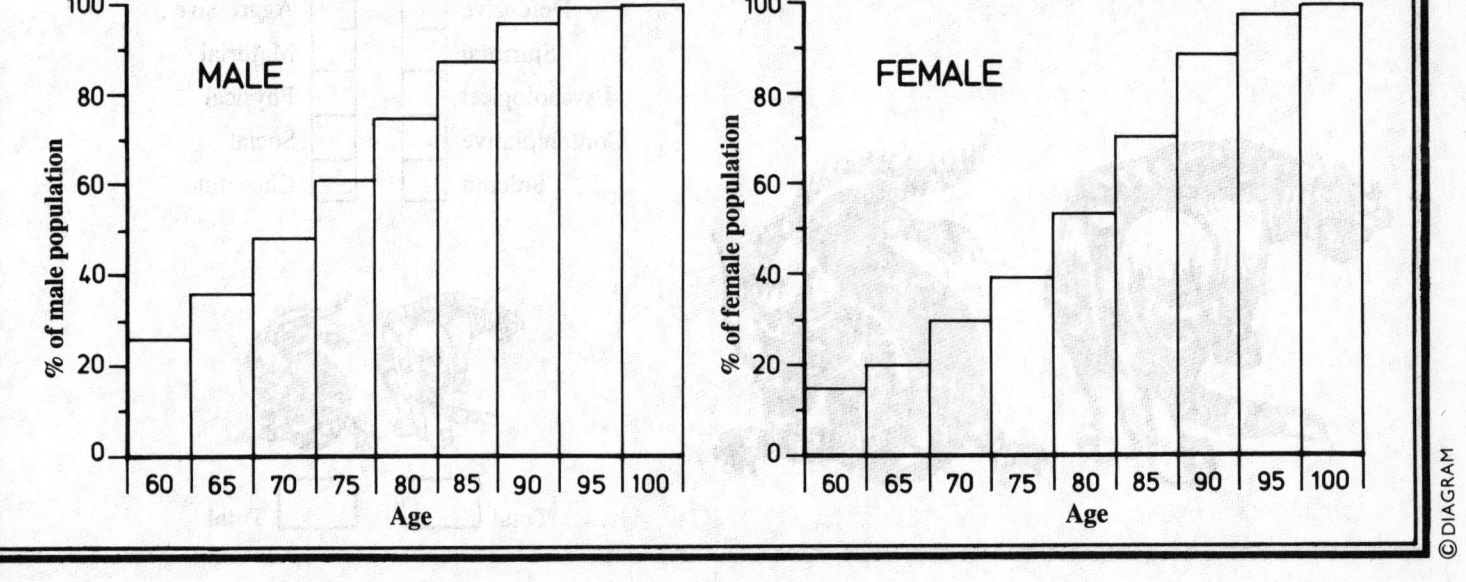

Are you *yin* or *yang*?

Do you have a balanced personality, or is one aspect of it stronger than the others – and why? And does your body affect your personality, or is it your personality that affects your body? Philosophers and scientists have been trying to answer these questions since ancient times. Today we know that the left and right halves of our brains work in independent but complementary ways (see pages 72–73); in medieval times they considered the balance between different fluids in the body (see pages 70–71.) But the earliest theories come from the Far East, and are still in practical use today, forming the basis for acupuncture, shiatsu, and other healing arts. In oriental philosophy, everything can be attributed to two opposing but complementary principles called *yin* ("the dark side of the hill") and *yang* ("the sunny side of the hill"). The traditional diagram (*right*) called the *T'ai Chi T'u* ("diagram of the Supreme Principle") shows the relationship between them. The black area represents *yin*, and the white *yang*: as one grows larger, the other grows smaller but is never completely replaced. They combine in different proportions to produce different results, different personalities, different physical natures. The contrasting small circles indicate that nothing is ever entirely *yin* or entirely *yang* – each always contains something of the other. Nor does anything ever contain exactly equal amounts of both – one or other is always in excess.

Yin and *yang* are considered to be different but equal, and it is the balance between them that is important. This balance is a dynamic balance that keeps subtly shifting and altering (perfect equilibrium is held to lead to stagnation). Everyone should have something of both in their makeup, but there should never be too great an excess of either one. Imbalance is the suspected root of all physical and psychological illnesses. One suggested way of modifying such an imbalance is by changing your eating patterns: if you need more *yin*, you simply eat more *yin* foods, and if you need more *yang*, you eat more *yang* foods.

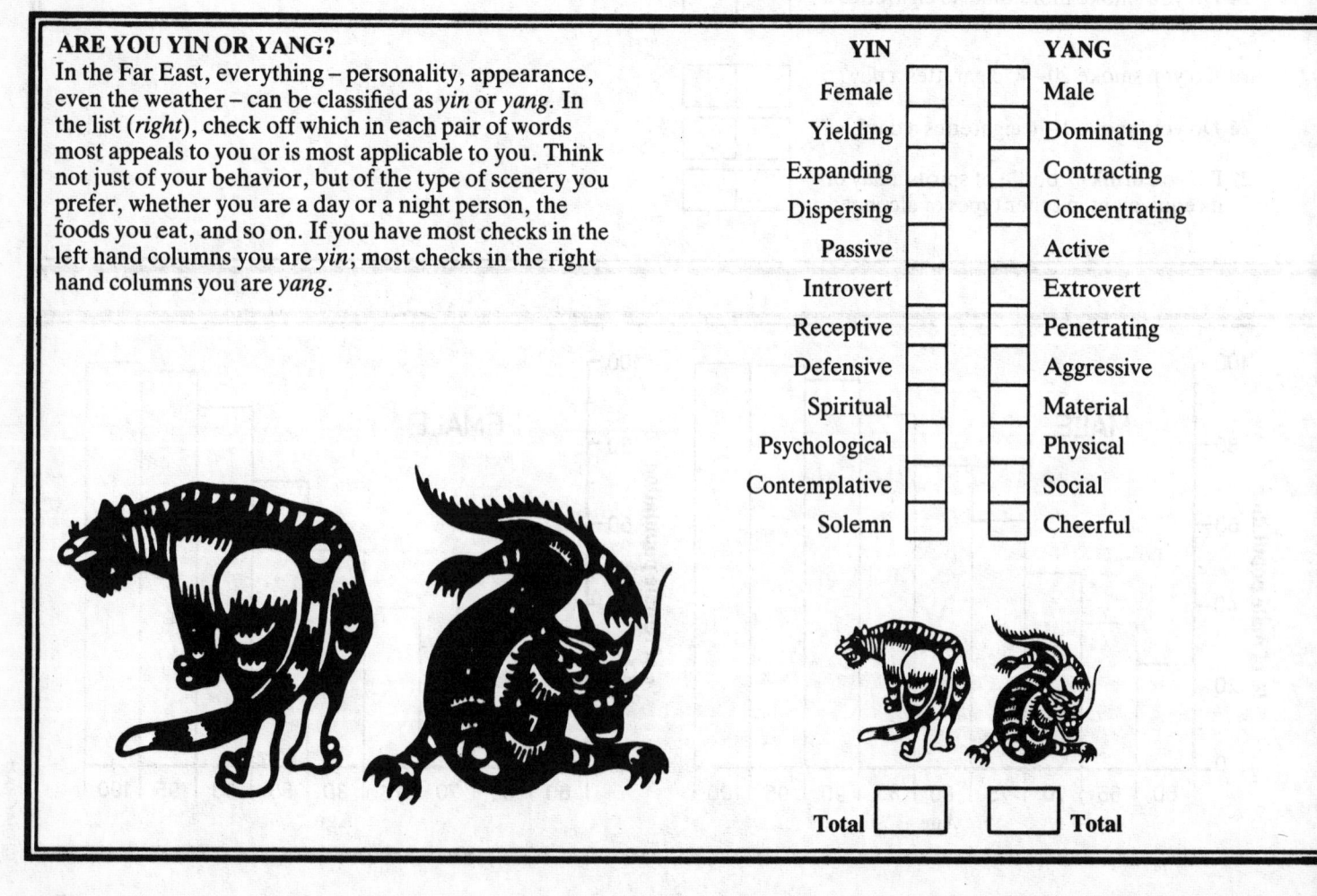

ARE YOU YIN OR YANG?
In the Far East, everything – personality, appearance, even the weather – can be classified as *yin* or *yang*. In the list (*right*), check off which in each pair of words most appeals to you or is most applicable to you. Think not just of your behavior, but of the type of scenery you prefer, whether you are a day or a night person, the foods you eat, and so on. If you have most checks in the left hand columns you are *yin*; most checks in the right hand columns you are *yang*.

YIN			YANG
Female			Male
Yielding			Dominating
Expanding			Contracting
Dispersing			Concentrating
Passive			Active
Introvert			Extrovert
Receptive			Penetrating
Defensive			Aggressive
Spiritual			Material
Psychological			Physical
Contemplative			Social
Solemn			Cheerful
Total			**Total**

Tiger and Dragon
The T'ai Chi T'u is shown (*above*). The White Tiger (*left*) is the symbol of the *yin* principle; the Green Dragon (*right*) is the symbol of the *yang* principle.

YIN		YANG		YIN		YANG		YIN FOODS
Flexible	☐	Inflexible	☐	Moon	☐	Sun	☐	Alcohol
Calm	☐	Movement	☐	Night	☐	Day	☐	Sugar
Universal	☐	Specific	☐	Winter	☐	Summer	☐	Spices
Future	☐	Past	☐	Cold	☐	Heat	☐	Fruit
Negative	☐	Positive	☐	Humidity	☐	Drought	☐	Milk
Life-sustaining	☐	Killing	☐	Valleys	☐	Mountains	☐	All liquids
Large	☐	Small	☐	Earth	☐	Sky	☐	Green, blue, and purple vegetables
Plump	☐	Slender	☐	Water	☐	Fire	☐	
Resilient	☐	Delicate	☐	Vegetable	☐	Animal	☐	
Muscular	☐	Slight	☐	Wet	☐	Dry	☐	
Short	☐	Tall	☐	Low	☐	High	☐	YANG FOODS
Soft	☐	Hard	☐	Slow	☐	Fast	☐	Meat
Dark	☐	Light	☐	Hollow	☐	Solid	☐	Poultry
								Cheese
								Eggs
								Caviar
								Salt
								Fish
Total ☐		☐ Total		Total ☐		☐ Total		Red, orange, and yellow vegetables

© DIAGRAM

69

Are you in a good humor?

The word "humor" originally meant simply "moisture" or "fluid." The ancient Greek physician and philosopher Hippocrates suggested that the human body contained four basic fluids – blood, phlegm, yellow bile, and black bile. The body of a healthy person was thought to contain a well-proportioned mixture of all four humors. Too much of any one humor was thought to cause illness: a cure could be found by diagnosing which humor was in excess and then reducing the amount of it in the body.

Another Greek physician, Galen, extended Hippocrates' theory to cover personalities. Galen suggested that there were four basic "temperaments" or personality types – the sanguine, the phlegmatic, the choleric, and the melancholic – each produced by an excess of one of the humors. The sanguine temperament was produced by an excess of blood; the phlegmatic by an excess of phlegm; the choleric by an excess of yellow bile; and the melancholic by an excess of black bile.

The humoral theory of personality remained popular until the seventeenth century. In medieval times each humor also became associated with one of the four astrological elements (air, water, fire, earth) and its related signs of the zodiac, and with particular "seasonal states" (cold, hot, dry, and wet). External physical characteristics were also associated with the four temperaments: for example, it was thought that you could tell a man's humor by the color of his complexion. The engraving (*right*) dates from the sixteenth century. Listed around it are the details of the four classical temperaments – which one most closely matches your personality?

THE CLASSICAL TEMPERAMENTS

THE PHLEGMATIC TEMPERAMENT
Humor Phlegm
Element Water
Signs of the zodiac Cancer, Scorpio, Pisces
Seasonal state Cold, wet
Complexion Pale
Character Slow, strong, calm, undemonstrative, lazy, stolid

THE SANGUINE TEMPERAMENT
Humor Blood
Element Air
Signs of the zodiac Gemini, Libra, Aquarius
Seasonal state Hot, wet
Complexion Ruddy
Character Quick, weak, optimistic, cheerful, enthusiastic, changeable

THE MELANCHOLIC TEMPERAMENT
Humor Black bile
Element Earth
Signs of the zodiac Taurus, Virgo, Capricorn
Seasonal state Cold, dry
Complexion Dark
Character Depressed, weak, pessimistic, sour, sad, slow to react

THE CHOLERIC TEMPERAMENT
Humor Yellow bile
Element Fire
Signs of the zodiac Aries, Leo, Sagittarius
Seasonal state Hot, dry
Complexion Sallow
Character Excitable, strong, hot-tempered, jaundiced, proud, quick to react

THE MODERN TEMPERAMENTS

Echoes of the four classical temperaments can still be found in our language – we talk about people being good- or ill-humored, or refer to someone as phlegmatic. The psychiatrist Hans J. Eysenck has used the names of the four classical temperaments to describe some modern personality types. In Eysenck's terms, the sanguine person is a stable extrovert; the phlegmatic person a stable introvert; the choleric person an unstable extrovert; and the melancholic person an unstable introvert.

Eysenck's research has shown that these personality types predominate in certain areas of work and social behavior. For example, successful sportsmen and women and army commandos tend to have sanguine personalities; scientists, mathematicians, and businessmen and women tend to have phlegmatic personalities; criminals tend to have choleric personalities; and people whose behavior is neurotic tend to have melancholic personalities.

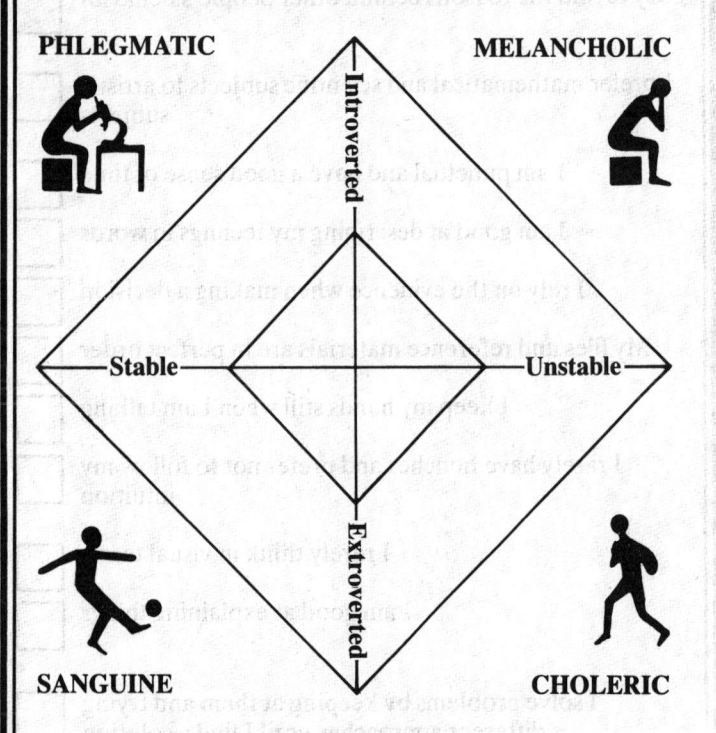

PHLEGMATIC   **MELANCHOLIC**

Introverted

Stable   Unstable

Extroverted

SANGUINE   **CHOLERIC**

To discover your modern temperament, choose one word or phrase from each group of four listed (*right*) that most closely applies to your personality. Check either **a, b, c,** or **d** for each group. You may not choose more than one word or phrase from each group. Then total the scores in each column.

Scoring
If your highest score is in:
column **A**, you probably have a melancholic personality;
column **B**, you probably have a phlegmatic personality;
column **C**, you probably have a sanguine personality;
column **D**, you probably have a choleric personality;

A	B	C	D	
				a Moody
				b Calm
				c Easy-going
				d Aggressive
				a Anxious
				b Even-tempered
				c Lively
				d Touchy
				a Rigid
				b Controlled
				c In charge
				d Changeable
				a Sober
				b Reliable
				c Outgoing
				d Restless
				a Pessimistic
				b Careful
				c Carefree
				d Optimistic
				a Reserved
				b Thoughtful
				c Responsive
				d Impulsive
				a Unsociable
				b Passive
				c Sociable
				d Active
				a Quiet
				b Peaceful
				c Talkative
				d Excitable
				Totals

©DIAGRAM

Are you of two minds?

"I'm of two minds about it." We've probably all said that at one time or another without realizing that in some ways it is literally true. Researchers have discovered that the two halves of the human brain – the left hemisphere and the right hemisphere – work in very different ways. They can work together, each hemisphere contributing its own special abilities to the task in hand, or they can work separately, or they can even work in opposition to each other. As the left hemisphere controls the right hand, and the right hemisphere controls the left hand, there may well be times when the right hand does not know what the left hand is doing. In most people one hemisphere tends to dominate the other: the test (*right*) will show you whether you are right-brained or left-brained. Try to do it before you read the details about the different modes of thinking used by the two hemispheres, or you may affect your results.

To find out whether you are a left brain or a right brain thinker, read through the pairs of statements (*right*). Check the statement from each pair that is most typical of you. If your score in the left hand columns is much higher than your score in the right hand column, then you are a left brain thinker. If your score in the right hand column is much the higher, then you are a right brain thinker. If the scores are roughly equal then neither hemisphere predominates in your case.

Right-brained or left-brained
If you are a predominantly right brain thinker, you tend to be intuitive and think in pictures. You are probably artistic or musical. You see things as a whole, and your leaps of insight enable you to create new combinations of ideas.
If you are a predominantly left brain thinker, you tend to be logical and to verbalize your ideas. You are probably skilled with numbers or with words. You analyze things, and arrive at new ideas by working through the information you have and reaching a rational conclusion.

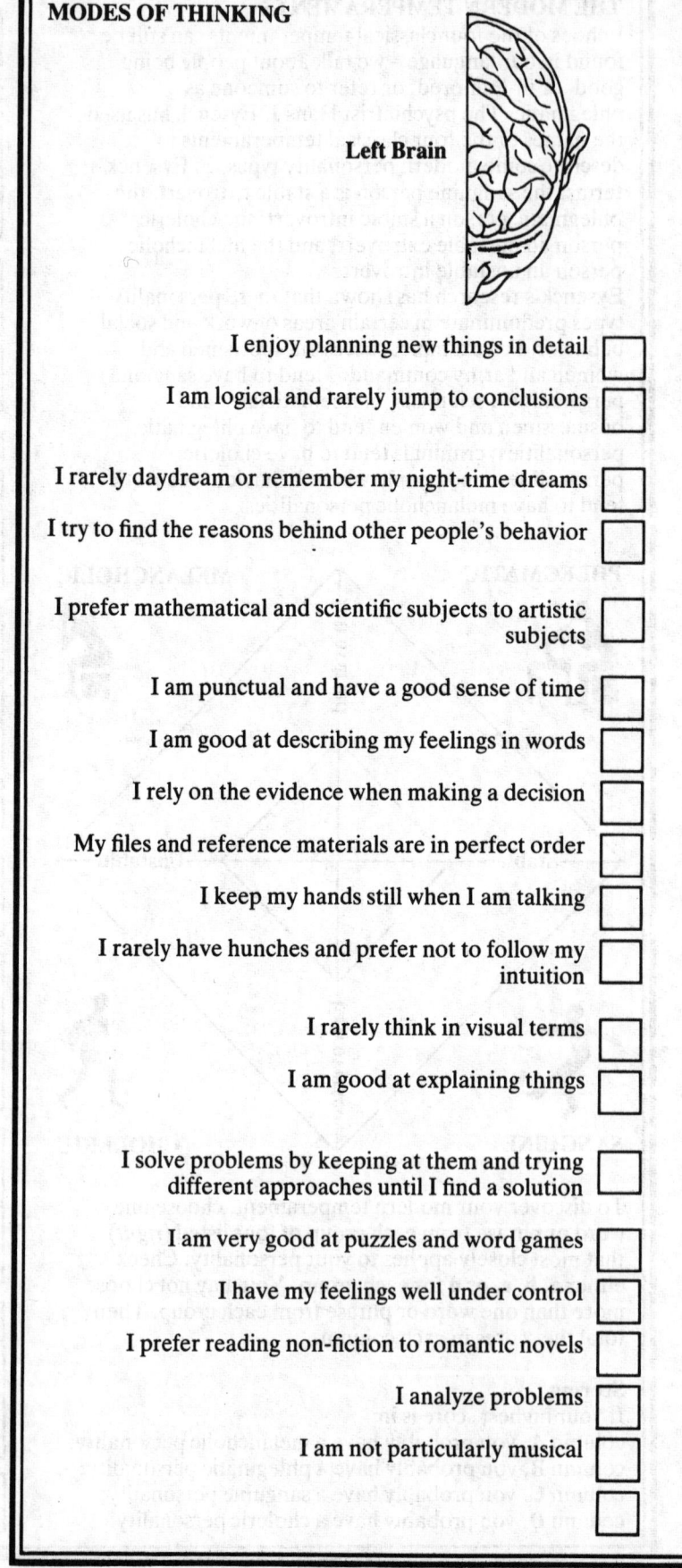

MODES OF THINKING

Left Brain

I enjoy planning new things in detail ☐

I am logical and rarely jump to conclusions ☐

I rarely daydream or remember my night-time dreams ☐

I try to find the reasons behind other people's behavior ☐

I prefer mathematical and scientific subjects to artistic subjects ☐

I am punctual and have a good sense of time ☐

I am good at describing my feelings in words ☐

I rely on the evidence when making a decision ☐

My files and reference materials are in perfect order ☐

I keep my hands still when I am talking ☐

I rarely have hunches and prefer not to follow my intuition ☐

I rarely think in visual terms ☐

I am good at explaining things ☐

I solve problems by keeping at them and trying different approaches until I find a solution ☐

I am very good at puzzles and word games ☐

I have my feelings well under control ☐

I prefer reading non-fiction to romantic novels ☐

I analyze problems ☐

I am not particularly musical ☐

☐

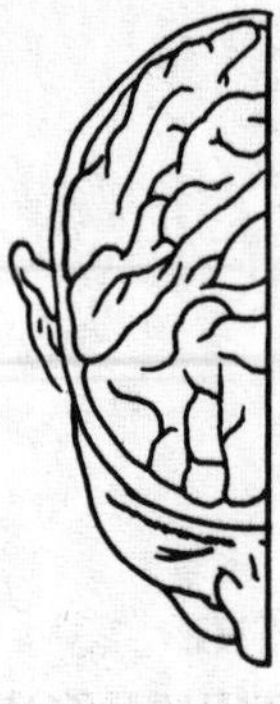

Right Brain

☐ I enjoy doing new things on the spur of the moment

☐ I can reach conclusions without following all the details of an argument

☐ My dreams are very vivid and I often daydream

☐ I can rarely see the motivation behind other people's behavior

☐ I prefer artistic subjects to mathematical and scientific subjects

☐ I am rarely punctual and have a poor sense of time

☐ I find it difficult to put my feelings into words

☐ I rely on my feelings when making a decision

☐ I rarely bother to file things

☐ I gesture a lot when I am talking

☐ I rely on my instincts and follow my hunches

☐ My impressions and thoughts often appear as pictures

☐ I can understand what someone means without being able to explain it

☐ I solve problems by putting them to the back of my mind and waiting for a solution to come up

☐ I do not enjoy puzzles and word games

☐ I let my feelings show

☐ I prefer reading romantic novels to non-fiction

☐ I deal with a problem as a whole

☐ I am very fond of music

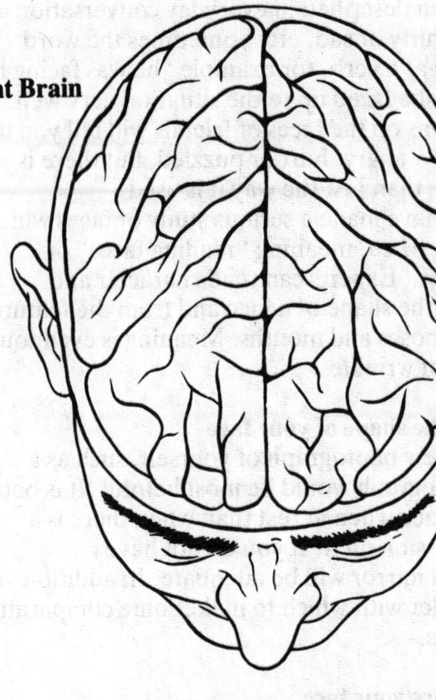

☐

Right Brain   **Left Brain**

MODES OF THINKING

Left brain	Right brain
Deals with verbal ideas and uses words to describe things	Aware of things but does not connect them with words – uses gestures or pictures in description
Analyzes: breaks things down into their constituent parts	Synthesizes: puts parts together to form a whole
Uses symbols to represent things	See things as they are
Abstracts relevant pieces of information from the whole	Makes analogies and sees likenesses
Good sense of time	Poor sense of time
Relies on facts and reasoning	Relies on intuition and instinct
Good sense of number	Poor sense of number
Poor sense of spatial relationships	Good sense of spatial relationships
Logical	Intuitive
Thinks linearly – one idea follows another	Thinks holistically – sees patterns linking ideas as a whole

© DIAGRAM

73

Which shape is your face?

Faces are often described in everyday conversation as kind, open, shifty or sad, etc. Sometimes the word "face" is used as a verb, for example "he was facing the window" or "she faced up to the situation very well." The expressions on the faces of friends will tell you if they are happy, angry, hurt or puzzled, but there is more to a face than just the way it is used.

The Chinese have made a serious study of faces which is called *Siang Mien,* meaning "reading faces" or "physiognomy." Experts can read character and attitude from the shape of a face and from the features such as eyes, noses and mouths. Meaning is even found in the tiniest of wrinkles.

How to read the shape of your face

A full front view photograph of yourself, such as a passport photograph would be most helpful. It is better to read your face when at rest than when there is a fleeting expression on it. If you do not have a photograph, a mirror will be adequate. In addition you will need a ruler with which to make some comparative measurements.

How to measure your face

Measurements are only needed for comparison; the actual sizes are not needed. If using a photograph, draw dotted lines across it as shown in diagrams **A** and **B**. If using a mirror, stand very still and, with one eye closed, mark the dotted lines on the mirror with a water-based felt-tip pen so you can clean it later. Enter your measurements in the spaces provided (*below*).

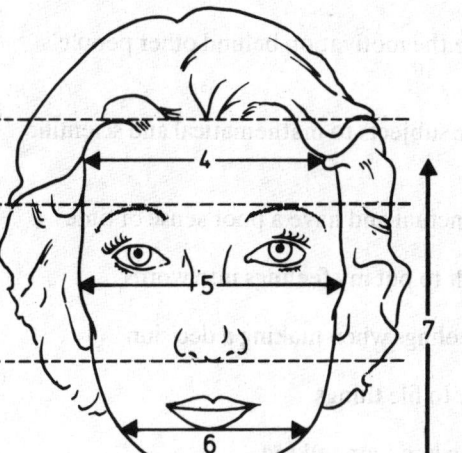

A THE THREE ZONES
1 Forehead zone
2 Cheek zone
3 Jaw zone

B THE THREE WIDTHS
4 Forehead width
5 Cheekbone width
6 Jawbone width
7 Face length

A THE THREE ZONES

Forehead zone is the length from your hairline to the top of your eyebrows.

Cheek zone is the length from your eyebrows down to the tip of your nose.

Jaw zone is the length from the tip of your nose to the edge of your chin.

B THE THREE WIDTHS

Forehead width is the distance from one temple to the other across the middle of the forehead zone.

Cheekbone width is the distance from one cheekbone to the other across the middle of the cheek zone.

Jawbone width is the distance across your jaw in the middle of the jaw zone.

Face length is from the middle of the forehead zone to the bottom of the jaw zone.

YOUR THREE ZONES AND YOUR FACE SHAPE

First compare the lengths of the three zones, and read the interpretations (*below*). The seven main face shapes are illustrated on the next few pages, beginning with the Iron face (*opposite*). Read each one to discover which is yours. You may like to measure the faces of your friends too.

Forehead zone . . . learning.
If longest: logical, a good memory; decisive.
If shortest: disorganized thinking; forgetful; passive and dreamy.

Cheek zone . . . development.
If longest: persistent; control of money and emotional problems.
If shortest: gives-up easily; lack of control.

Jaw zone . . . maturity.
If longest: wisdom and success; self-reliance.
If shortest: maturity is delayed; tendency to rely on others.

The tree and wall faces

The Iron Face

The iron face of Sir Winston Churchill

The iron face is square in shape.
The three widths are about equal and are the same as the length of the face.

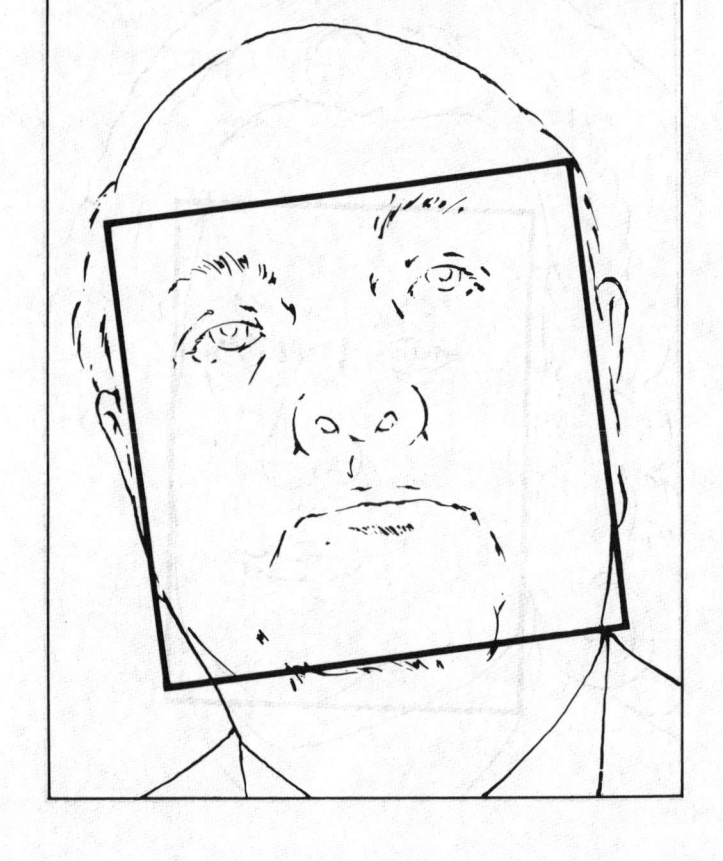

The meaning of an iron face
Tough and hard, iron faces tend to be immobile until they are softened by the heat of great energy from their owners. People with iron faces know when to be tough and when to soften their approach. This is the face typical of political ability; the face of leadership, especially in a crisis when the person can apply the qualities of iron to situations that need both careful decisions and careful handling. Once a decision has been made, iron-faced people carry out their intentions without wavering.
Stable, honest and dedicated to whatever is believed to be the right course of action, iron faces can arouse enthusiasm in others and equally irritate some people with their hard-headed ideas.
An iron face with a short forehead zone would indicate someone whose ideas are rather illusionary. Those whose forehead zone is the longest of the three zones, as is Sir Winston's, can be relied upon to weigh matters carefully before taking any action. Iron-faced people can make their partners feel valued and thus gain the support they need themselves.

The tree and wall faces

The Tree Face

The tree face of J. S. Bach

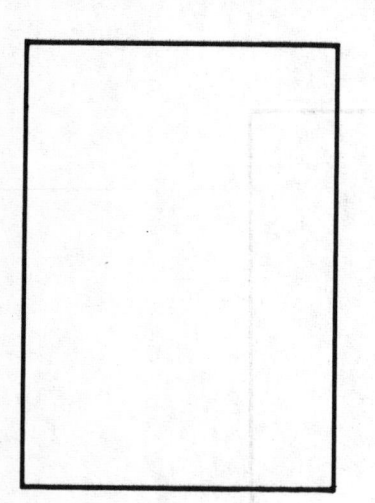

The tree face is a tall
rectangle in shape.
The three widths are about
equal but the length of the
face is greater than the
width.

The meaning of a tree face
In general, although the length may only be slightly
greater than the width, tree faces give the impression of
being longer than wider. Tree faces, like trees, mature
slowly over the years and learn as they mature. Old,
craggy trees show many knots and markings on their
barks...so it is with tree faces. People with tree faces
show, on their faces, the signs of their sufferings more
than most of us.
Tree-faced people can brave any kind of storm,
bending when necessary for survival and can protect
others under their wide, spreading branches. Like
mature trees, tree people generally bear fruit later in
life.
People with tree faces develop slowly and are naturally
assertive and even aggressive at times. They do not like
to be trapped in unsatisfying situations, including
boring marriages! They are unlikely to give other
people thanks for help received, but with freedom to
grow, they will blossom and repay everyone with fruit
at harvest time.

The Wall Face

The wall face of Mohammed Ali

The wall face is a wide rectangle in shape.
The three widths are about equal but the length of the face is shorter than the width.

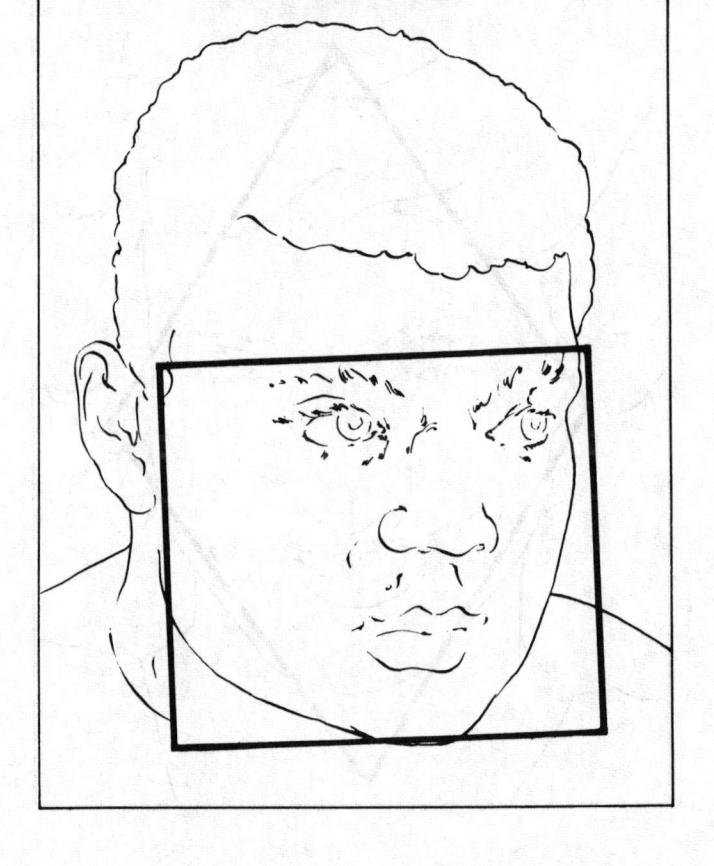

The meaning of a wall face
It is said that walls have ears and certainly people with wall faces can sense danger and are sensitive to what others may be discussing. Walls are built to keep danger out, but more than that, to keep something **in**, like the Berlin wall. Although they can be impulsive and fairly quick to lose their tempers, wall people are guarding themselves. They can consequently show a solid front when under attack and take time to marshal their own counter-attack.
Full of wonderful ideas and great dreams, many wall people find it difficult to plan ahead properly, so are inclined to either ignore problems or be forced into reacting without too much thought. They live very much for the moment and are usually more aware than most of the immediate situation and feel passionately about it. A broad view with strong feelings about the here and now is the face of a person of power. Some others may feel that relating to a wall person is rather like "banging your head against a brick wall."

The jade and fire faces
The Jade Face

The jade face of HRH Princess Diana

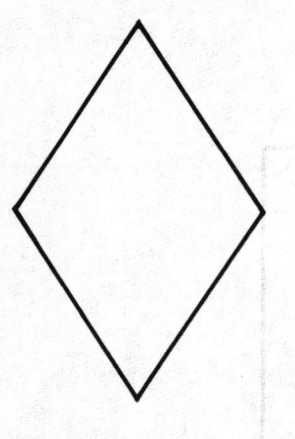

The jade face is diamond shaped.
The cheekbone width is greater than either of the other two, which both point towards the top and bottom of the face. The cheekbones of a jade face are usually high and clearly seen.

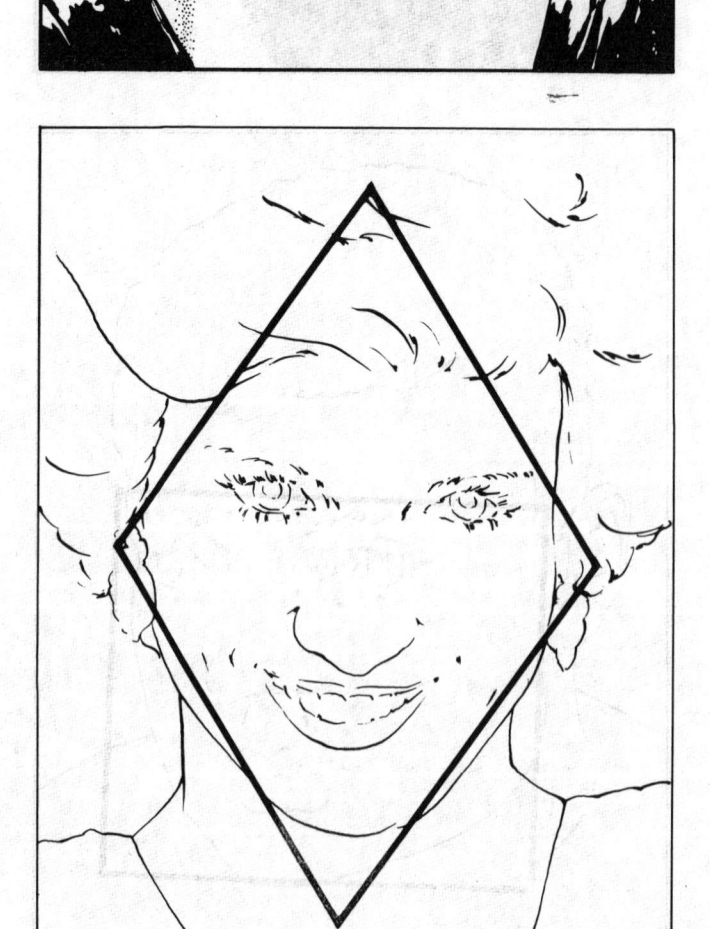

The meaning of a jade face
A traditional symbol of good fortune, jade is valued for its beauty and rather mystical qualities. The face of Venus on Botticelli's famous painting "The Birth of Venus" is jade-shaped. Jade faces are very attractive, in both men and women of any race, but like jade itself they may have mixed fortunes early in their lives. Jade has to be dug from the earth, fashioned and polished before its great beauty can be seen. So it is with jade people. Many have difficulties early in life, or rise to fortune later in life.
Although they may be unappreciated before they have fully developed their talents, jade people are tough and durable with a strong will to survive. They can be sharp and uncompromising and make possessive partners. They are more interested in doing things than in thinking and have a firm sense of duty.
People, like Princess Diana, who have some irregular features, usually have irregular fortunes. Ears and eyes of different sizes show that there have been upsets or difficulties earlier in life. Ears that stick out from the head belong to a person who has to draw on inner reserves. Diana has slightly protruding ears as does her husband, Prince Charles.

The bucket and earth faces

The Fire Face

The fire face of Joan Collins

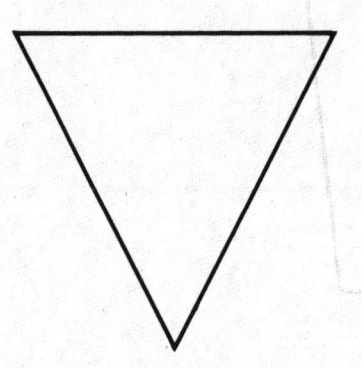

The fire face is triangular. The forehead is wide and so is the cheekbone area which has prominent cheekbones. The jaw slopes smoothly down to a point . . . the point of the triangle shape.

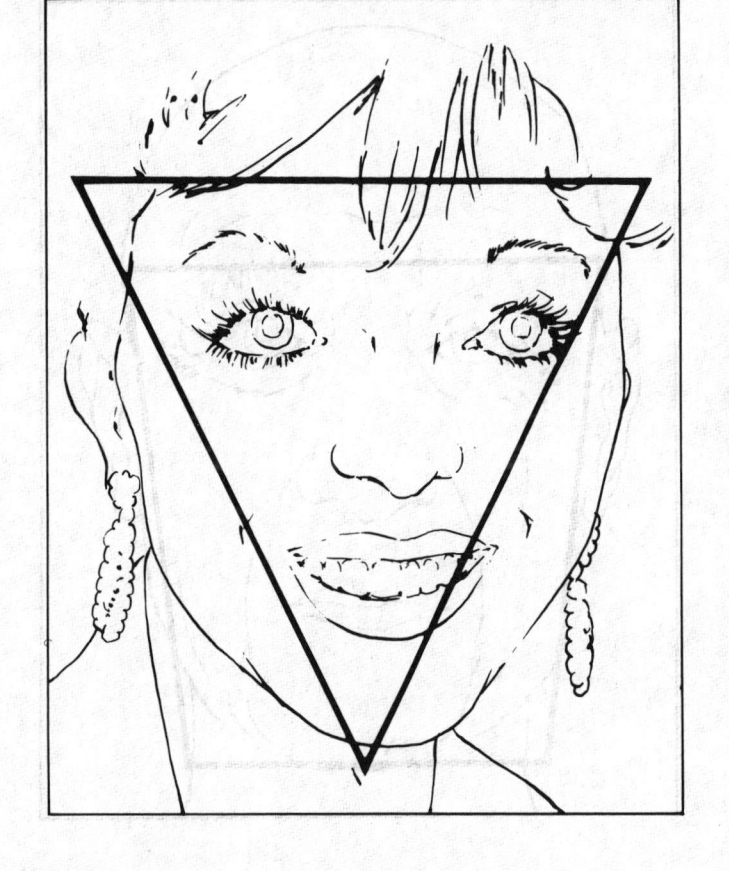

The meaning of a fire face
Bright, sparkling and burning with ambition, like fire, the fire face is that of a person who is very quick to learn, although mistakes may often be made by burning too brightly and too quickly.
Many fire people find it very difficult to trust as they are never sure of the motives of others. This may be because fire people themselves are never quite certain of their own motives. Often they choose quite unsuitable partners, or end up changing their partners. Fire people are sensitive and sexually passionate. In the case of Joan Collins, the actress, her half-moon shaped eyebrows enhance her passion. People with fire faces have great, radiant, power and like to be out there either at the forefront of things or in the limelight; they can be blunt, arrogant or quietly self-centered. Those with large mouths, like Joan Collins, are usually good communicators and make contact easily with others. If the gums show when a person smiles, as in the drawing of Joan Collins, then this is the mark of a generous personality.

© DIAGRAM

79

The bucket and earth faces

The Bucket Face

The bucket face of Pablo Picasso

The bucket face is the shape of a bucket. Each of the three widths is less than the one above it, giving a wide forehead, a slightly narrower cheekbone width in which the bones are not usually prominent, and a narrower but not pointed chin.

The meaning of a bucket face

Like a bucket, people with this face are sometimes empty and sometimes full; their fortunes vary from time to time. As one setback appears after another, they work at re-building their resources. This is the way in which they acquire inner strength and use the mental capacity shown in the wide forehead.

Given the right opportunities, many of these people have quite brilliant ideas and are very creative too. They are given many burdens to carry . . . a full bucket is heavy and has to be carried carefully. A sense of balance comes with maturity. Rarely do they lose their outward appearance of calm and stability, although when they are pouring the water of life from their buckets, it may seem that there is a temporary upset; the bucket may swing and sway a little before becoming stable once more.

From the outside, buckets don't look particularly attractive but they are kind people, although they have a clear sense of their own importance. Those who love bucket people must look within or they will feel rejected; nobody really knows what goes on inside bucket people, who have alternate periods of ecstasy and gloom.

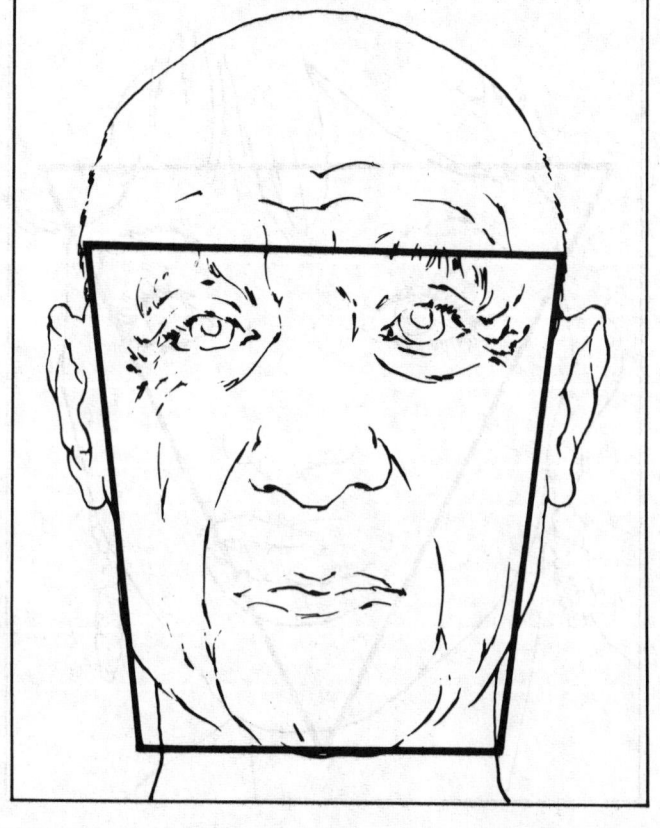

The Earth Face

The earth face of Rembrandt

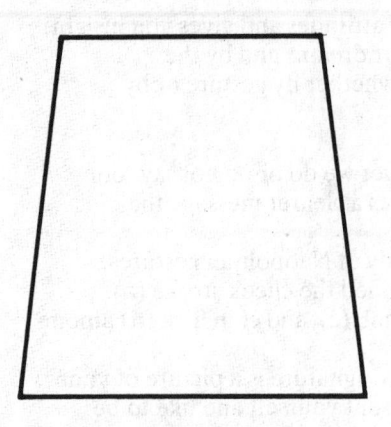

The earth face is shaped
like a mound of earth or a
roof with a flat top.
Each of the three widths is
more than the one above,
resulting in a forehead that
is narrower than the jaw
width.

The meaning of an earth face
Pragmatic and very down-to-earth, people with an
earth face are probably the most determined and
stubborn of all. Earth is stable unless weakened by
flood or earthquake, but even these upheavals are of a
temporary nature. Earth will settle down to rebuild its
own shape no matter what happens to it. Resilience is a
feature of the earth person.
Most earth people are self-made one way or another.
They are capable of achieving impossible tasks but are
equally capable of great self-undoing. In a hurry to
succeed, they may make rash decisions sometimes, but
are usually, though not always, willing to admit their
mistakes. Earth people are ambitious and demanding
both at work and in personal relationships.
They can be relied upon to persist in any chosen task
with the inevitability of a steamroller. Loyal to one
project at a time they are often sensual and may have a
dry wit or a satirical sense of humor. Earth-faced
people like to build a reputation or a project. When
they want their way, they usually go out to get it, slowly
but surely.

©DIAGRAM

Chapter 3

YOUR REVEALED SELF

Experience shapes your attitudes and gives you insight. You are revealed by your dreams and by the movements you make, whether by gesture or by handwriting.

1 Irrespective of whatever we do or do not say, our body language often gives a clearer message than words.

2 Andrea de Jorio's study of Neopolitan gestures, published in 1832, examined the cheek stroke (**a**), eyelid pull (**b**), nose thumb (**c**), and chin flick (**d**) among many others.

3 To graphologists, your signature is a picture of your self-image, how you present yourself and like to be seen by others.

4 One well-known personality test is the Hermann Rorschach ink-blot test – what do *you* see in these blots?

5 An eighteenth century engraving by the Spanish artist Goya representing the fantastic nature of dreams (**a**), whereas a nineteenth century engraving visualizes Dickens's claim that many of his characters appeared before him while he was daydreaming (**b**).

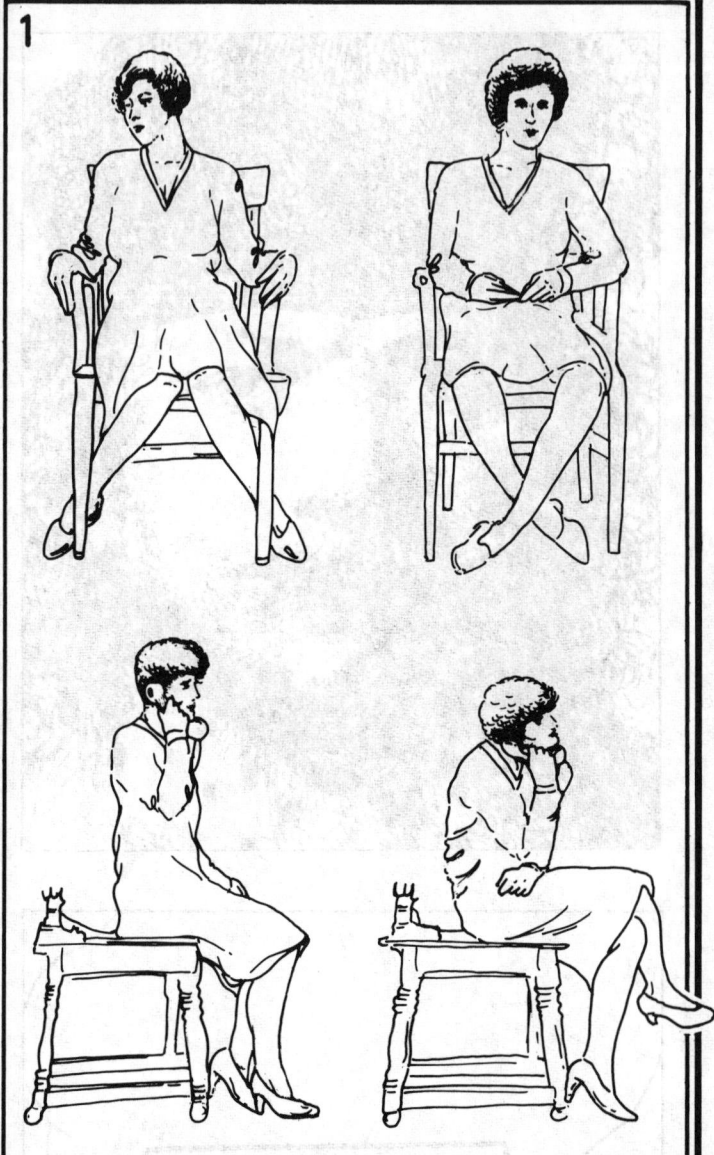

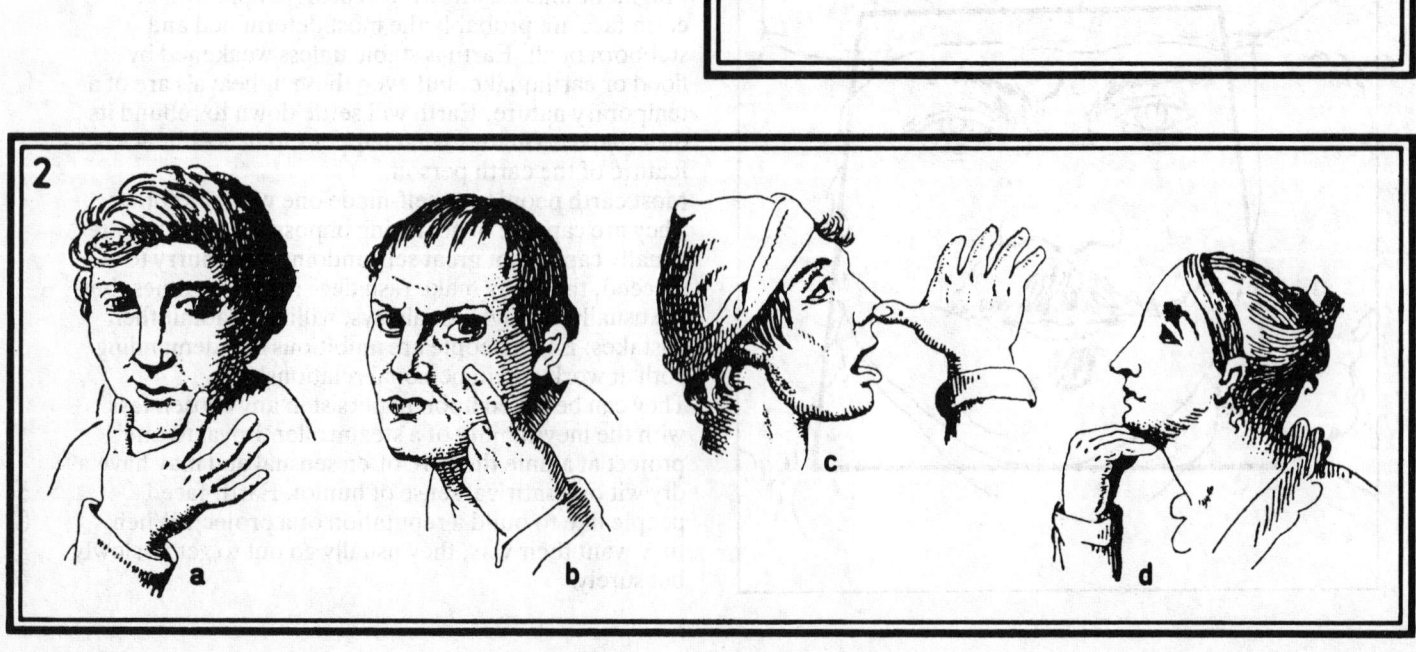

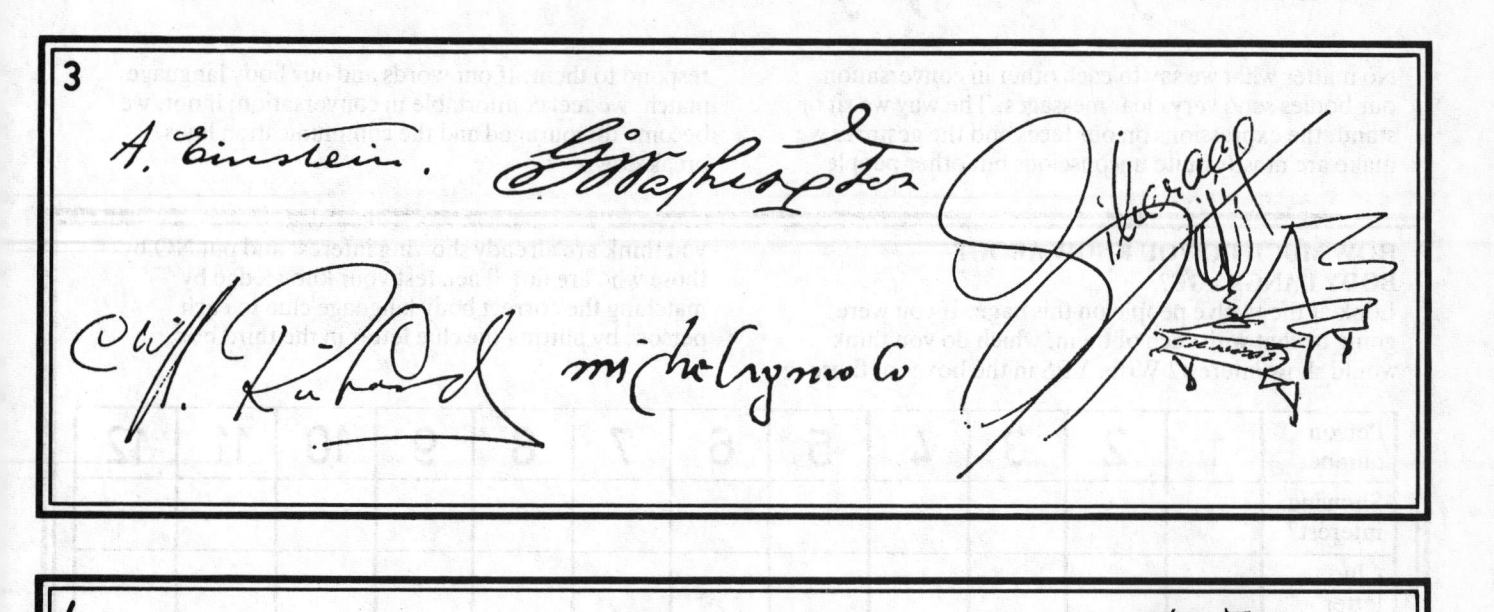

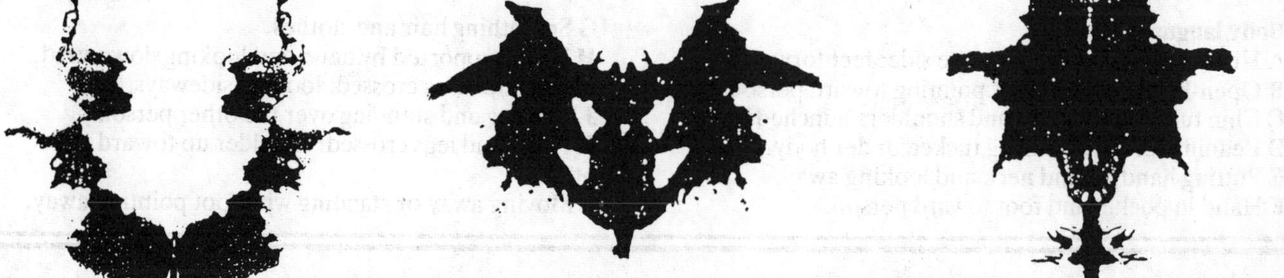

Would you enjoy a chat?

No matter what we say to each other in conversation, our bodies send very clear messages. The way we sit or stand, the expressions on our faces and the gestures we make are mostly quite unconscious but other people respond to them. If our words and our body language match, we feel comfortable in conversation; if not, we become discouraged and the communication lines break down.

HOW MUCH DO YOU KNOW ABOUT BODY LANGUAGE?

Look at the twelve people on this page. If you were going to chat with each of them, which do you think would show interest? Write YES in the boxes of those you think are already showing interest and put NO by those who are not. Then test your knowledge by matching the correct body language clue to each person, by putting the clue letter in the third box.

Person number	1	2	3	4	5	6	7	8	9	10	11	12
Showing interest?												
Clue letter												

Body language clues

A Head nodding or tilted to one side; feet forward.
B Open-hand gesture; foot pointing toward person.
C Chin tucked into chest and shoulders hunched.
D Leaning forward with leg tucked under body.
E Putting hand behind neck and looking away.
F Hand in pocket and foot toward person.
G Smoothing hair and clothes.
H Head supported by hand and looking downward.
I Legs and arms crossed; looking sideways.
J Pointing and standing over the other person.
K Arms and legs crossed; shoulder up toward the other.
L Moving away or standing with foot pointing away.

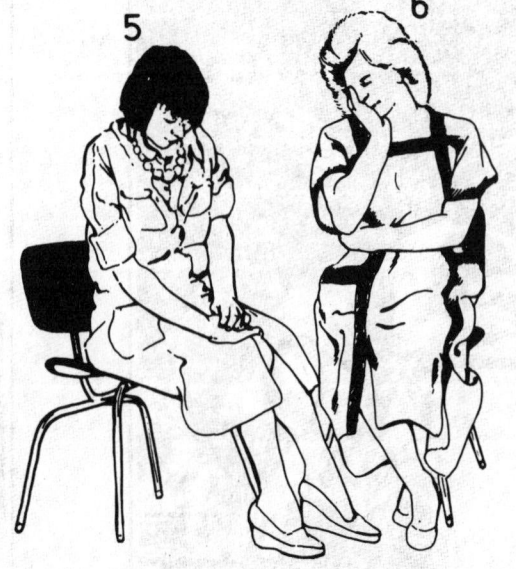

WHICH MESSAGE IS EACH PERSON GIVING?
Write the person's number in the box next to the message you think is most descriptive of the body signals.

☐	**M** I don't like this so I'm leaving.
☐	**N** I'm interested and ready to listen.
☐	**O** Oh, you're such a pain in the neck.
☐	**P** I like you and feel relaxed with you.
☐	**Q** So do I.
☐	**R** I'm attracted to you; is my dress O.K.?

☐	**S** I feel quite open towards you.
☐	**T** I'm terribly shy and embarrassed.
☐	**U** Let me point out to you . . .
☐	**V** I just don't want to talk to you.
☐	**W** I'm so bored I'm falling asleep.
☐	**X** Huh, you don't impress me.

©DIAGRAM

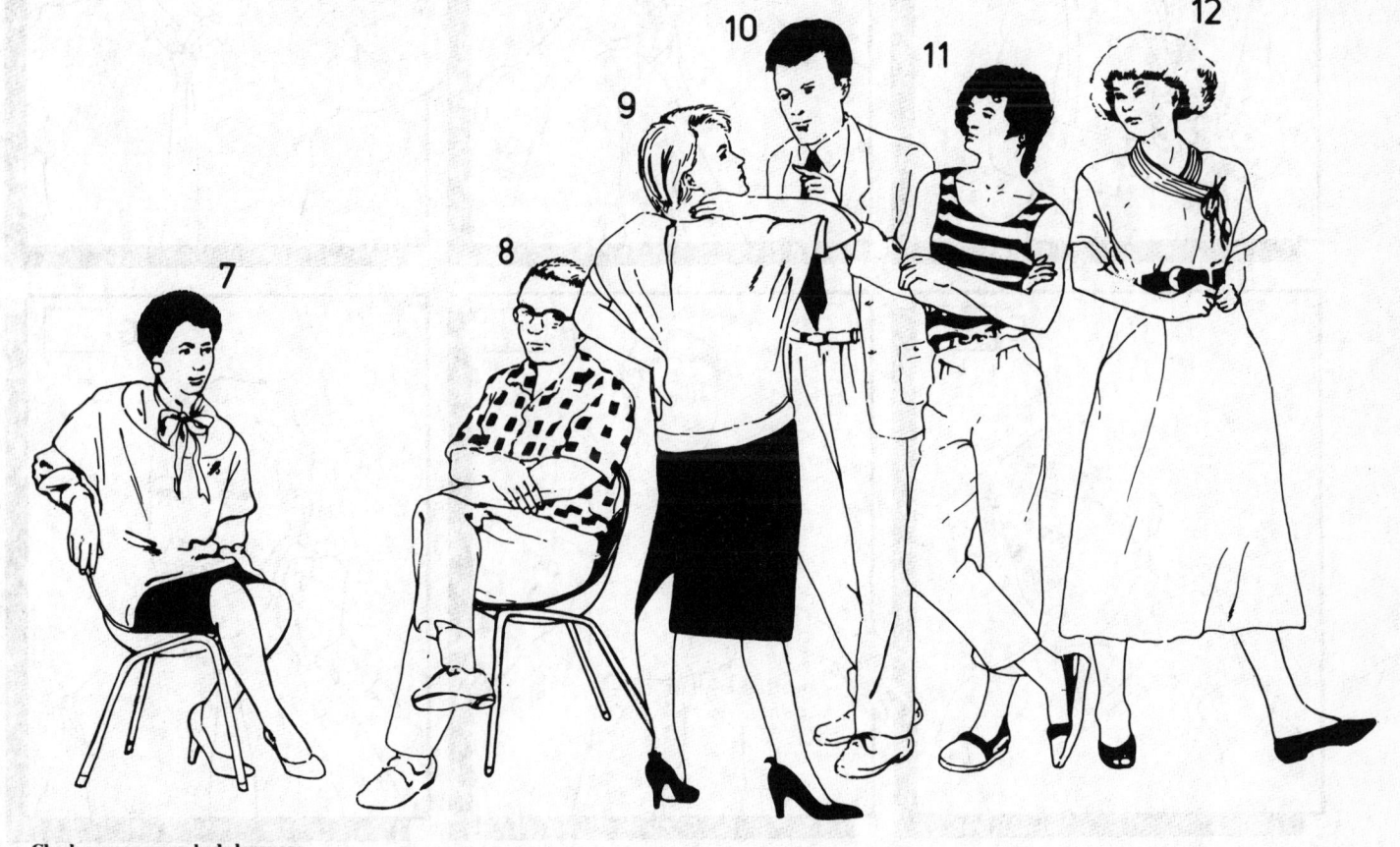

Check your answers: body language.
1 YES A; **2** YES F; **3** YES B; **4** YES G; **5** NO C; **6** NO H; **7** YES D; **8** NO I; **9** NO E; **10** NO J; **11** NO K; **12** NO L.
Which message?
M–12; **N**–7; **O**–9; **P**–1; **Q**–2; **R**–4; **S**–3; **T**–5; **U**–10; **V**–8; **W**–6; **X**–11.

Communication without words

Can you read the body signals of your boss, your clients and other people with whom you work? Here are some common, non-verbal signals which can give you a clearer message than words. Which of these messages do you think each person is giving? Put the numbers in the boxes with each drawing. The solutions are at the bottom of the page (*opposite*).

1 I don't have a clue about what's going on.
2 I feel confidently safe behind these flowers.
3 I neither agree with you nor like you.
4 It's a lie when I say I can deliver in two weeks.
5 Goody, I'm going to get just what I want.
6 I'm still listening, but I've already decided.
7 You'll have difficulty altering my viewpoint.
8 I'm confident and in charge here.
9 I suspect you aren't being totally honest.
10 I don't really want to hear any more.
11 Hmmm... I'm not sure I agree with you.
12 I'm thinking and making my decision.
13 I really feel like punching you.
14 Oh no! Not another mess-up!
15 Help, I'm feeling very insecure!
16 I'm far superior to you in every way!

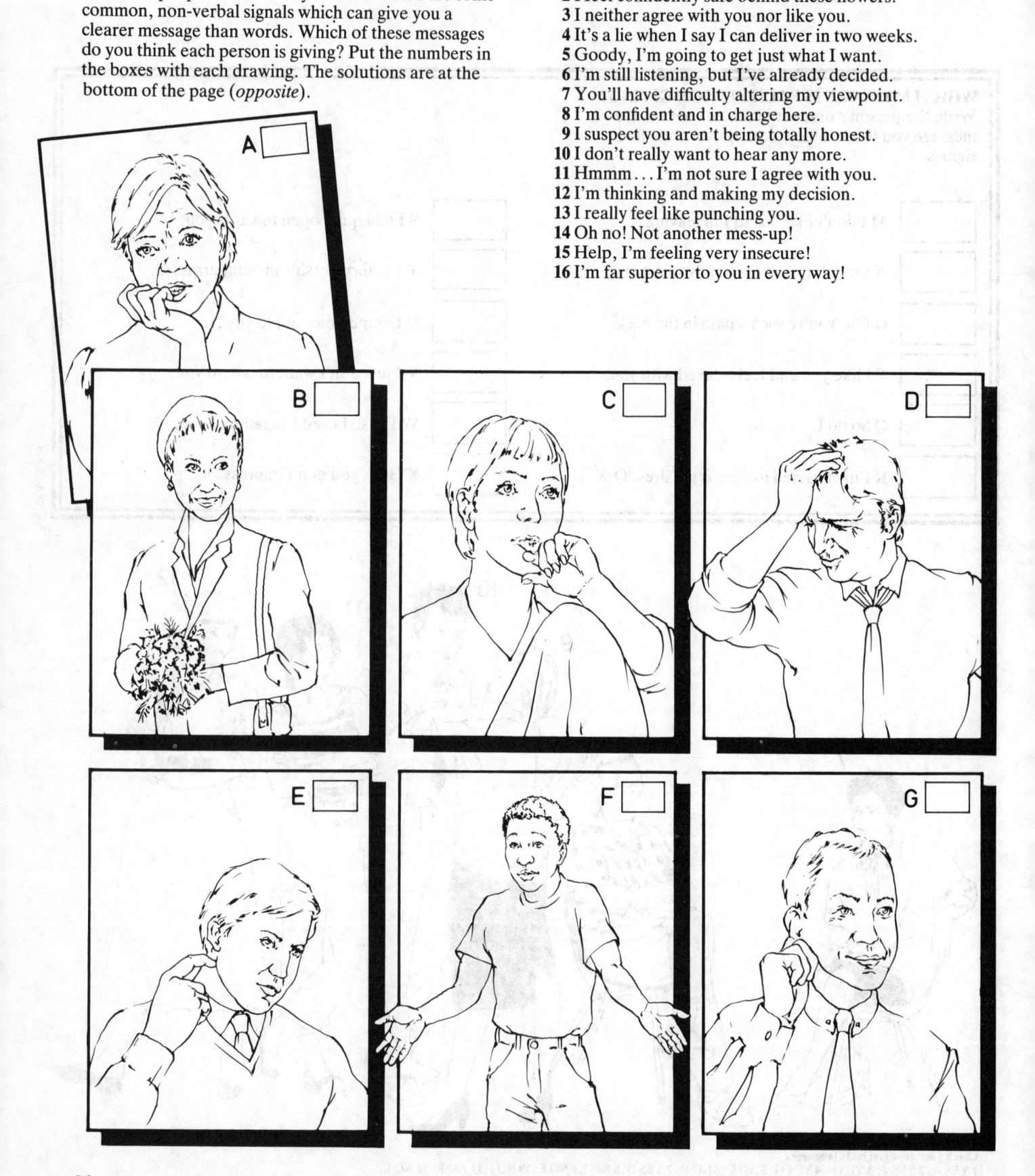

Solutions A–15; B–2; C–12; D–14; E–10; F–1; G–11; H–9; I–4; J–8; K–13; L–16; M–3; N–5; O–6; P–7.
How many did you get right? 11 to 16 EXCELLENT; 5 to 10 GOOD; less than five? Use these drawings to help you learn more about body language!

Would you believe it?

When people give the same message their body is giving, you can generally believe they mean what they say. If the body language contradicts the words, then a double message is likely and you should be cautious. Communication can be improved by checking if you have read body signals correctly. Be very careful to allow for habits and for any nervousness if you decide to begin reading body language regularly!

Would you believe what these people are saying? Read the words being said by each person and then answer the question under each picture.

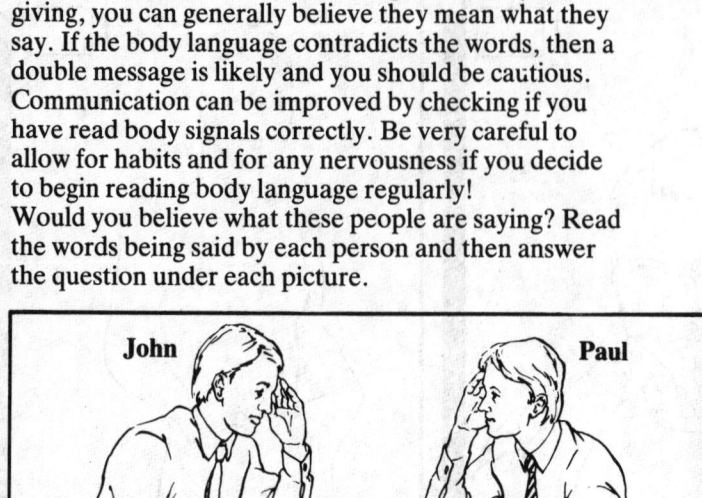

John: I think we could cooperate on this, don't you?
Paul: Yes, I agree, we could.
A Does Paul agree?

YES ☐   NO ☐

Michael: I hope we are able to meet again sometime.
June: Yes, I'd like that very much.
B Does June want to meet Michael?

YES ☐   NO ☐

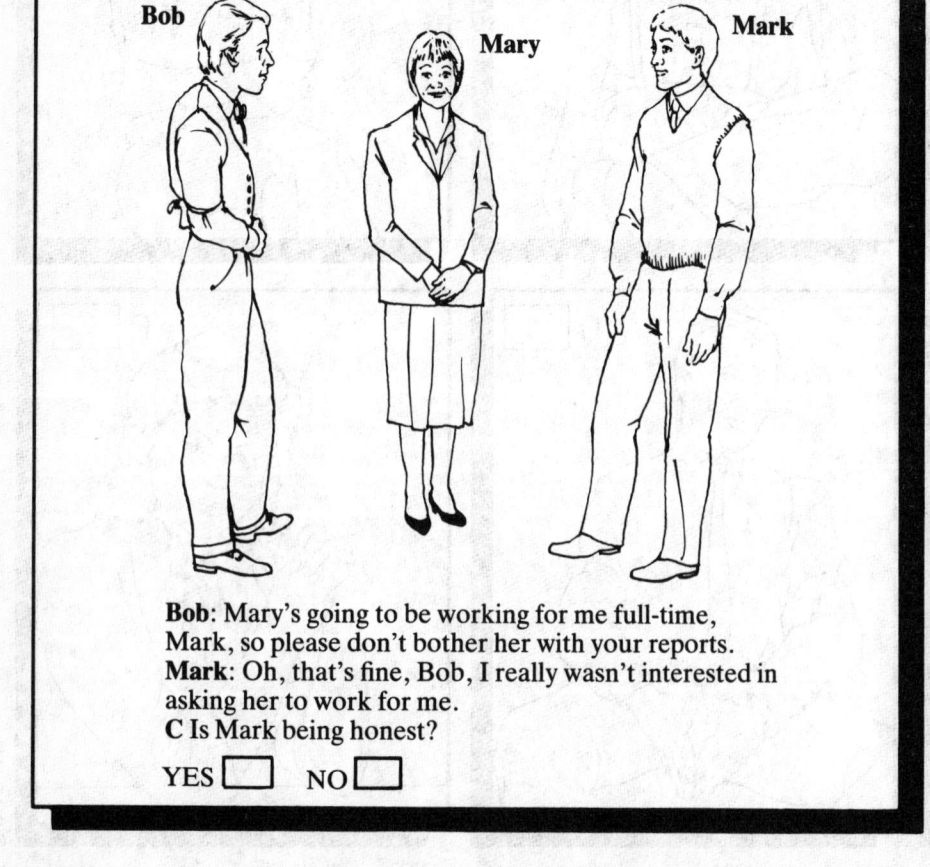

Bob: Mary's going to be working for me full-time, Mark, so please don't bother her with your reports.
Mark: Oh, that's fine, Bob, I really wasn't interested in asking her to work for me.
C Is Mark being honest?

YES ☐   NO ☐

Barbara: I'm not at all happy with this situation.
D Is Barbara being honest?

YES ☐   NO ☐

George: I really don't know when Mr. Smith will return.
E Is George honest?

YES ☐ NO ☐

Montague: My dear, I adore your paintings.
F Is Montague honest?

YES ☐ NO ☐

Lawyer: Your honor, I humbly submit . . .
G Is he humble?

YES ☐ NO ☐

Deborah: Thankyou, I'd love to see you soon.
H Is Deborah honest?

YES ☐ NO ☐

Geoffrey   Bill

Bill: I'm eager to start the project soon.
Geoffrey: Bill, I don't think you are fully committed.
I Is Geoffrey speaking his mind?

YES ☐ NO ☐

©DIAGRAM

Solutions Check each one with which you agree.

A YES ☐
B NO ☐
C NO ☐
D YES ☐
E NO ☐
F NO ☐
G NO ☐
H YES ☐
I YES ☐

What was your score?
6–9 Excellent
4–5 Good
0–3 You need some practice in reading body language. Of course, gestures don't always mean the same thing in every situation. It is much easier to learn to read body language by watching people who are in conversation, so you can see the complete movements and expressions in action.

Did you spot the body language?
A Paul agreed with similar body language to John.
B June's arms are crossed and her feet forward.
C Mark *is* interested in Mary, his right foot says so.
D Barbara's crossed arms and legs show displeasure.
E Rubbing closed eyes is a sign of dishonesty.
F Montague shuts out the paintings with closed eyes!
G Nose in the air, hand on collar and thumb up are signs of superiority not humbleness!
H Tipped head, hand stroking thigh and foot kicking shoe are female courting gestures.
I Bill rubs his nose, a sign of dishonesty and his casual way of sitting shows lack of concern. Geoffrey picks his sleeve, "picking holes in Bill."

Are you in touch?

Touching and being touched is healthy and relaxing. All human beings need it, but it is a touchy subject for many people. Touch stimulates feeling and demands a response, as in physical love which depends entirely on the sense of touch.

Two people shaking hands can be in touch on equal terms (**A**). Do you shake hands on equal terms? You can analyze your handshakes on the page (*opposite*). The quality of touch can range from love to hate and both can be fairly hot! Less involving touches are much cooler but still contribute to the sense of aliveness that being in touch gives us.

Do you keep in touch?

It is not the amount but the quality and regularity of touching that has a positive effect on the nervous system. You may like to keep a record over a week or so, then you can check for yourself if you are keeping in touch. You can always take action to improve your situation such as touching yourself with pleasure or stroking the cat more often. Yes, stroking pets has been found to reduce the chance of heart attacks. Put a check for pleasant touches and a cross for unpleasant touches, each time a touch occurs, separating those you receive from those you give. The results may surprise you.

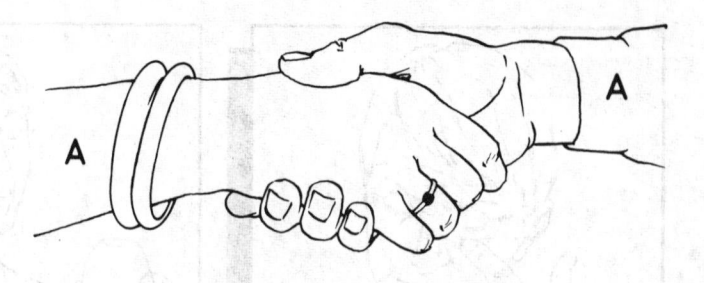

MY TOUCH RECORD	Touches I received	Touches I gave
People I love		
Friends		
Others		
Animals		
Myself		

DOMINANT GREETINGS

It is generally acceptable to touch the arm of an acquaintance but the person who is touching is taking a dominant position when touching accompanies a handshake, as shown here. Do you use any of these?

1 The elbow grab.   **2** The wrist clasp.
3 The arm squeeze.   **4** The shoulder hold.

Are you aware of subtle cultural differences?

Britons and Americans have a friendly habit of holding your right arm to control your response. Indians would be deeply insulted by these left-handed touches. West Indians would most likely reciprocate with enthusiasm and the French would disarm you with a kiss on both cheeks as well!

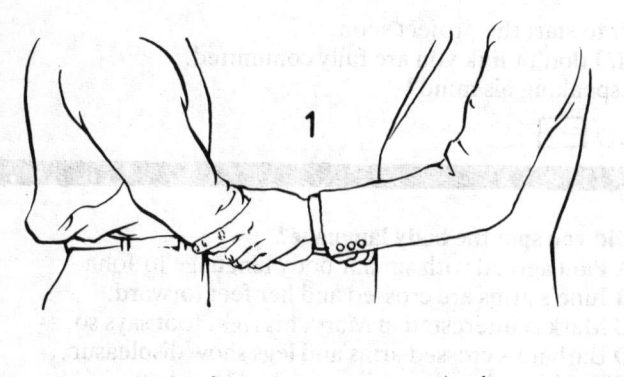

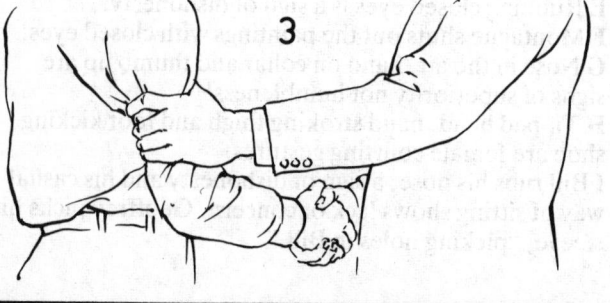

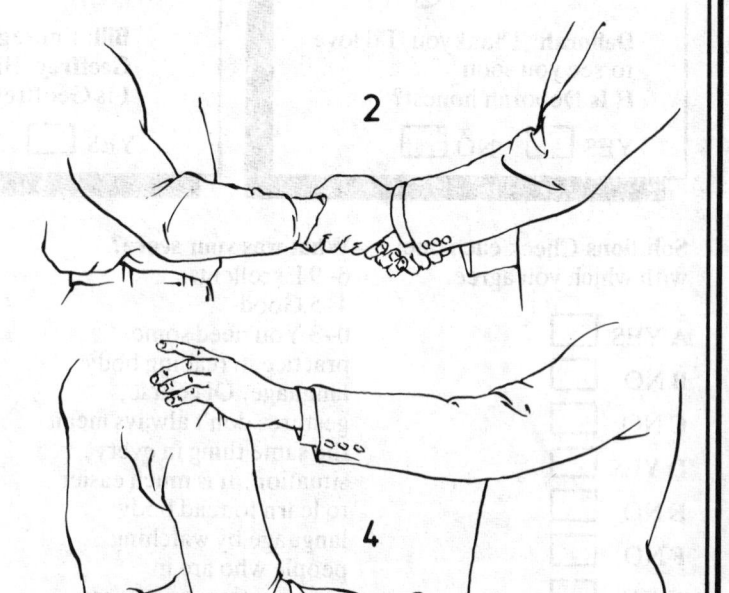

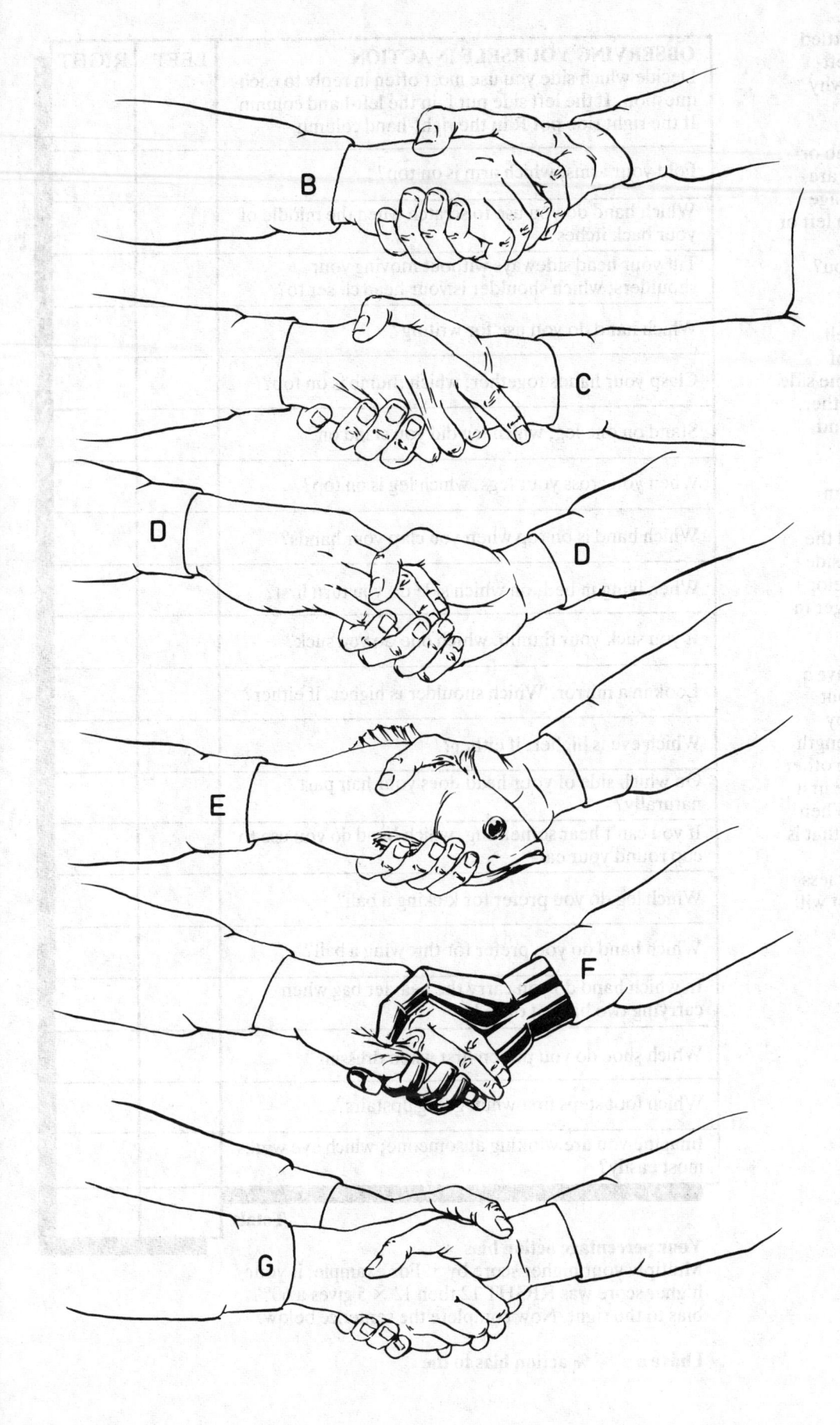

WHAT KIND OF HANDSHAKE?
Study these to discover what kind of handshakes you give. You may need to make some adjustments to yours, unless you already shake hands on equal terms.

A Equal terms (*opposite*)
Both hands are vertical, with thumbs together and the shake is firm but relaxed.

B Taking control
Hands are turned so that the controlling hand is on top of an open palm. Fine for lovers, but not so good in business.

C The pull
Pulling a person closer may mean a lack of confidence or a need for closer contact.

D Fingers only
Either given or taken, this is the shake of someone who holds back and doesn't give themselves.

E The cold fish
Floppy, cold or damp, this handshake is unmistakable and uninviting. Ask your friends to check if you do it unwittingly.

F The clamping vice
Ouch! is the usual response. Used by aggressive people who like to appear tough.

G The protector
A double hand-clasp is warm between friends but implies a need to ingratiate from a stranger. Many politicians use this one.

From which side does your body speak?

By the age of five we have settled down to becoming right-or left-handed. Nobody yet knows why. About 10% of the world's population are left-handed. Whether you are right-handed or left-handed it is unlikely you are exclusively either. The language your body speaks may have a left or a right bias, but just how left-bodied or right-bodied are you?

On this page are questions to answer as you observe yourself doing some of the hundreds of actions which involve using one side of your body more than the other. By adding these up you can find your action bias.

On the page (*opposite*) you can confirm your bias by taking measurements on the left and the right sides of your body. The side used more often tends to develop more muscles and thus be larger in measurement.

Did you also know that you have a dominant eye? You can find out which eye is more dominant by raising your thumb at arm's length and covering a spot across the other side of the room with it. Close first one eye and then the other. When your dominant eye is the one that is open, your thumb will still be covering the spot. When your less dominant eye is open, the spot will be at one side of your thumb.

OBSERVING YOURSELF IN ACTION Decide which side you use most often in reply to each question. If the left side put L in the left-hand column. If the right side put R in the right-hand column.	LEFT	RIGHT
Fold your arms; which arm is on top?		
Which hand do you use to scratch when the middle of your back itches?		
Tilt your head sideways without moving your shoulders; which shoulder is your head closer to?		
Which hand do you use for writing?		
Clasp your hands together; which thumb is on top?		
Stand on one leg; which leg did you stand on?		
When you cross your legs, which leg is on top?		
Which hand is on top when you clap your hands?		
When lying in bed, on which side do you turn first?		
If you suck your thumb, which one do you suck?		
Look in a mirror. Which shoulder is higher, if either?		
Which eye is higher, if either?		
On which side of your head does your hair part naturally?		
If you can't hear something, which hand do you use to cup round your ear?		
Which leg do you prefer for kicking a ball?		
Which hand do you prefer for throwing a ball?		
In which hand do you carry the heavier bag when carrying two bags at once?		
Which shoe do you put on first when dressing?		
Which foot steps first when going upstairs?		
Imagine you are winking at someone; which eye winks most easily?		
Totals		

Your percentage action bias
Multiply your higher score by 5. For example, if your higher score was RIGHT 12 then 12 × 5 gives a 60% bias to the right. Now complete the sentence below.

I have a   % action bias to the

YOUR BODY MEASUREMENTS
Measure exactly each part of your body as listed down BOTH sides and write the measurements in the spaces provided. Be consistent as you will need to compare them later.

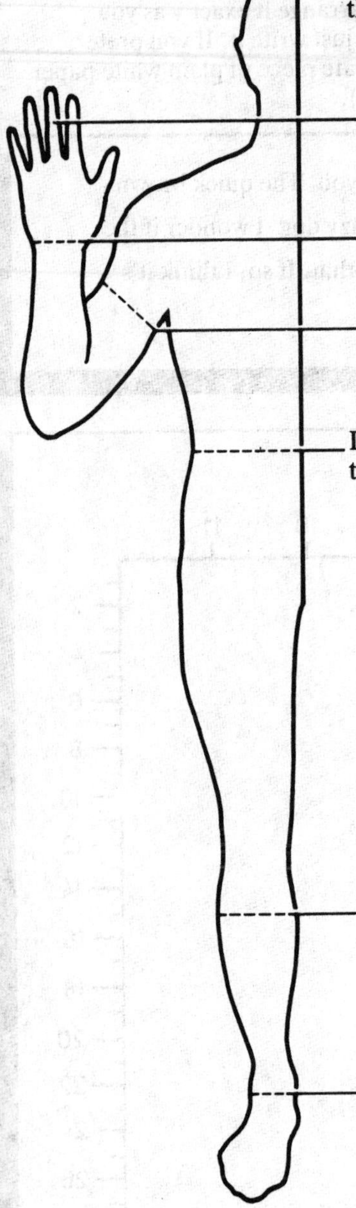

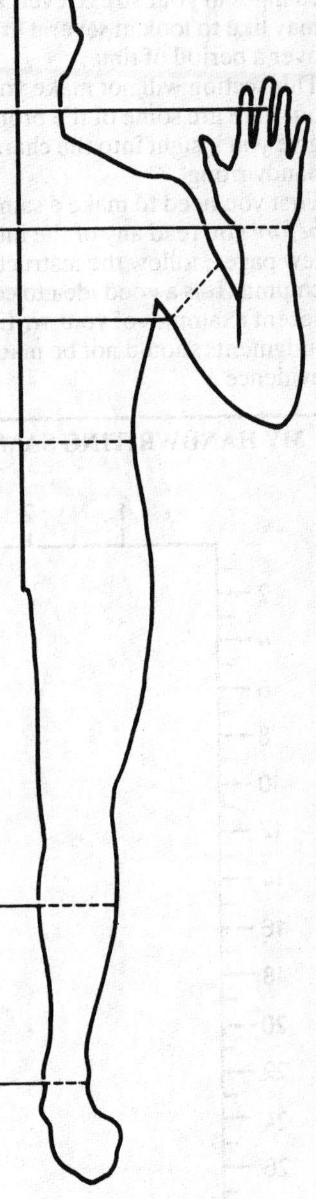

YOUR LEFT SIDE	YOUR RIGHT SIDE
Length of second finger from crease at base to tip.	Length of second finger from crease at base to tip.
Distance around wrist.	Distance around wrist.
Distance around upper arm	Distance around upper arm.
Left hip from spine around to navel.	Right hip from spine around to navel.
Finger span (*see below*).	Finger span (*see below*).
Hand span (*see below*).	Hand span (*see below*).
Foot length (*see below*).	Foot length (*see below*).
Distance around calf.	Distance around calf.
Foot span (*see below*).	Foot span (*see below*).
Distance around ankle.	Distance around ankle.

My left side physical bias Total

My right side physical bias Total

Hand span: place your hand palm down, fingers closed on paper. Draw a line on each side. Measure widest part. Use the same method for **foot span** and **foot length. Finger span:** spread fingers as wide as you can, measuring from tip of thumb to tip of little finger.

How to analyze your physical bias
Compare each pair of measurements: **a** left with **a** right; **b** left with **b** right and so on. Draw a circle round the larger measurement of each pair. Count up the number of circles on each side and enter the totals in the appropriate physical bias box.

I have a   % physical bias to the

Your percentage bias
Multiply your higher score by 10. For example if your higher score was LEFT 7 then 7 × 10 gives a 70% bias to the left. Now you can compare this physical bias with your action bias. Are they similar?

©DIAGRAM

93

What can your handwriting tell you?

How you form letters and generally arrange your handwriting reflects your personality and your emotional attitudes. While the style of your writing remains the same, changes in pressure and flow show changes in your stress levels and general health; you may like to look at several examples of your writing over a period of time.

This section will not make you a qualified graphologist but here are some of the properly researched facts to give you insight into the characteristics of your handwriting.

First you need to make a sample of your normal writing *before* you read any of the interpretations on the next few pages; follow the instructions at the top of the next column. It is a good idea to collect together other recent examples of your writing for comparison as judgments should not be made on only one piece of evidence.

How to make your handwriting sample
Use whichever writing tool you would normally choose, such as pen or pencil. Select the color you normally use. Copy the short paragraph from this small box into the large box below; arrange it exactly as you like. Don't think about it, just write it. If you prefer, you could write on a separate piece of plain white paper 6″ × 5″ (152mm × 126mm).

A Happy Birthday to you. The quick brown fox jumped over the lazy dog. I wonder if the Man in the Moon saw that. If so, I think it's all a fairy story.

MY HANDWRITING SAMPLE   DATE WRITTEN:

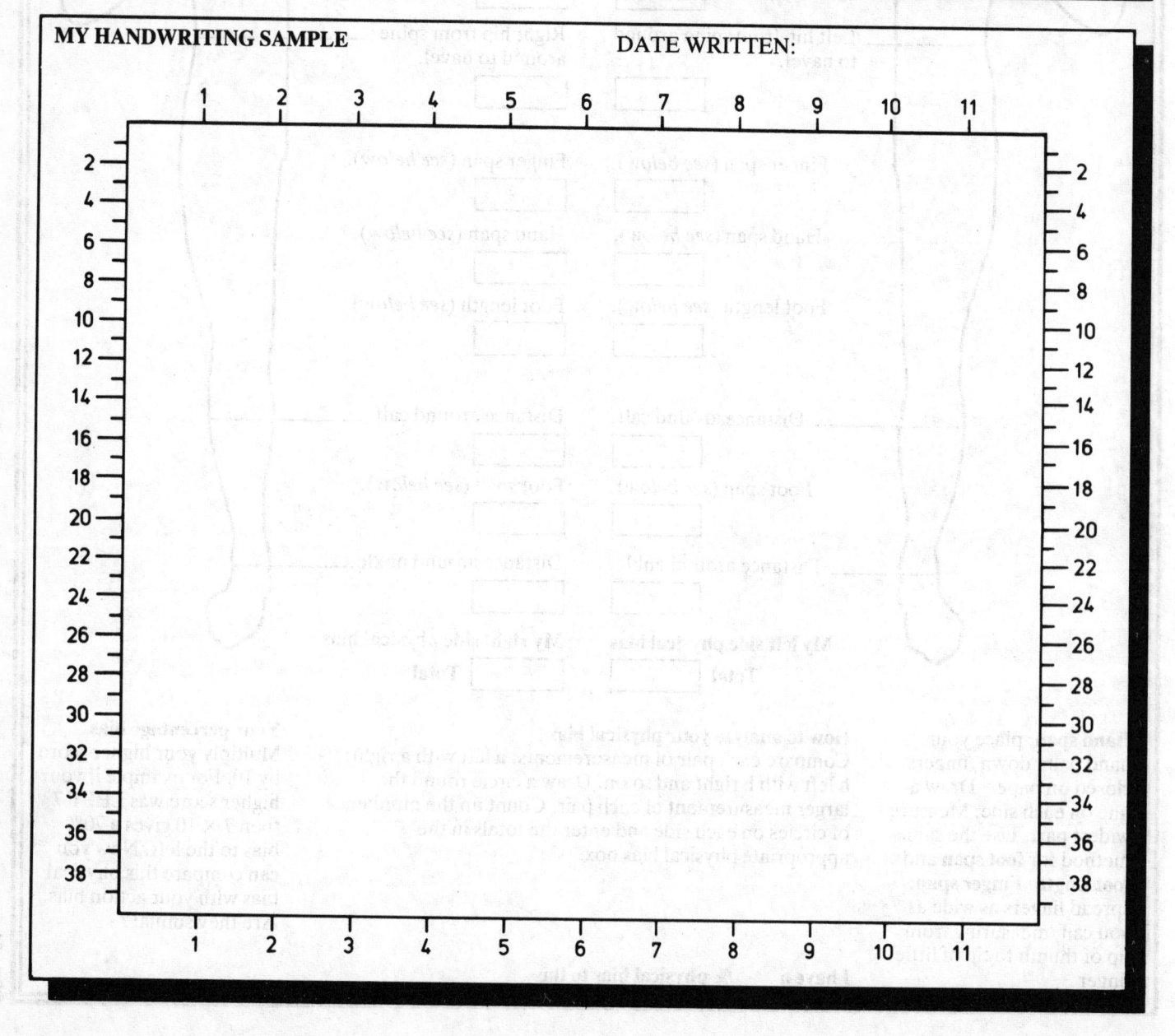

How to analyze your handwriting sample
On this and the following pages you will find some questions to answer. Use your sample throughout and if in doubt refer to other examples of your handwriting.

A characteristic missing from your handwriting does not mean you do not have it, but the consistent presence of a handwriting characteristic means there is a 90% certainty it is part of your personality.

WHICH IS YOUR COLOR?
When you write, which color do you choose most often? If you use two or more colors regularly, mark them in order of preference; then read the interpretations.

Blue ☐
Black ☐
Brown ☐

Red ☐
Green ☐

Violet ☐
Yellow ☐

Color interpretations
Blue You are warm, loyal, sincere and sympathetic.
Black You are assertive, bold and a leader.
Brown You have a strong sense of responsibility.
Red You like to be seen as authoritative.
Green An individualist; you are artistic.
Violet You are fussy; a bit of a show-off.
Yellow You are rather passively aggressive.

HOW WELL ORGANIZED ARE YOU?
Look at the general layout of your sample and compare it with the examples given in the illustrations on this page. Check which is most like the way you have organized your sample and read the interpretation. You may like to use these examples to compare with the way you write the address on an envelope too.

Near the top
You are a dreamer with your head in the clouds and perhaps careless.

Near the bottom
You are a realist, a materialist and a bit pessimistic perhaps.

Top left
You are reflective, secretive, egocentric and perhaps shy.

Top right
You are an idealist, and do not like to conform.

Bottom left
You are cautious, even suspicious, preferring facts to fiction.

Bottom right
Materialism is your way of escape. You have no illusions.

Central
You are well organized, considerate and have a good aesthetic sense.

Towards the left
You are self-reliant, conservative and slow to seek advice.

Towards the right
You are adaptable and forward-looking but slow to take the initiative.

In columns
You are very insecure and compulsively ordered.

Diagonally left to right
You are reticent and unsure; imaginative but seek security.

Filling the space
You are obsessional, dominating or perhaps have inner conflicts.

©DIAGRAM

Your handwritten character profile

No one characteristic describes your personality. You are a combination of many parts, both expansive and contained. In this section you can make a profile of your general characteristics... are you a high energy person, but somewhat restricted, an outgoing, sociable type but gentle and considerate or are you a strong, silent time-bomb? How do *you* channel your energy? First you need to prepare your sample for analysis and understand a few technical words as illustrated in the sample (*below*), which has been reduced in size from the original. Then answer the six questions, carefully examining your own sample.

A HANDWRITING SAMPLE PREPARED FOR ANALYSIS

a Horizontal lines. **d** Ascenders.
b Vertical lines. **e** Tails.
c Base-line.

How to prepare your sample for detailed analysis
Using a fine pencil and a ruler, lightly draw horizontal lines across the box, one line for each line you have written. Start each line just touching the underneath of the first small letter at the left-hand end of the writing and continue all the way across until you meet the right-hand side of the box. Use the numbered scales down each side to make sure your lines are drawn horizontally.
Now draw vertical lines in pencil from top to bottom of the box, this time joining the pairs of numbers one to eleven.
Finally, under the second and third line of your sample, draw base-lines in pencil. These should start under the first small letter on the left, as before, but should continue until they just touch the underneath of the last small letter on the right. If you have only made two lines of writing, use these two. Now your sample is ready for analysis.

Analyze and check off the correct answers
1 Look at the base-lines of your sample. Are they:

A Rising above the horizontal lines?

C Falling below the horizontal lines?

B About level with the lines?

D Wavy, rising up and falling down?

2 Compare the ascenders and tails with the vertical lines. Does your writing:

C Slope to the left?

A Slope to the right?

B Remain more or less upright?

D Vary between left, right and upright?

3 Ignoring the capitals, how many of your letters fit between two of the vertical lines on average?

A Three or less on average.

B Four on average.

C Five on average.

D Six or more on average.

4 Compare the spaces between your words with the width of your letter o. How many o's could you fit in the spaces between your words, on average?

A One or less on average.

B Two on average.

C Three on average.

D Four or more on average.

5 Look at the tails on your letters p, y, q, j, f and g. How long are the tails compared with the scales marked down the sides of your sample box?

D About half a unit or shorter.

C About one unit long.

A About two units long.

B About three or more units long.

6 Compare your sample with the pressure index (*above right*). Is the pressure and intensity of your writing:

C Fairly light?

B Easy to read with little variation.

A Fairly heavy and can be felt on the back?

D Variable in pressure and intensity?

PRESSURE INDEX

C Peace on earth to you all.

B Peace on earth to you all.

A Peace on earth to you all.

D Peace on earth to you all.

	Number	Value	Score	Total Scores
A		2		
B		1		
C		1		
D		2		

How to score your answers
Enter the number of **A**, **B**, **C** and **D** answers in the
appropriate box (*above*). Multiply by the value. Add **A**
and **B** scores: **C** and **D** scores. Starting from the middle
of the profile scale, fill in one block for each point scored.

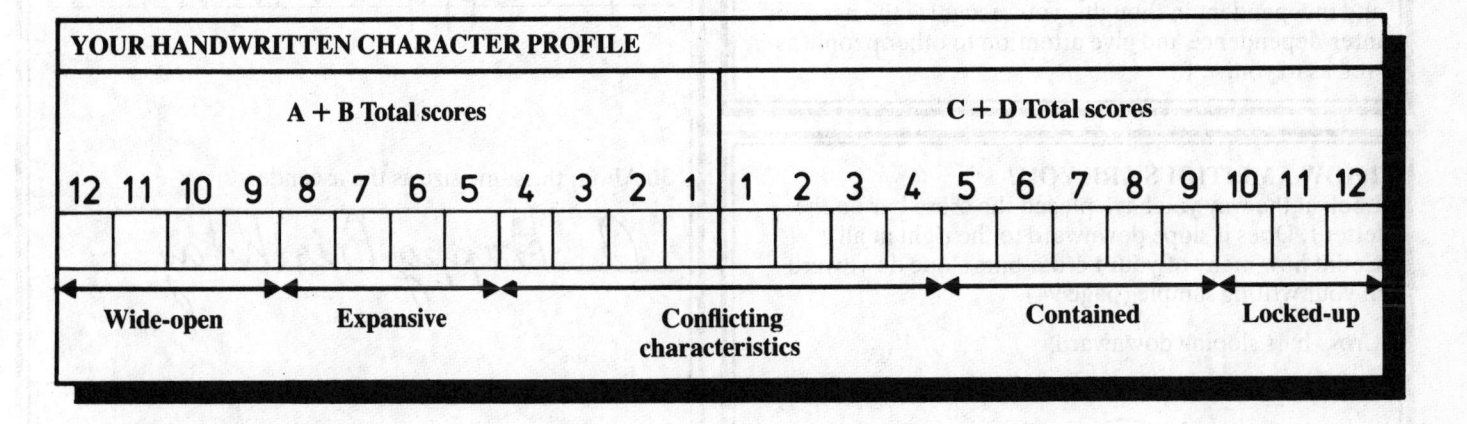

YOUR HANDWRITTEN CHARACTER PROFILE

A + B Total scores	C + D Total scores

12 11 10 9 8 7 6 5 4 3 2 1 | 1 2 3 4 5 6 7 8 9 10 11 12

Wide-open   **Expansive**   **Conflicting characteristics**   **Contained**   **Locked-up**

INTERPRETING YOUR CHARACTER PROFILE

The more evenly spread your scores are on either side
of the central line, the more difficult you find it both to
keep your inner desires under control and to give full
expression to your natural interests and drives.
Conflicting characteristics If your scores fall within
this band you show some of the "time-bomb"
characteristics: well-organized and middle-of-the-road
on the surface but potentially explosive once someone
or something lights your fuse. Many of your conflicts
are unresolved and possibly unconscious. You tend on
the whole to be rigid and restrained.
Expansive or contained If your scores have moved into
either of these bands, you have found ways to create a
reasonable balance between your energy drives and
acceptable ways of expressing yourself. Expansive
types tend to be more sociable, outgoing and enjoy
movement, physical activity and taking the initiative.
Contained types tend to be less sociable, more pensive·

and ready to follow somebody else's lead. Their outlet
is likely to be more mental than physical. Both types
have usually found outlets and occupations that are
satisfying and can cope with adversities on the whole.
Wide-open or locked-up If your scores have moved into
either of these extremes you should take warning that
there is likely to be a high-stress situation in your life
that needs attention. Wide-open types burn up their
energy yet feel unsatisfied, while locked-up types tend
to withdraw into isolation. In either case there is a
tendency to flip suddenly to the opposite extreme.

What's your style?

How you form letters shows how you express yourself. Qualities such as rebelliousness, ambition, assertiveness, aggression and originality can all be reflected in the manner in which you write. Examples of letter styles are given (*below* and *opposite*) so that, by referring back to your own handwriting sample (page 94), you can determine to what degree, if any, you possess these qualities.

1 ARE YOU A REBEL?

In your sample (page 94), eight of the letters needed a dot. Count how many dots you have included and read which interpretation is appropriate.

0–3 dots
The lower your score the more independent and rebellious you are likely to be. Geniuses, anarchists and anyone who is kicking against conformity come into this group. You are resilient, resourceful and aloof; nobody tells you what to do. You are unlikely to feel guilt or to be afraid of the future.

4–8 dots
The higher your score, the less rebellious you are. People who dot all their letters are stable, reliable and have a sense of rightness. While you may be creative and independent in thought, you recognize the need for inter-dependence and give attention to other people as well as to yourself.

2 HOW AMBITIOUS ARE YOU?

Look at the way you have placed the cross-bar on the letter t. Does it slope downward to the right at all? Count how many of your t cross-bars slope downward in your writing sample (page 94).

Cross-bars sloping downward.

to   ñe   story

to   Tc   the

to

8–10 You are very ambitious and take life fairly seriously. Work or business comes before pleasure.
4–7 You have ambitions but some doubt about how committed you are to them, lacking follow-through.
0–3 Whatever ambitions you may have, they never take all your attention. You always have alternative interests.

3 ARE YOU ASSERTIVE?

Look at the first line of your sample (page 94); compare the heights of the capital letters **A**, **H** and **B** with the heights of the ascenders (upper parts) of the small letters **h** and **d**: "**A H**appy **B**irt**hd**ay to you."

Are the capital letters:

3a Smaller than the ascenders?

A Happy Birthday

3b About the same size as the ascenders?

A Happy Birthday

3c Taller than the ascenders?

A Happy Birthday

3a You are rarely assertive and find it difficult to take an authoritative position or to get your wishes accepted. You tend to adjust to what comes rather than go out for what you want.
3b You are one of the half of the population who are able to express your wishes and opinions when necessary and get what you want within reasonable expectations.
3c You are assertive and confident in most situations, able to approach people easily and persist regardless of criticism that comes your way. You have leadership ability and usually liven-up social gatherings.

4 HOW AGGRESSIVE ARE YOU?

Read each question, comparing your sample (page 94) with the features marked with arrows in the diagrams. Then choose your answer and check the appropriate boxes (*below*).

4a Do your cross-bars have sharp points?
4b Do you make long, straight upstrokes that start below the base-line of the writing?
4c Do you finish words with some end-pressure?
4d Do you begin words with sharp ticks?
4e Do you use lateral (sideways) pressure?

	Always	Sometimes	Never
4a Cross-bars with sharp points. 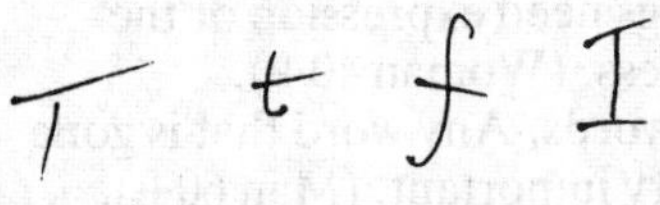			
4b Long, straight upstrokes. 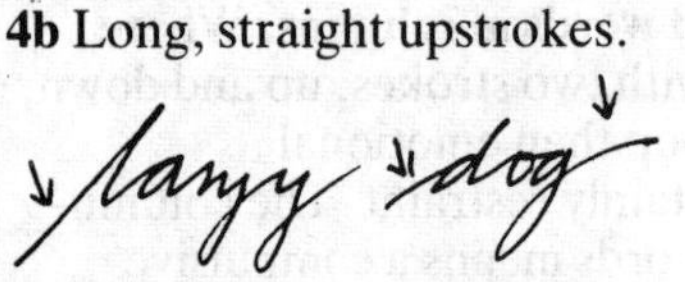			
4c Words finished with end-pressure. 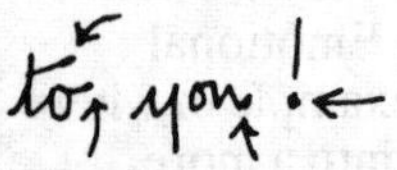			
4d Words begun with sharp ticks. 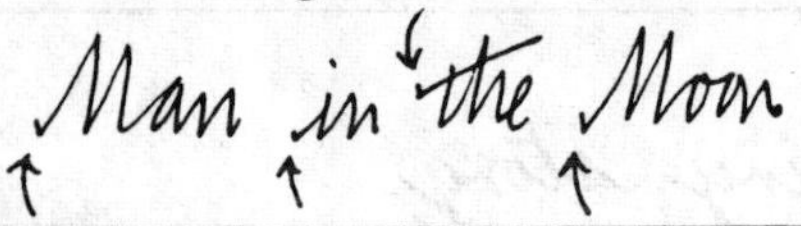			
4e Lateral pressure. 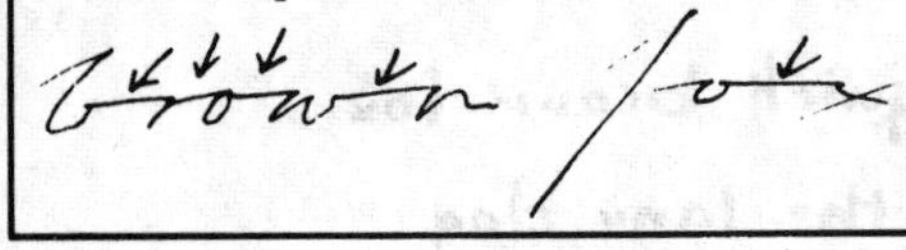			

Scoring

When you have calculated your total for each column, multiply the three figures as follows: Always × 5, Sometimes × 3, Never × 0. Then add up your new total to give your aggression score.

Total			

Total Aggression score

Interpreting your aggression score

16–25 You are a very dominating and aggressive person.
10–15 You make your zest and drive go to work for you.
6–9 You can show aggression when confronted.
0–5 You are happy, low in energy or hiding aggression.

5 HOW ORIGINAL ARE YOU?

Originality and intelligence are shown by the many ways letters are simplified which leads to ease of movement and increased speed of writing. Providing the writing is still easy to read, a very original person can introduce dozens of simplifications over the years. There are hundreds of possibilities. The more you find in your sample (page 94), the more original you are. Five different examples would be a good score, ten an excellent score. Arrows point to examples of simplification in the diagram.

Simplifications showing originality.

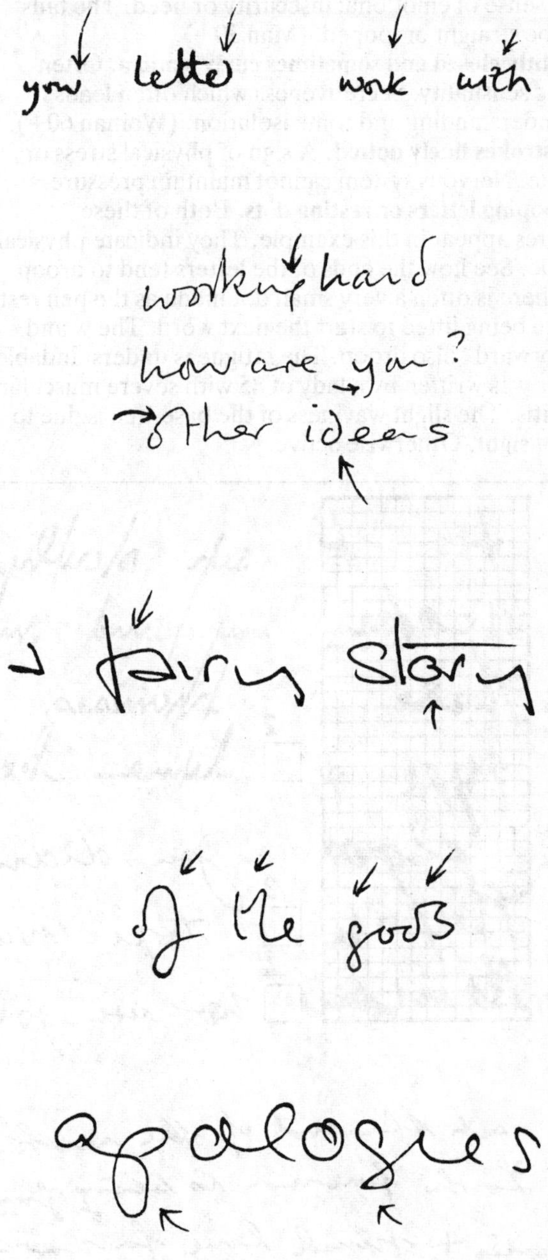

Is your writing in good health?

Changes, illness, stress, aging and long-term emotional reticence and suppression all show up in your handwriting. Some of the common features shown here may appear or disappear as your life-conditions change. If they appear, or are permanently resident in your writing, then you would be wise to be aware and take steps to reduce stressful situations in your life. It is as well to note that we often place unnecessary stress upon ourselves through such things as lack of sleep, compulsive busyness and never crying or laughing.

COMMON HANDWRITING FEATURES

Compare these examples with your sample and check the boxes if you find any of these features.

1 Letter t like a cross. A sense of duty and obligation; fear of putting a foot out of place; a symbol of protection against calamity. (Man 40+).

2 Tails touching or overlapping the writing below. A deep sense of emotional insecurity or need. The tails may be straight or looped. (Man 30+).

3 Tightly closed and sometimes curly o and a. Often hiding sensuality. Secretiveness which often leads to misunderstanding and some isolation. (Woman 60+).

4 Upstrokes finely dotted. A sign of physical stress or fatigue. Nervous system cannot maintain pressure.

5 Drooping letters or resting dots. Both of these features appear in this example. They indicate physical fatigue. See how the ends of the letters tend to droop and there is often a very small dot made as the pen rests before being lifted to start the next word. The w and r of "forward" also droop. The fatigue is understandable as this was written by a lady of 85 with severe muscular arthritis. The slight waviness of the base-line is due to loss of sight. Otherwise active.

6 Rounded anchors begin the words. A conformist tendency with a need for emotional security. (Woman 30+).

7 Cut-off endings and disappearing letters. Emotional constipation. Under pressure, mostly from own fears of appearing "weak." Feelings need expression or the result may be physical illness. (Woman 40+).

8 Overwriting of emotive words. Any word that is gone over more than once is very important. (Man 60+).

9 Narrow upper loops and words in columns. Where the ascenders are made with two strokes, up and down, if the result is a narrow loop then emotional suppression is likely. Certainly restraint. The column-like arrangement of the words means a compulsive need for orderliness and a fear of letting go. (Man 40+).

10 Lurching letters or lurching words. Emotional disturbance and upheaval. This is an example of where emotions need control or channelling into a more satisfying activity. (Woman 30+).

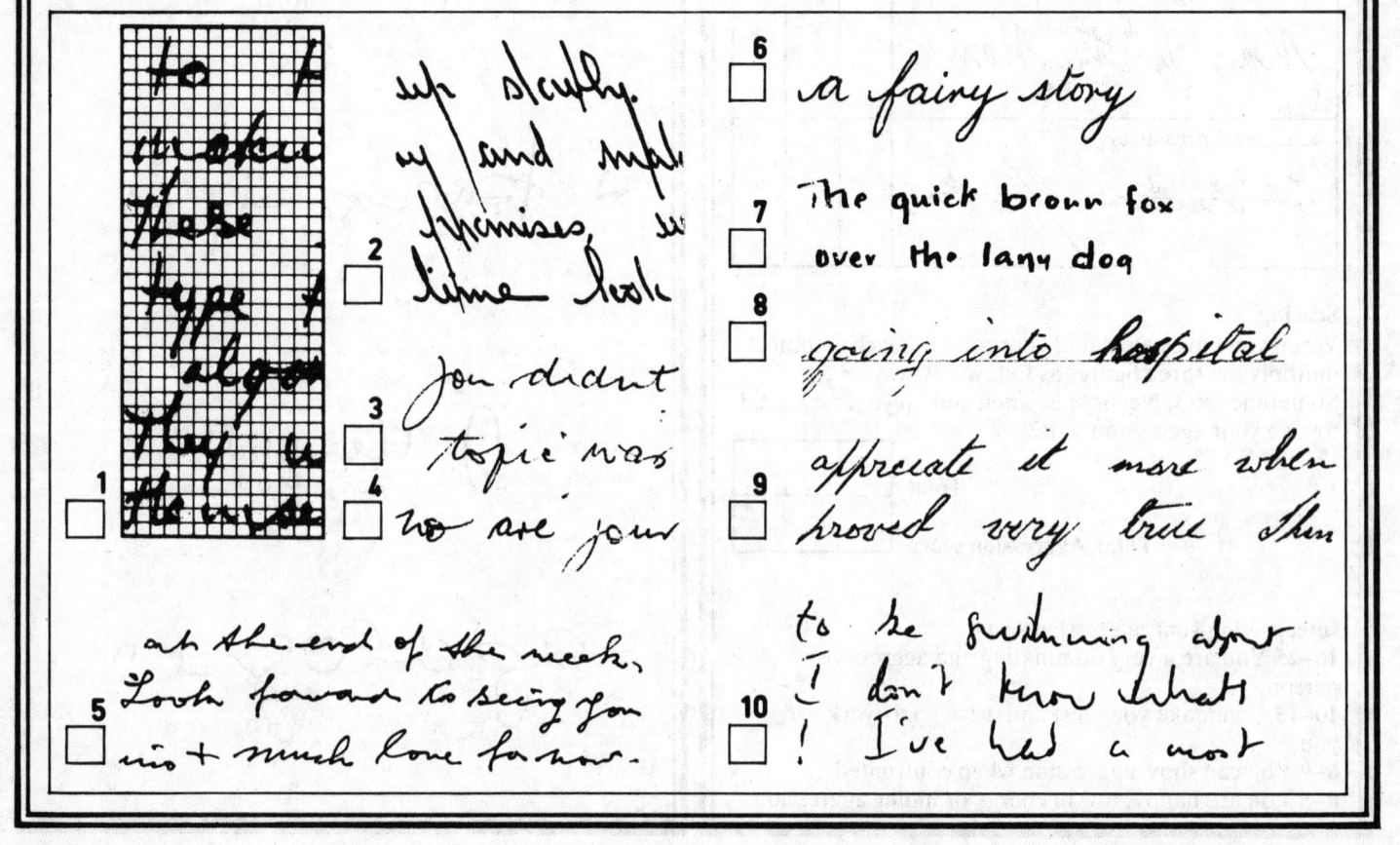

WHAT CAN YOUR CAPITAL I TELL YOU?

In general the top of the capital I represents your head, your intellect, illusions, imagination, hopes and fears. The bottom represents your reality-base, how you make yourself feel secure; the earthy, emotional part of you. Height, width, slope and pressure should all be taken into account. As with all your writing, the capital I is a little drawing of yourself and every drawing tells a different story. There are three in your sample; compare them with these twelve examples and read the stories they tell. Are any of these your story? Take your sense of humor with you.

1 Without money I'm nothing. (Large reversed dollar sign is crossing out a small capital I.)

2 I've got a firm footing, but I'm keeping the lid on my own development. I'm split three ways. (Notice that the ascenders are much taller than the I.)

3 Here I am, so take notice. I haven't a firm base because I move on quickly, so I won't let you see what's going on in my head

4 I don't seem to have a leg to stand on; I am cut off and out of touch so I have to reduce my size to stay upright, but I have a sharp brain to see me through.

5 I'm sharp even though I'm not showing how clever I really am. I usually hold myself back.

6 Come to me, I'll protect and care for you, because can't you see I too need protection? (Curled inwards.)

7 I have emotions down there, but hold myself straight up above them and hang my head in shame.

8 The question is, do I really need someone else? (I looks like 2, Q or ? and words have wide spaces.)

9 There are two of me and I dislike being alone. I've a good head so I can keep myself busy and make money to protect myself. (Lower part is £ sign.)

10 I'm cracking under the pressure but I must be rational and keep my feelings to myself. Emotions are a sign of weakness! I can just stay upright so long as I don't grow any "taller."

11 I'm doing all right for now and sharpening up my ideas before I decide what to do next.

12 Bottom heavy and emotionally open, I need to stop and think before following my heart blindly.

1	I was
2	I've decided
3	If So, I think
4	I am still
5	I took
6	I was
7	If
8	I can't begin
9	In
10	In a moment
11	I am
12	I'm

WHAT CAN YOUR CAPITAL M TELL YOU?

Is the first leg of your capital M shorter or taller than the second leg?

a and b First leg shorter. You tend to hold yourself back either because you are uncertain of yourself or because you are anxious in positions of success.

c and d First leg taller. You are not afraid to express yourself and have a sense of self-worth.

a	Man	c	Mary
b	Mary	d	Molly

©DIAGRAM

What does your signature reveal?

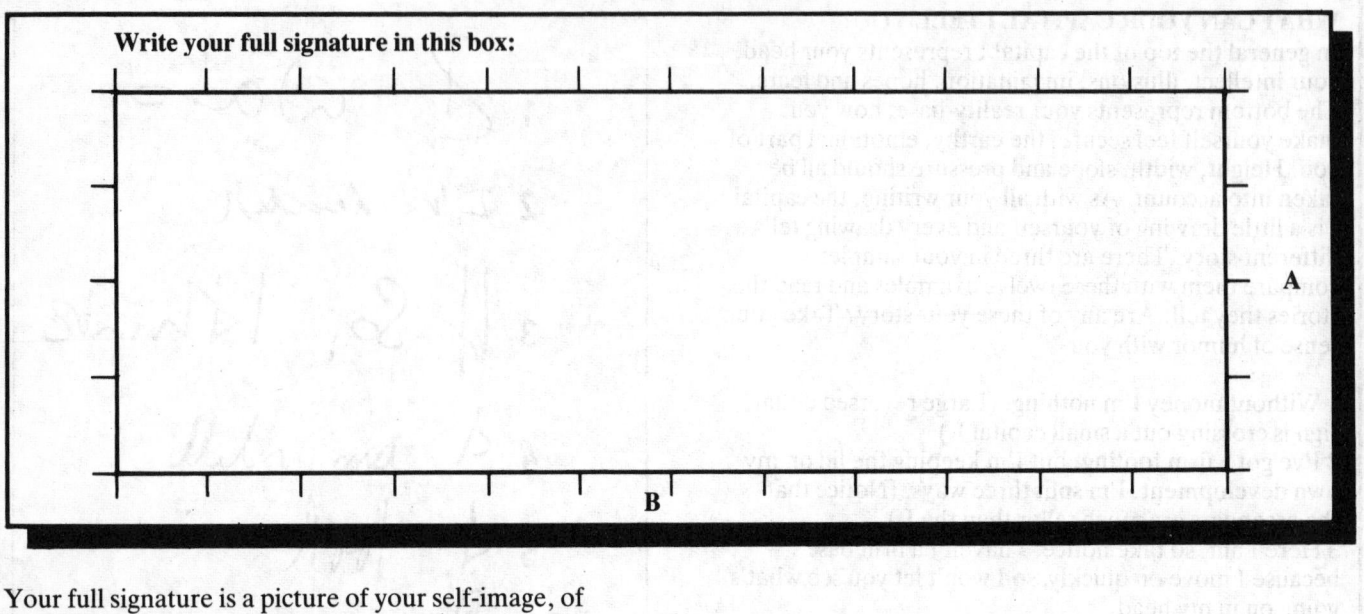

Write your full signature in this box:

A

B

Your full signature is a picture of your self-image, of how you present yourself and like to be seen by others. To analyze it, use all the features on previous pages plus the two tests on this page: size and formality.

Size Using the marks around the signature box to keep your lines horizontal and vertical, draw a box enclosing your signature, just touching the top, bottom and sides and including any underlining (*see examples opposite*). Allowing part of a space as one whole space, count how many spaces down side **A** and across **B** your box occupies. Multiply **A** and **B** to obtain your score. Is your signature tiny, small, average, large or enormous?

My Score is ⬜

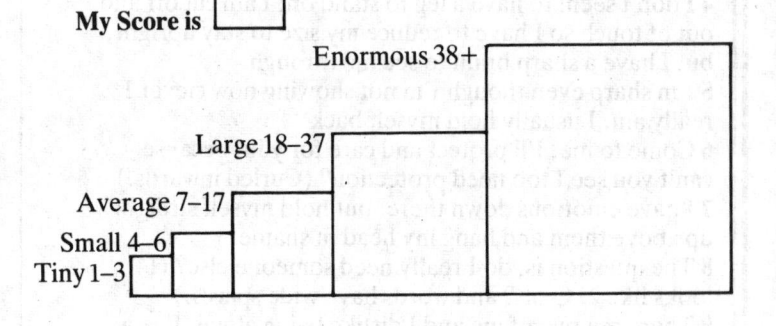

Enormous 38+

Large 18–37

Average 7–17

Small 4–6

Tiny 1–3

YOUR SIGNATURE SIZE

Tiny You are intellectually inclined and may be very bright with academic interests. It is likely that you prefer to work as part of a team but need time alone to concentrate. You tend not to take credit for your own ideas and may be prepared to make excuses for others and never reveal your own true feelings. You need praise and even flattery. Your strength seems to come from keeping a low profile and not taking too much initiative openly. You do not make contact with others easily and wait for them to come to you. Sexually you may be passive or need reassurance.

Small You have some of the above characteristics but are less likely to be emotionally reticent and more able to enjoy social contacts easily.

Average You maintain a balance between the characteristics of small and large signatures, being adaptable and more able to accept your own strengths and weaknesses without having to either diminish yourself or blow yourself up. However, if you have gained an average score by using large capitals, but really have very small writing, you should read the comments for tiny signatures.

Large You have many of the characteristics of

enormous writing, but with a less fragile ego. You are less dominating and can cooperate as well as take the lead. You have energy and can put it to good use.

Enormous You need to lead an active life. If the self-esteem indicated by the size of your signature is relative to your actual importance, then you are not a person to be trifled with. However, you should beware of putting too much energy into defending your position as you have a very weak and vulnerable spot in your ego. You need recognition and do not like to be put in a position where you feel pushed, under pressure or criticized. You take any kind of rejection badly. You can be highly creative, very sociable and adventurous. You are competitive and have a great need to prove yourself in every way, especially sexually, as you fear being found inadequate.

Variations in signature size

These may occur as your circumstances change. The most important points to watch for are the stress signs. Enlargement may be contrary, i.e. due to feeling less important. However, shrinking signature size is usually due to loss of self-esteem.

The size of a signature is not necessarily related to the length of a name, nor is it related to the sex of the writer, as illustrated by these examples from two men and two women who have the same names.

1 Ted Hall Score $6 \times 5 = 30$. Size **Large**. This Ted takes more space with a rising base-line, a long T-bar and underlining. The straight lines enclose his name; while appearing correct and upright he keeps his real self hidden. The long, tall T-bar shows he dominates even his family, since it is taller than his surname. Outgoing and active, he likes to come first and create an image of importance and success.

2 Ted Hall Score $2 \times 2 = 4$. Size **Small**. This Ted presents a much smaller self-image than the other Ted and is much less likely to try dominating anyone; nor does he find it easy to assert himself, since his capitals are smaller than his ascenders. However, he does have energy and occasionally expresses it. He is more likely to watch a football match critically than go out and run around himself.

1 Sally Whittington Score $5 \times 6 = 30$. Size **Large**. Ebullient and active, she draws attention to herself by making her first name larger than her surname, which tails off at the end. She draws further attention to herself by crossing out the g of her surname and pointing to her own y. However, she also cancels out the round, sensual part of her S with a straight, driving line, aiming for some goal.

2 Sally Whittington Score $1 \times 3 = 3$. Size **Tiny**. A much more intellectual lady, but with emotional constipation shown by the cut-off y, g and final n. However, she too gives herself more importance than her family name.

HOW FORMAL ARE YOU?

Take a piece of plain paper and sign your name once for each of these situations:

1 You are signing a cheque or a withdrawal form.
2 You are signing a letter to your lawyer.
3 You are signing a license or credit card.
4 You are signing a letter of complaint.

Compare the styles you have used with the examples (*below*), multiply the number of times you have used a particular style by the value, enter your score and find your total formality rating.

Which style?	Examples	Value	Score
Name in full	Mary Brown	1	
Initials and surname	M. Brown M. T. Brown	3	
Name, initial and surname	Mary T. Brown T. Mary Brown	2	
		Total	

What is your formality rating?

Total 4–5: **Informal** You are honest, open-minded and forward-looking, probably enjoying the latest fashions in activities of interest to you. Sympathetic to minority groups you may be idealistic and impractical.

Total 6–8: **Average** You have a practical approach to life and tend to adapt to circumstances as you see it may be to your advantage. Maybe you can't make up your mind.

Total 9–12: **Formal** You have a rather fatalistic view of things and dislike too many changes or new ideas; you prefer to stick to the known and tested. It may take a lot to make you laugh and let your hair down.

Now that you have completed the analysis of your own handwriting, do remember that a feature missing from your writing does not mean it is missing from your personality.

©DIAGRAM

103

Extrovert or introvert?

In a questionnaire the style or phrasing of the questions may offer you enough clues to enable you to choose the right answers, i.e. to match your answers to the personality you might choose to have rather than to your actual personality. Because of this your quick reaction to abstract shapes can sometimes give a truer indication of the real you. The 10 sets of pictures on this page will help you discover if your personality tends towards the extrovert or the introvert. Extroverts are confident, demonstrative, aggressive, outgoing, active, impulsive and enjoy being the center of attention. Introverts are careful, reserved, peaceful, passive, controlled, and tend to avoid the limelight. People who display both extrovert and introvert qualities are known as ambiverts.

Here are 10 groups of abstract shapes. Choose the picture in each group that most appeals to you and make a note of its identifying letter. Do this as quickly as possible – do not attempt to choose the right shape. There are no right or wrong shapes, just as there are no right or wrong personalities. IT IS IMPORTANT THAT YOU DO NOT LOOK AT THE ASSESSMENTS BEFORE MAKING YOUR CHOICES.

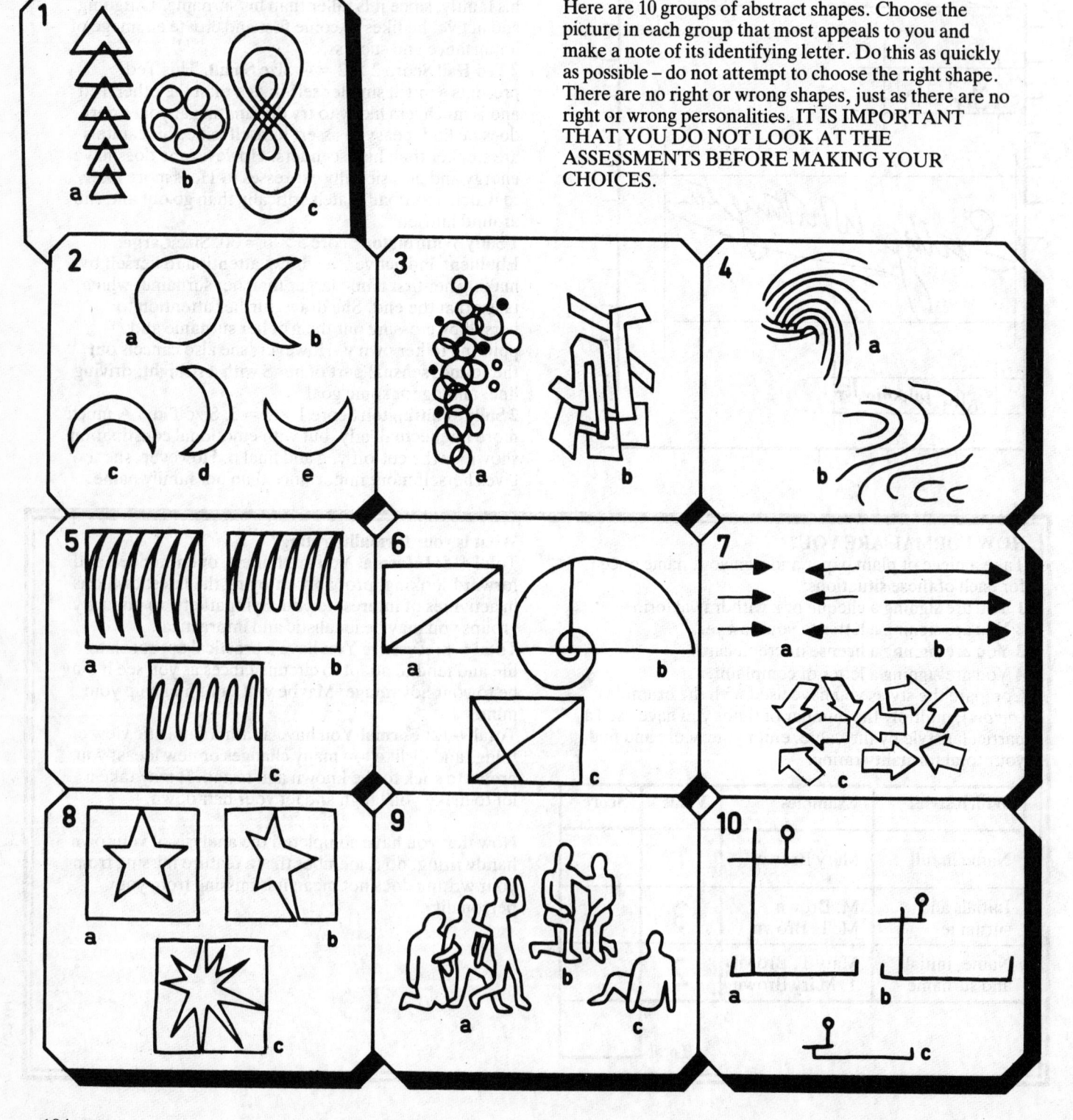

Scoring

Circle the letters of the pictures you have chosen on the profile sheet (*below*). Join the circled letters by a series of straight lines, as if you were joining up the points on a graph. The resulting profile will show if you tend towards extroversion or introversion. Sample profiles are shown for a person who tends to be extroverted (**A**) and a person who tends to be introverted (**B**).

	EXTROVERT				INTROVERT
1	a		c		b
2	d	b	a	c	e
3	b				a
4	a				b
5	a		b		c
6	b		a		c
7	a		b		c
8	c		b		a
9	c		a		b
10	a		b		c

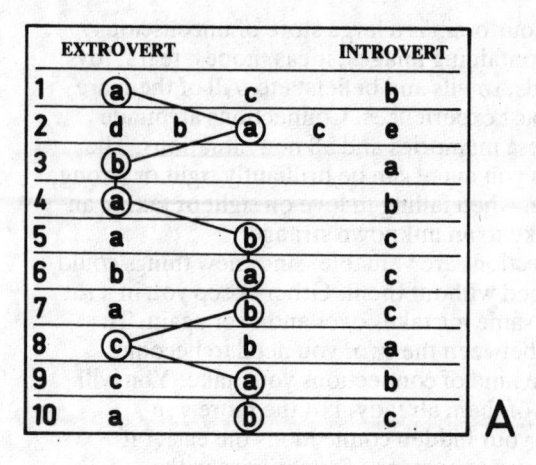

A

	EXTROVERT				INTROVERT
1	a		c		b
2	d	b	a	c	e
3	b				a
4	a				b
5	a		b		c
6	b		a		c
7	a		b		c
8	c		b		a
9	c		a		b
10	a		b		c

B

ASSESSMENTS

1 Very self-confident people tend to choose **a**; those who lack confidence in themselves tend to choose **b**; self-reliant but unambitious people tend to choose **c**.

2 People with a strong sense of their own humility tend to choose **e**, while those with strong, aggressive personalities tend to choose **d**. Ambitious people who use acts of humility as part of their plan to be successful tend to choose **b**; those who expect to gain attention through their acts of humility tend to choose **a**; protective people who expect respect and gratitude for their acts of humility tend to choose **c**.

3 People who choose **b** tend to be more vulnerable to emotional disappointment and more easily swayed by the arguments of others than those who choose **a**.

4 People in positions of leadership and who are outgoing in their relationships tend to choose **a** in preference to **b**.

5 People who can speak their mind when necessary but who are also capable of keeping quiet to avoid upsetting others tend to choose **b**. Those who consistently avoid taking a stand which could possibly irritate someone else tend to choose **c**, while those who consistently assert themselves tend to choose **a**.

6 People who enjoy facing challenges and using their initiative tend to choose **b**; those who are prepared to be creative when it is necessary but do not seek out opportunities to do so tend to choose **a**; those who avoid challenges and are timid about using their initiative tend to choose **c**.

7 Aggressive people tend to choose **a**; well-organized people tend to choose **b**; nervous people tend to choose **c**.

8 People who feel themselves somewhat inferior to others tend to choose **a**; those who feel that they are roughly on a par with others tend to choose **b**; those who feel themselves somewhat superior to others tend to choose **c**.

9 People who enjoy being the center of attention tend to choose **c**; those who are willing to be either performer or audience tend to choose **a**; those who actively avoid the limelight tend to choose **b**.

10 People who will take a risk whatever the odds tend to choose **a**; those who are prepared to take a calculated risk tend to choose **b**; those who prefer to avoid taking risks at all tend to choose **c**.

© DIAGRAM

Making connections

Hidden in your brain is a large store of unconscious memories containing images, ideas, hopes, fears, joys, loves, sounds, smells and beliefs, etc. All of them are from your past experiences. Connections are made between these memories and all new situations. The connections you make can be brilliantly right or wrong, for example, when falling in love on sight or taking an instant dislike to an unknown stranger.

Some connections are valuable, since new things could not be learned without them. Others keep you in a rut making the same mistakes over and over again. To distinguish between the two, you need to become aware of the kind of connections you make. You will know some of them already, but the more you understand your hidden connections the easier it becomes to use your store of experience with confidence.

What kind of connections do you make?

In the box (*below*) are the first-name signatures of 24 people, presenting themselves on paper. Look at them as if they were little drawings in an exhibition.

1 Which signatures do you instantly like most of all? Choose the six which you prefer and check their names in the list (*opposite*). MAKE YOUR CHOICE QUICKLY, DON'T ANALYZE THE WRITING.

2 Write M for male and F for female by the six names you have selected. Since some of the names are used by both sexes, say which sex you assumed they were.

3 Sign your own first-name signature, as you would for a friend, in the space given.

4 Analyze your choice by answering the questions.

1 FIRST NAME SIGNATURES WRITTEN BY 24 DIFFERENT PEOPLE

2 CHECKLIST IN ALPHABETICAL ORDER

Alan	Eileen	Margaret	Shirley
Andy	Elaine	Maya	Sue
Daniel	Garry	Nick	Ted
Denis	Jackie	Paul	Terry
Di	Jim	Rose	Tony
Doreen	John	Sandy	Wendy

3 YOUR FIRST-NAME SIGNATURE:

4 ANALYZING YOUR CHOICES

In choosing signatures, you have made some complex personal connections with visual images, handwriting styles, gender and associations with the names. In doing so, you have also made some value-judgments. To find out which of two main value-systems you tend to use, read these ten pairs of statements.

Decide which of each pair of statements has more truth in it for you and give it a score as follows:
If a statement is largely true, score 5.
If a statement is untrue, score 0.
If you think there is some truth in both of a pair, give one statement a score of 3 and the other 2.
THERE ARE NO RIGHT OR WRONG ANSWERS.

At least two of my choices are those of people I know or like.	At least two of my choices are those of people I admire or respect.
At least four of my choices are the same sex as I am.	At least four of my choices are of the opposite sex to me.
The writing style of at least four of the names is rather similar to mine.	The writing style of at least four of the names is very different from mine.
The ones I chose look familiar as if we might have something in common.	The ones I chose offer me some kind of challenge or stimulation.
The ones I have chosen give me a feeling of warmth.	The ones I have chosen give me a good impression.
My choice of people was made because I think I would like them.	My choice of people was made because I think they would like me.
The writing size of at least four of the names is about the same as mine.	The writing size of at least four of the names is larger or smaller than mine.
I am more interested in the shape and flow of the signatures.	I am more interested in the proportions and detail of the signatures.
The names I have chosen have happy and pleasant associations for me.	The names I have chosen have important and satisfying associations for me.
When I say the names I have chosen I enjoy the sound of them.	The look of the name is more important to me than the sound of it.
Total for value-system A	**Total for value-system B**

The higher score shows which value-system you have mostly used when making connections between the signatures and your store of experiences.

Value-system A
You tend to value emotional connections with the signatures and ignore your own objective experience. You look for those which you identify as similar in feeling to your experience. You are visually aware of movement, general impressions and color. You are able to adapt easily in new situations but may make mistakes by failing to connect with detailed information and overlooking important facts "out there."

Value-system B
You tend to value intellectual connections with the signatures and ignore your own subjective experience. You look for those which appear to be similar to your ideas of how they are. You are visually aware of proportion, perspective and details. You are able to control your response in new situations but may make mistakes by failing to connect with the whole picture and ignoring important feelings "inside yourself."

You may find it interesting to analyze the writing of the signatures you chose, using the Graphology section.
Did your preferred value-system reject any signatures?

©DIAGRAM

Big trees grow slowly!

Before you read anything else on this page, draw a tree in the space (*right*).

THIS IS NOT A DRAWING TEST

Take as much time as you like. It can be any kind of tree and you can add anything you like to it.

When you have finished your tree, answer the questions (*opposite*) by checking the correct answers. Then read the interpretations (*below*).

A Swiss psychologist said that when we draw a tree, we symbolically draw an image of how we see ourselves. This is a simple way of drawing from your unconscious a view you have of yourself.

MY DRAWING OF A TREE   Date:

Interpreting your tree

1 The size of your tree indicates how you see your place in the world. The more space you take, the more you may be unsure of where you end and the rest of the world begins. People who draw small trees (**1a**), may be unwilling to expand their horizons fully, whereas those who draw bigger trees (**1b** and **1c**) may be bursting with ideas, talents and energy they need to express fully.
2 The lack of a base (**2a**) may mean you feel insecure deep inside and tend to be out of touch with your inner energy source. When some ground is shown (**2b**) there is a sense of self, while roots and ground (**2c**) show a firm base in reality, both inner and outer.
3 Left-sidedness (**3a**) means a tendency to hold on to the past and withdraw from the present and the future. Centrally placed trees (**3b**) are drawn by people who live more in the present than the past or future. Right-sidedness (**3c**) shows an inclination to escape from the present by always looking ahead to the future.
4 The trunk symbolizes the body; any markings on it are related to bodily awareness. The top of the tree represents the head or mind. People who relate to the world mostly through their intellects usually draw tall thin trees (**4a**). Balanced trees (**4b**) are drawn by

people aware of their intellectual, emotional and physical lives. Thick trunks with smaller tops (**4c**) are often drawn by those who are more interested in physical and emotional matters than in using their brains to best effect.
5 If a line separates the top of the tree from the trunk (**5a**) thoughts are often disconnected from feelings. Where the trunk and branches are continuous (**5b**) then felt messages are getting through from the body to the head, although sometimes we may be unconscious of them. Branches chopped off (**5c**) usually mean being held back or frustrated by outer events. Chopped off branches aren't a disaster... they can sprout new growth, as trees do.
6 Bare branches (**6a**), as in winter, mean ideas haven't yet been given expression. Growth may be dormant for all kinds of reasons... usually because the tree hasn't yet decided to break into leaf! Leaves (**6b**) show there is growth and satisfaction. Flowers and fruit (**6c**) speak for themselves and show an abundant life full of interest and energy. Too many fruits and flowers may mean a need to prove oneself.
7 Things fallen off are losses or endings.
8 Other additions are of personal significance.

1 How much of the given space does your tree occupy?
1a Less than half the space
1b About half the space
1c Almost all the space

1a ☐   1b  ☐   1c ☐

2 What is at the base of your tree?
2a Open base or standing on the outline
2b Some ground indicated
2c Roots or grass shown

2a ☐   2b  ☐   2c ☐

3 Where is your tree placed and does it lean?
3a On the left or leaning to the left
3b In the middle and upright
3c On the right or leaning to the right

3a ☐   3b  ☐   3c ☐

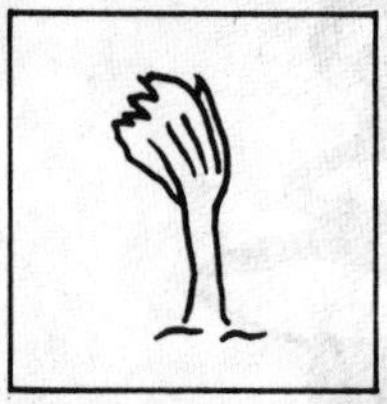

4 How long and wide is the trunk compared with the branches?
4a Taller or thinner
4b About equally balanced
4c Thicker or shorter

4a ☐   4b  ☐   4c ☐

5 How have you drawn the top of the tree?
5a With a line between the trunk and the top
5b Trunk continuous with branches or foliage
5c Branches with chopped-off ends

5a ☐   5b  ☐   5c ☐

6 Are the branches of your tree:
6a Bare and empty;
6b Covered with leaves;
6c Covered with leaves, flowers, fruits or birds?

6a ☐   6b ☐   6c ☐

7 Has anything from your tree fallen to the ground?
7a Yes
7b No

7a ☐   7b ☐

8 Have you added any other trees, a background or some people?
8a Yes
8b No

8a ☐   8b ☐

© DIAGRAM

109

Images from your unconscious

These blots have been made by dabbing ink onto paper and folding it in half. You can make your own blots later if you wish.

What you see when you look at these blots will tell you a great deal about the depths of your hidden self. Just by looking at these blots you can connect with your inner attitudes.

Look at each one in turn for as long as you like and write down whatever you see in the blot. Use the boxes on the page (*opposite*). If at first you can make nothing of a particular blot, leave it and return to it later. Just muse upon them casually; trying hard to think usually inhibits. Let your imagination roam. THERE ARE NO RIGHT OR WRONG IDEAS AND FRIENDS MAY SEE QUITE DIFFERENT THINGS FROM WHAT YOU SEE IN THE BLOTS.

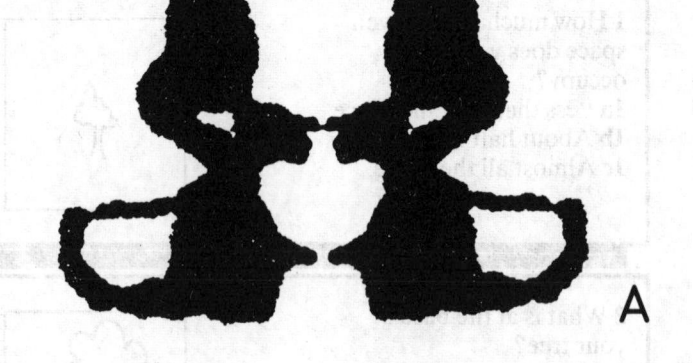

A

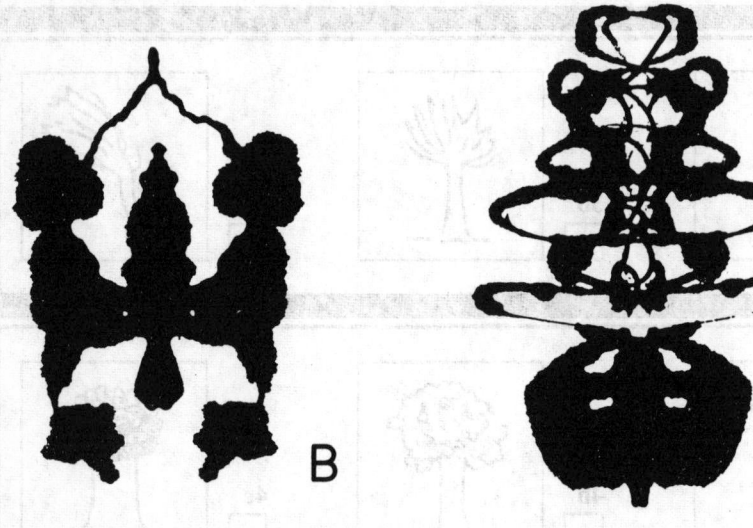

B

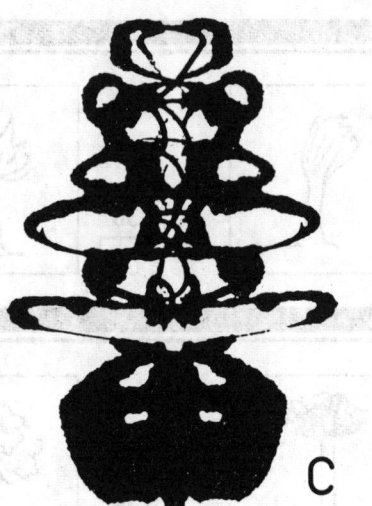

C

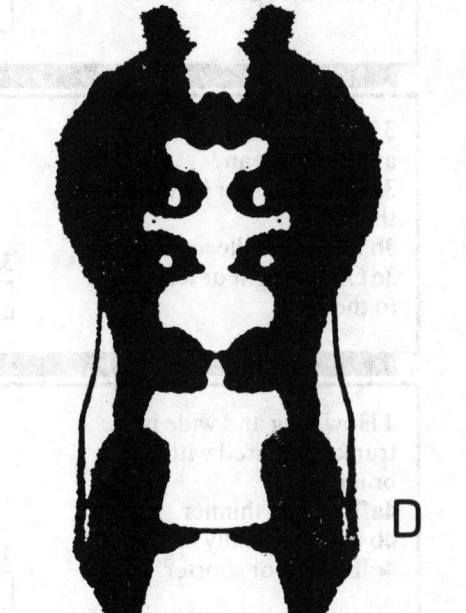

D

E

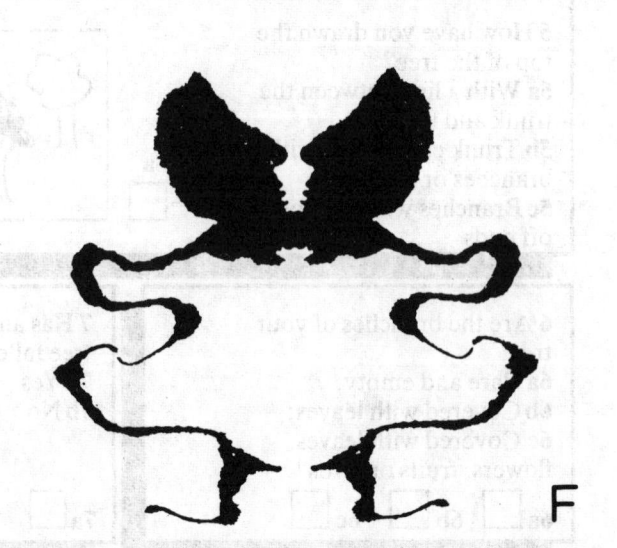

F

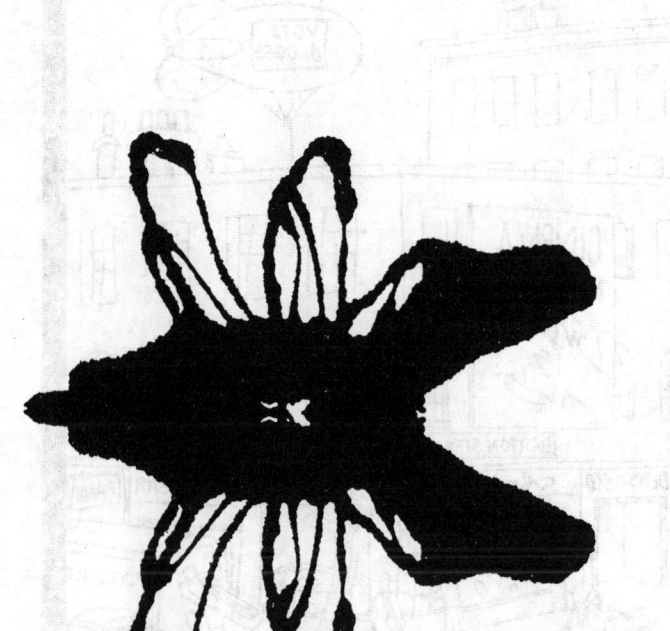

G

H

WHAT I SEE IN THE BLOTS	Number of images
A	
B	
C	
D	
E	
F	
G	
H	
Total	

How many different ideas did you have altogether?
Count them up. More than 16? You have a rich
imagination. 8 to 15? You have a good imagination. 4
to 8? Well, that is a fairly good number of ideas. Try
some blots of your own. Less than 4 means your
unconscious is not easily accessible, perhaps you are a
little nervous?

WHAT KIND OF IMAGES CAME FROM YOUR UNCONSCIOUS?
Write down the number of times each of the following
occurred in your list (*above*).

Skeletons or other dead things. Objects that
are standing still. Illness, disabilities or decay.
Disasters, wars, tragedies, monsters.

If you score more in this section, you are rather
negative or pessimistic. Perhaps you need an outlet
such as writing, singing, dancing, sport or drama. Go
out and find some good friends and share your fears.

Animals, people, plants, living things.
Objects that are moving or performing.
Health, fun, humor, growth, love.
Fantasies, dreams, food and drink.

If you score more in this section, you are positive and
optimistic. You love life and do not let your fears and
upsets get you down for long and can always find new
interests.

©DIAGRAM

111

Can you remember what you see?

Your ability to be a reliable witness depends on your personal viewpoint, how much you noticed, what you thought important, how you interpreted what you saw and your memory. It isn't surprising that different people give different accounts of the same situation. Here you can test your short-term observation and memory. You will need a watch and two pieces of paper.

COVER THE OPPOSITE PAGE WITH A PIECE OF PAPER

For two minutes only, study the street scene (*below*) in detail; then cover this page.
Leave the book for fifteen minutes...do something else.
When you return, leave the picture covered, uncover and answer the questions as accurately as you can, taking as much time as you like.

Answer these questions without looking at the picture	Write your answers here	
1 Name the film that is showing at the cinema.		
2 Exactly what is written on the news-stand billboard? You must write down the complete message.		
3 Is the pedestrian crossing warden male or female?		
4 How many oranges could you get for $1?		
5 There are four cars visible. Is this correct?		
6 On which street is Den's Disco?		
7 Where did you see a man carrying a briefcase under his arm? Describe his location exactly.		
8 On which street would you find the bank?		
9 What are the removal men carrying?		
10 Name the two streets at the junction of which there is a telephone booth.		
11 What time is it?		
12 How many children are actually on the crossing?		
13 Who wants your vote?		
14 How many people are on the pavement outside the coffee shop and which sex are they?		
15 Could the window cleaner see the mail-box?		
16 How many children are carrying balloons?		
17 Could the woman with a feather in her hat catch a train at 3.25?		
18 Could the garbage collectors see the window-cleaner?		
19 Which shop name or names have not been mentioned?		
20 How many miles is it to Cambridge?		

Total number of correct answers, maximum 20:

©DIAGRAM

Checking your accuracy
Look again at the picture and examine the factual accuracy of your answers, checking those that are completely correct. Add up the number of checks.
How observant are you?
Score 16–20 Excellent observation and memory.
    12–15 Good observation and fair memory.
      8–11 Average all round.
      4– 7 Not at all good.
      0– 3 You need more practice, unless you are

over the age of 70. If you are elderly, try waiting a month before answering the questions as long-term memory improves with age, just as short-term memory deteriorates with age.

Reality or illusion?

On the whole a healthy pair of eyes will see what is on the paper but our brains sometimes interpret incorrectly. The visual illusions on these two pages are examples. Even if we *know* the reality, our brains often refuse to believe it. Without using tools to check them out, look at each drawing and try to answer the questions (*below*). Write your answers in the spaces below each question.

1 Which line is longer, **a** or **b**?

2 Which line is shorter, **a** or **b**?

3 There are three ways of "seeing" this drawing; what are they?

4 Could you construct this skeleton cube?

5 Which pairs of lines are parallel to each other: **a** and **b**; **c** and **d**; or **e** and **f**?

6 What can you see in this drawing?

7 Would it be possible to construct this in wood?

8 What can you see in this drawing?

9 Focus on the center point and move the page from side to side. What happens?

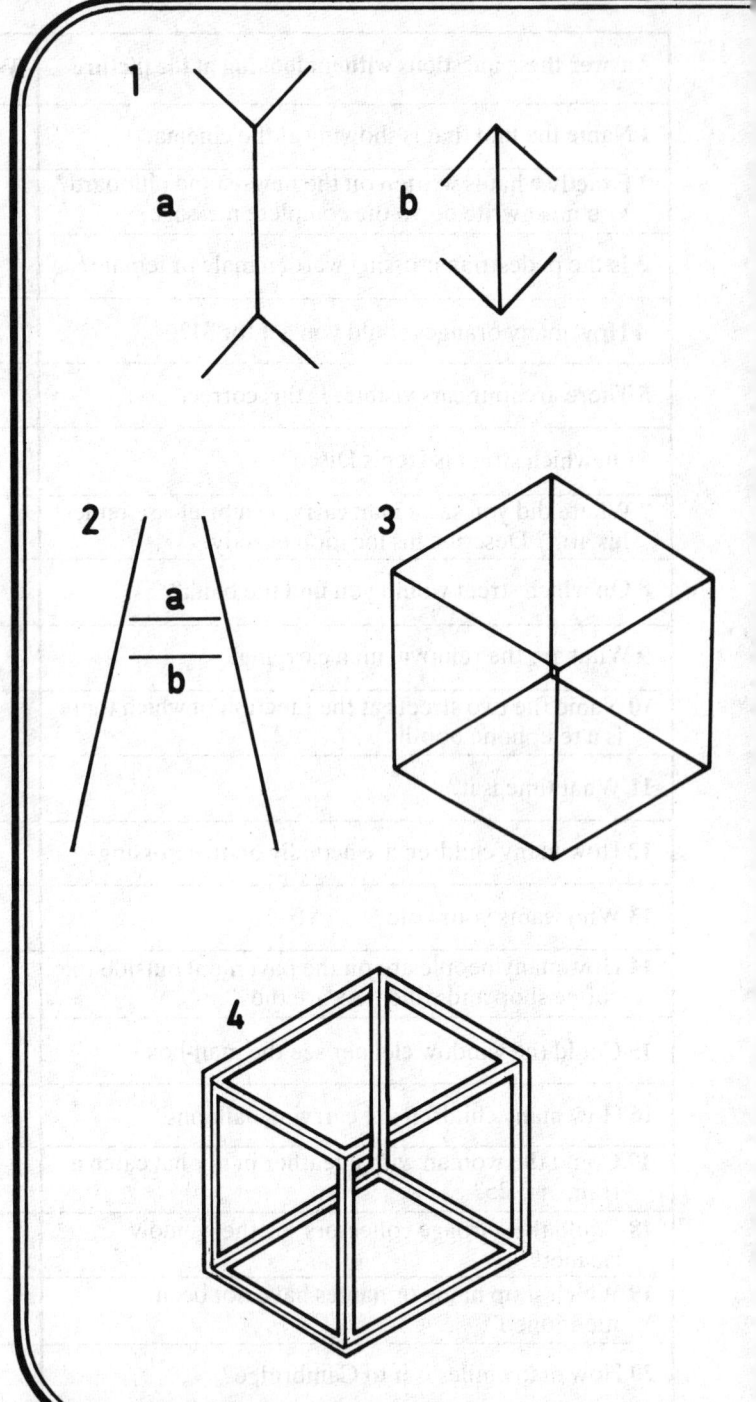

Four kinds of visual illusions
Distortion occurs when it is difficult to judge length, width or position correctly.
Ambiguity occurs when it is possible to interpret the drawing in two or more different ways.
Paradoxical drawings of three dimensional objects do not make sense until you realize they are **drawings.**
Fictional illusions happen when we see things that are not really there, even on the drawing.

Which kind of illusions are the ones on these pages?
Write the correct numbers by each type.

Distortion	
Ambiguity	
Paradox	
Fiction	

5

c   d

e   f

a   b

6

8

7

9

Answers to the questions

1 Neither; **a** and **b** are the same length.

2 Neither; **a** and **b** are the same length.

3 A pattern of six triangles; a cube viewed from the top; a cube viewed from underneath.

4 No, one upright overlaps an edge in the drawing that it would have to pass behind in three dimensions.

5 All the pairs of lines, **a/b, c/d, e/f** are parallel, i.e. equal in distance from each other.

6 A black vase and the white profiles of twins looking at each other.

7 No, the corners could be made but not connected.

8 A white triangle on top of the one outlined in black.

9 The wheel appears to spin round.

Distortion: 1, 2 and 5. **Ambiguity:** 3 and 6.

Paradox: 4 and 7. **Fiction:** 8 and 9.

What kind of dreamer are you?

Are you dreaming your life away or are you using your dreams to get the most out of life? Our dreams tell us what is needed to restore a balance in our lives; to become whole, *not* perfect. Dreaming itself can slowly change our attitudes. Over a long period of time, a personal pattern becomes clearer and these dream-patterns can give us insight into the neglected parts of ourselves. Every dream has a purpose and is entirely honest. While we are awake we may pretend, but while we are asleep there are no deceptions. Dreams are part of our inner lives, akin to intuition, fantasy, imagination and those inner urges, desires and needs of which we may be only vaguely aware.

It is said that, on average, everybody dreams four times each night. Researchers have discovered that people who normally cannot remember dreaming are able to recall dreams if they are woken during those periods of sleep that are accompanied by rapid eye movements (called REM sleep). Almost anything can stimulate dreaming, especially unusual events that take place during the evening – but remember that a regular intake of alcohol depresses REM sleep and may deprive you of essential dream periods.

REMEMBERING AND CHANGING YOUR DREAMS

The Senoi people of SE Asia meet each morning to discuss their dreams. They believe that remembering, understanding and changing dreams contributes to good health. The Senoi learn from childhood to recall dreams, to repeat enjoyable ones and to dream happy endings to nightmares. You can also learn to remember and change your dreams.

Keep a notebook and pencil by your bed. The moment you wake up in the morning, write down anything at all that you remember, before it fades. Even just noting the way you feel will give you some insight into the kind of dreams you have had. These feelings are the first clue to your inner life. Do you wake up feeling sad, happy, angry, bored, lively...?

Learning to recall a whole dream will take a little time and patience. Relax in bed each night and tell yourself "When I wake up, I shall remember my dream." Note down *exactly* whatever you begin to remember; it may seem like nonsense, but images from our unconscious are rarely logical. As you become more familiar with your own dream patterns, you will discover they are full of intuitive wisdom.

To repeat a dream you particularly enjoyed, use the same kind of self-suggestion. As you relax before sleeping, describe quietly to yourself how the dream began. This same method can be used if you want to finish an incomplete dream or to change the ending of an unsatisfactory or frightening dream. For example, have you ever woken up in a sweat while dreaming of falling? The Senoi people use self-suggestion to change the fears of falling into pleasures – "As I fall I will change into a great bird and fly across the valley to..." or "I will begin to float down to earth as gently as a feather and land in the sunshine on..." You can fill in your favorite places. Some people discover that they can redirect events during the dream itself. However, it is very important that you do not use self-suggestion to try and change your dreams until you have first brought any inner conflicts they represent to consciousness. Only if you deal with the conflicts first will you avoid putting extra stress on yourself.

DREAM PERSONALITIES

What kind of dreamer are you? And does your dream personality reflect your waking personality? Find out by answering the questions (*below*).

Check one answer to each question. Choose the answer that is most typical of you during the last three years. Then enter your scores into the scoring boxes.

How often are you aware that you have been dreaming?

	A	Rarely
	F	At irregular intervals
	C	Once a week
	D	Once a month at the most
	E	Every day
	B	When I'm on holiday

When can you recall a dream most clearly?

	E	Immediately on waking
	D	I know I have dreamed, but I can't recall it
	C	Whenever I choose
	A	During routine work or traveling
	B	When something else reminds me of it
	F	When I have a similar dream

How do you prefer to sleep?

	D	In complete darkness or in a fairly dark room
	C	With a light on inside the house or out
	B	With a light switch handy

How do you react if you are short of sleep or under stress?

	D	I sleep for 24 hours or more
	B	I catnap during the day
	E	I sleep restlessly and wake frequently
	A	I sleep heavily for 10–12 hours
	F	I daydream a lot
	C	I have very vivid dreams for several nights

What are your waking-up habits?

	A	I wake up at the same time every morning
	B	I wake up when the alarm goes off
	C	I wake up at different times each day
	D	I find it hard to change my wake-up time
	E	I can decide at what time to wake up
	F	I always need an alarm clock

How would you describe your sleep?

	E	I am a light sleeper
	A	I am a deep sleeper
	F	I am an average sleeper

A	B	C	D	E	F

Add your **A** score to your **D** score to find your total passive score.

Add your **B** score to your **F** score to find your total conditional score.

Add your **C** score to your **E** score to find your total active score.

The highest score – passive, conditional, or active – shows your main dream personality. Read the description (*right*) and decide how well it matches with your waking personality. (If it does not match at all, you may be one of the rare breed of mainly contrary dreamers, or you may have a distinctly Jekyll and Hyde personality!) If you scored the same in two categories, read the descriptions of both and decide which seems most appropriate. Fairly even scoring usually indicates a conditional dreamer.

Passive dreamer This type of dreamer is hardly aware of dreams, and can gain by learning to recall and understand them. If this is your dream personality, you are interested in worldly things, fairly controlled, and you like to take the lead and to plan changes. You are logical, enjoy intellectual pleasures, try to avoid conflicts, and are usually very sensible and reasonable.

Conditional dreamer This type of dreamer is aware of dreams but usually ignores them, and can gain by recording their dreams and taking notice of them. If this is your dream personality, you are interested in balancing things, fairly flexible, and you like to go your own way and resist changes. You are pragmatic, enjoy practical pleasures, try to neutralize conflicts, and are usually very inventive and dogmatic.

Active dreamer This type of dreamer is very aware of dreams and makes use of them, and can gain by finding his or her own personal dream pattern. If this is your dream personality, you are interested in emotional things, fairly spontaneous, and you like to follow a lead and to adapt to changes. You are intuitive, enjoy sensual pleasures, try hard to solve conflicts, and are usually very romantic and imaginative.

©DIAGRAM

What kind of dreams do you have?

TYPES OF DREAMS

It has been suggested by dream researchers that there are 11 types of dreams. No one dream or type of dream is more important than any other – it is the patterns that are revealed over a period of time that are important. Begin your dream interpretation by trying to identify the type of dream you have had – remembering that some dreams can combine several types. Dreams accompanied by strong feelings may show a conflict in urgent need of attention.

Contrary dreams are natural balancing dreams. During periods of great happiness we may dream of crying or during grief we may dream of laughing. Frequent contrary dreams indicate a lack of balance in life:

Insight dreams may include a flash of light or just a shadowy image showing a tableau that reveals your hidden motives concerning current activities.

Nightmares reveal your deepest fears and inner conflicts, particularly about sexuality. Childhood nightmares often include memories of birth.

Physiological dreams may restore a balance for you (as in sexual dreams), or may wake you up so you can urinate, keep warm, or relieve thirst, etc. Women can become aware of pregnancy very early on.

Problem-solving dreams show very clear solutions. Self-suggestion before sleeping is very helpful.

Repeating images are a clue to your basic conflicts and may be part of your longterm dream-patterns.

Residual dreams finish the day's affairs.

Sequential dreams, like nightly instalments, are an important part of your conflict patterns.

Transforming dreams in which you change things or are changed show a great desire to assert yourself.

Vigilant dreams keep you aware of your environment so that you notice things that go bump in the night or the sound of the alarm clock!

Wish-fulfilling dreams reveal your deepest yearnings and may need careful interpretation. Your personal word and image associations are very important here.

GENERAL INTERPRETATIONS OF COMMON DREAM IMAGES

The Swiss psychologist, Carl Jung described many dream images as part of the "collective unconscious" present in all of us. Some of these are "archetypes" – primordial images of ourselves – which also appear in myths, legends and fairy tales all over the world.

Accidents Self-punishment. Worry about accidents to others shows hidden aggression towards them.

Actors Parts of ourselves, often hidden talents.

Action Whatever happens in a dream has been solely invented by you and is totally your responsibility.

Aggression Repressed anger. If it is turned toward yourself you may have unnecessary guilt-complexes.

Animals Your own animal nature. Sometimes word associations can be involved, e.g. bear could indicate "overbearing" or "bear-hug."

Ascending or climbing Urge to succeed. Rhythmic climbing of stairs indicates sexual movements or needs.

Anxiety or emotions Felt during dreams these are real feelings that underlie your waking life.

Birds Imagination, freedom, the urge to escape. For men the feminine part; for women themselves.

Body and parts of the body Your inner view of yourself; health, sickness; gaining, losing; sexual conflicts.

Boxes or prisons Intolerable restrictions/inhibitions.

Buildings You, your body, the structure of your life, your attitude of mind. A stranger in a building is an unrecognized part of yourself; stairs are your sexuality.

Catastrophes The unconscious side of us that wants us to change. Old attitudes crumbling. Real tragedies may be re-run during dreams, or there may be dreams of happiness, relief, or revenge depending on your needs.

Caves or darkness Uncertainty; a need for security.

Chases Conflict between desires and fear of getting what you want. Try ending the dream differently.

Clocks Your heart's emotional needs and attitudes.

Color Your emotions – vivid, depressed, bright, etc.

Conflicts Confusion, stress, unhappiness; needs for decisions not yet brought to consciousness.

Crimes Oddly enough these are usually visual images of your emotions, so interpret them accordingly.

Crossing Satisfactory decisions made or about to be made. Cliffs may be obstacles to implementation.

Death If yours, a need for rest and retreat for a while. If another person's, hostility towards that person or towards that particular part of your personality.

Dirt or excrement Money, your ego, sex, rebellion. Try playing with it and enjoying it to resolve conflicts.

Falling Fear of giving in to pleasure and sexual feelings, both men and women. Fear of failure.

Fire Passions, desires, joy or threats and a sense of powerlessness. Word associations – "tongues of fire," etc.

Flowers Beauty, love, tenderness, the genitals.

Flying Desire for escape, freedom, sex, relief.

Illness A need for rest, attention, or appreciation.

Insects Something bothering you?

Journeys and transport Where you want to go and how. Which part of yourself wants to develop, e.g. cars – your sexuality; buses – social activities; gliders – your ideas; missing a train – reassurance you have plenty of time.

Machines Habits, routines, body language.

Money Time, energy, love, guilt, jealousy.

Paralysis Unresolved conflict between fear and desire.

People Themselves if you feel strongly towards them; otherwise parts of you, valuable objects, or events. Archetypal people are parts of yourself that either need recognition or are dominating your personality:
Mother, father, wise old man or woman – care, wisdom;
Witch, ogre, monster – possessiveness, oppression;
Prince, princess, youth, maiden – love, romance;
Prostitute, tramp, playboy, siren – eroticism;

Hero, heroine, amazon, hunter – intellectual affairs;
Priestess, wizard, angel – intuition and imagination;
Baby, cupid, elf, dwarf – sensuality, security;
Soldier, devil, thief – your negative feelings.
Places Your current state of mind and attitudes.
Perversions Ways you are avoiding a fulfilling love.
Sex A wish for love, a need for love; hunger, thirst.

Shadows Your own worst side you haven't yet accepted.
Smells and sounds Sensuality, longings, yearnings.
Time The time usually means the age you are in the dream.
Water Emotional needs. Usually a deep need for change. Use word associations, e.g. "out of my depth" and floods, flowing, semen, birth, etc.

INTERPRETING IMAGES AND EVENTS IN YOUR DREAMS

1 Never tell your dream to someone else until you have interpreted it yourself: other people will give you their own interpretations, which will almost certainly not be the same as yours! However, a friend who has learned to ask questions without "leading" you can be helpful during the gestalt process.
2 Write down exactly what happened in your dream, describe every image, and include the feelings you had.
3 Use the gestalt process to retell your dream. Using the first person, speak as if each item and action in the dream is speaking, and retell the dream from that point of view. For example, "I am a large house and …" or "I am a bus moving along a bumpy road …" Gestalting means taking a whole view, and as you retell the dream in the first person from varying points of view, your own inner need for wholeness will become clearer, showing you ways to develop the more neglected sides of yourself. Dreams come from the unconscious, so expect many surprises.

I am a tall, strong lighthouse. My light is always shining...

I am a battered, old bag full of useless bits of information...

Chapter 4

YOUR SOCIAL SELF

Making contact with others gives you choices and develops your character, adding variety to life. You are, indeed, involved with other people. Alone, with others or in love, you show the many different sides of yourself.

1 Our true feelings are often hidden by an assumed mask while we play various roles in life.
2 The stereotyped image of the happy family – the young married couple with child celebrating the joys of Christmas together.
3 On the other hand, togetherness is not always as untroubled as might be hoped for, as this illustration dramatically shows.
4 Since the fifteenth century we have celebrated St. Valentine's Day, and expressed our feelings, by sending either a gift or love token as illustrated here.
5 A typical social gathering, as sketched by the artist, at a Saturday market.
6 The everlasting kiss of lovers, caught in marble by Rodin.

3

5

4

Valentine Wishes for You!

6

Which you?

You will probably have come across some contradictions as you worked through this book. This should not surprise you; you are a very complex person. How many of you are there?
1 The one you are at heart.
2 The one you think you are.
3 The one you would like others to think you are.
4 The one others think you are.
5 The one you are afraid you might be.
6 The one you refuse to be.
7 The one you would like to be.

You may be different at home from how you are at work. You may feel very different when you are in familiar surroundings from when you are in strange surroundings. When you achieve something you hoped for, you are not the same person as when you are being rejected. In a strong position you may feel confident but in a threatening position you may feel weak. Here you can look at four sides to yourself: your strengths and weaknesses; your hopes and fears.

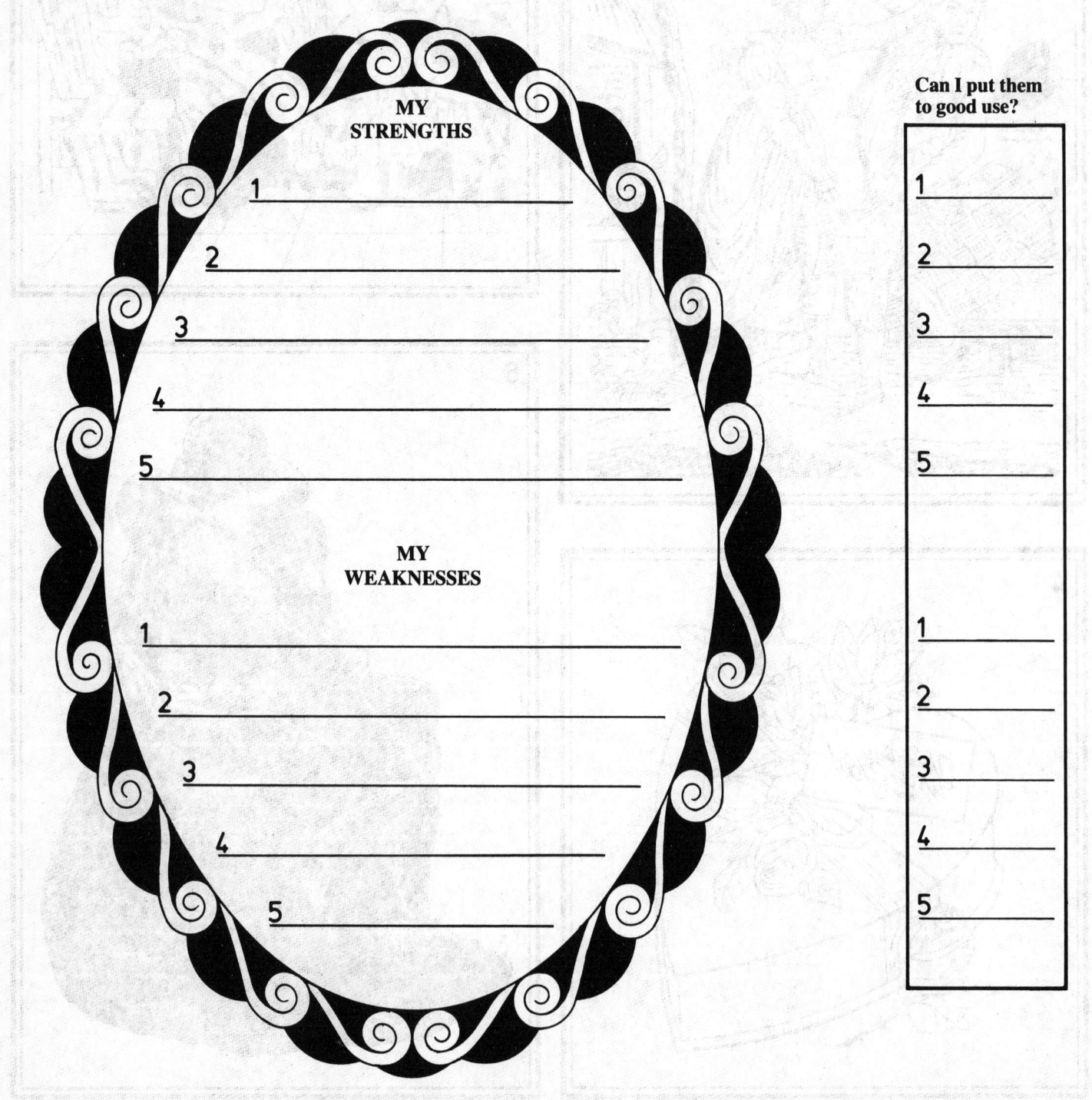

MY STRENGTHS

1 _____
2 _____
3 _____
4 _____
5 _____

MY WEAKNESSES

1 _____
2 _____
3 _____
4 _____
5 _____

Can I put them to good use?

1 _____
2 _____
3 _____
4 _____
5 _____

1 _____
2 _____
3 _____
4 _____
5 _____

Strengths and Weaknesses

Think of five things you do well or five parts of your personality that you like and write them down on the lines at the top of the left-hand mirror. For example, GOOD AT MIXING WITH PEOPLE or CAN FIX A SHELF. Then write down five weaknesses, for example, TALK TOO MUCH or WORK TOO HARD. Yes, what one person sees as a strength, another person might see as a weakness. Then check off in the column whether or not you put your strengths and weaknesses to some positive use.

Hopes and fears

Choose five of each and write them in the right-hand mirror, like the mirror of your soul! Then give a check or cross to show if you really think they are realistic or not. For example, a hope to WIN THE LOTTERY is unrealistic and a FEAR OF THE DARK is also unrealistic, unless you put yourself in danger. When you have completed this page, turn to the next section called: Who makes my decisions?

Are they realistic?

1 _____

2 _____

3 _____

4 _____

5 _____

1 _____

2 _____

3 _____

4 _____

5 _____

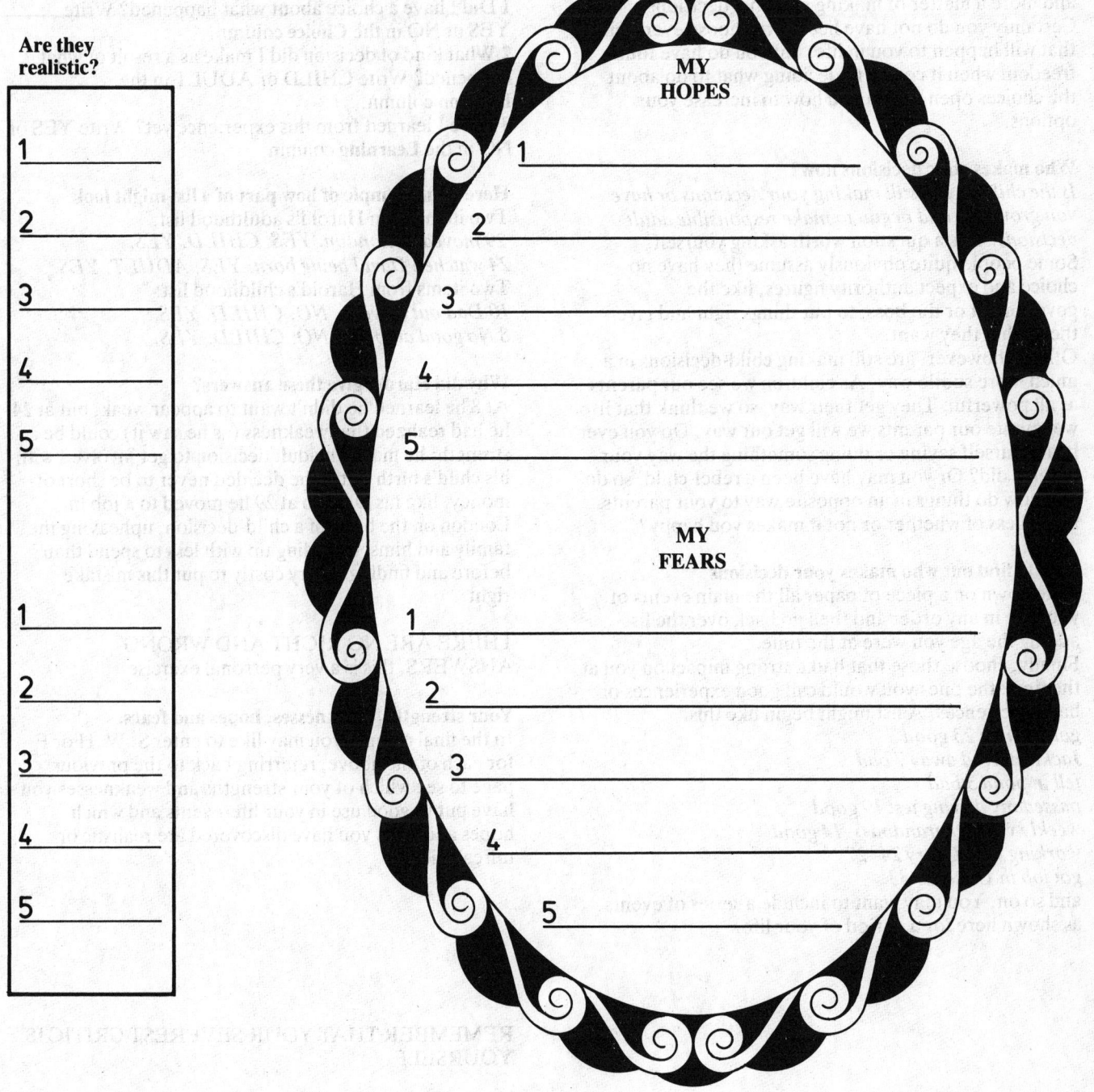

MY HOPES

1 _____

2 _____

3 _____

4 _____

5 _____

MY FEARS

1 _____

2 _____

3 _____

4 _____

5 _____

Who makes your decisions?

You were born with a set of genes that determined your inherited characteristics. Your upbringing affected your attitude to life and your attachments to people and places. During your childhood you realized you did not have much choice about important things such as where and when you were born, where you lived and what your parents and other adults did. As a result you made some important childhood decisions...mostly about how to get what you wanted. We all do it, one way or another. If you are a parent, you will know that your children do it too.

What happens during and after teenage becomes more and more a matter of making personal decisions. Certainly you do not have license to choose everything that will happen to you in life, but you do have total freedom when it comes to deciding what to do about the choices open to you and how to increase your options.

Who makes your decisions now?
Is the child in you still making your decisions or have you grown up and begun to make responsible adult decisions? It is a question worth asking yourself. Some people quite obviously assume they have no choice and expect authority figures, like the government or the boss, to put things right and give them what they want.
Others, however, are still making child-decisions in a much more subtle way. As children we see our parents as all powerful. They get their way, so we think that if we imitate our parents we will get our way. Do you ever hear yourself saying or doing something the way your parents did? Or you may have been a rebel-child, so do you now do things in an opposite way to your parents, regardless of whether or not it makes you happy?

How to find out who makes your decisions
Note down on a piece of paper all the main events of your life in any order and then go back over the list adding the age you were at the time.
Finally, choose those that had a strong impact on you at the time; the ones you would call good experiences or bad experiences. A list might begin like this:
got married 23 good
Jackie moved away 7 bad
fell in pond 3 bad
passed my driving test 19 good
weekly visits to grandpa 6–14 good
working with Garry 24–27
got job in Leicester 33
and so on. You may want to include a series of events, as shown here, or a period of your life.

Using the life-events table
Enter the events against which you wrote good or bad. Begin at the bottom of the page with the earliest, putting your age in the age column. Work upwards towards the top of the page.
Draw a line between each event and a colored line between your adulthood and your childhood, probably somewhere in your late teenage.

When your list of events is complete, think carefully about each one and answer these three questions about them all. Begin from the bottom of your list.

Questions to ask yourself
1 Did I have a choice about what happened? Write YES or NO in the **Choice** column.
2 What kind of decision did I make as a result of what happened? Write CHILD or ADULT in the **Decision** column.
3 Have I learned from this experience yet? Write YES or NO in the **Learning** column.

Here is an example of how part of a list might look
Two items from Harold's adulthood list:
29 moved to London. YES, CHILD. YES.
24 watched David being born. YES. ADULT. YES.
Two items from Harold's childhood list:
10 Dad out of work. NO. CHILD. YES.
8 No good at sports. NO. CHILD. YES.

Why did Harold give these answers?
At 8 he learned he didn't want to appear weak, but at 24 he had realized that weakness (as he saw it) could be a strength: he made an adult decision to get involved with his child's birth. At 10 he decided never to be short of money, like his Dad, so at 29 he moved to a job in London on the basis of a child-decision, upheaving the family and himself, ending up with less to spend than before and finding it very costly to put this mistake right.

THERE ARE NO RIGHT AND WRONG ANSWERS, this is a very personal exercise.

Your strengths, weaknesses, hopes and fears.
In the final column you may like to enter S, W, H or F for each of the above, referring back to the previous page to see which of your strengths and weaknesses you have put to good use in your life-events and which hopes and fears you have discovered are realistic or unrealistic.

REMEMBER THAT YOUR SEVEREST CRITIC IS YOURSELF

LIFE-EVENTS TABLE					
Age	Life-events	Choice	Decision	Learning	Analysis S/W H/F
	Now				
	Birth				

Are you satisfied?

Where are you now and are you satisfied with your position? This is the question you can answer if you take stock of your situation and consider all the parts of your life, including the people you love.

Drawing a flower of life is one way of making a visual picture on which you can clearly see where you are now, what satisfies you and which are the black spots in your life. George's flower (*below*), is an example.

How to draw your own flower

Using a pencil first of all, draw short lines from MYSELF NOW and write down all the main parts of your life. There is a list (*opposite*) of the kinds of things you might choose. George, who is a married man of 42, chose SELF, FAMILY, WORK and FUTURE because he saw these as most important for him. Next draw each "petal" by making lines that branch, each being a thought that occurs to you as you draw. Finally, add a spot to show your dissatisfactions and a star to show what satisfies you, or would satisfy you if you could do what you have written.

SAMPLE: GEORGE'S FLOWER OF LIFE

WHICH PARTS OF YOUR LIFE DO YOU WANT TO INCLUDE?
Here are some ideas to choose from but you may want to invent some of your own, for example, the name of a person or an activity.

SELF	WORK
CLOTHES	JOBSHARE
HEALTH	HOUSEKEEPING
KEEP FIT	VOLUNTARY WORK
HABITS	REDUNDANCY
HOBBIES	UNEMPLOYMENT
FRIENDS	RETIREMENT
LOVERS	RE-TRAINING
MATES	OWN BUSINESS
HOLIDAYS	EDUCATION
ADVENTURES	SCHOOL
FUTURE	COLLEGE
PAST	UNIVERSITY
FAMILY	D.I.Y.
SPOUSE	PETS
PARENTS	TRAVEL
CHILDREN	EMIGRATE
RELATIVES	PROBLEMS
HOME	AMBITIONS
MONEY	DREAMS

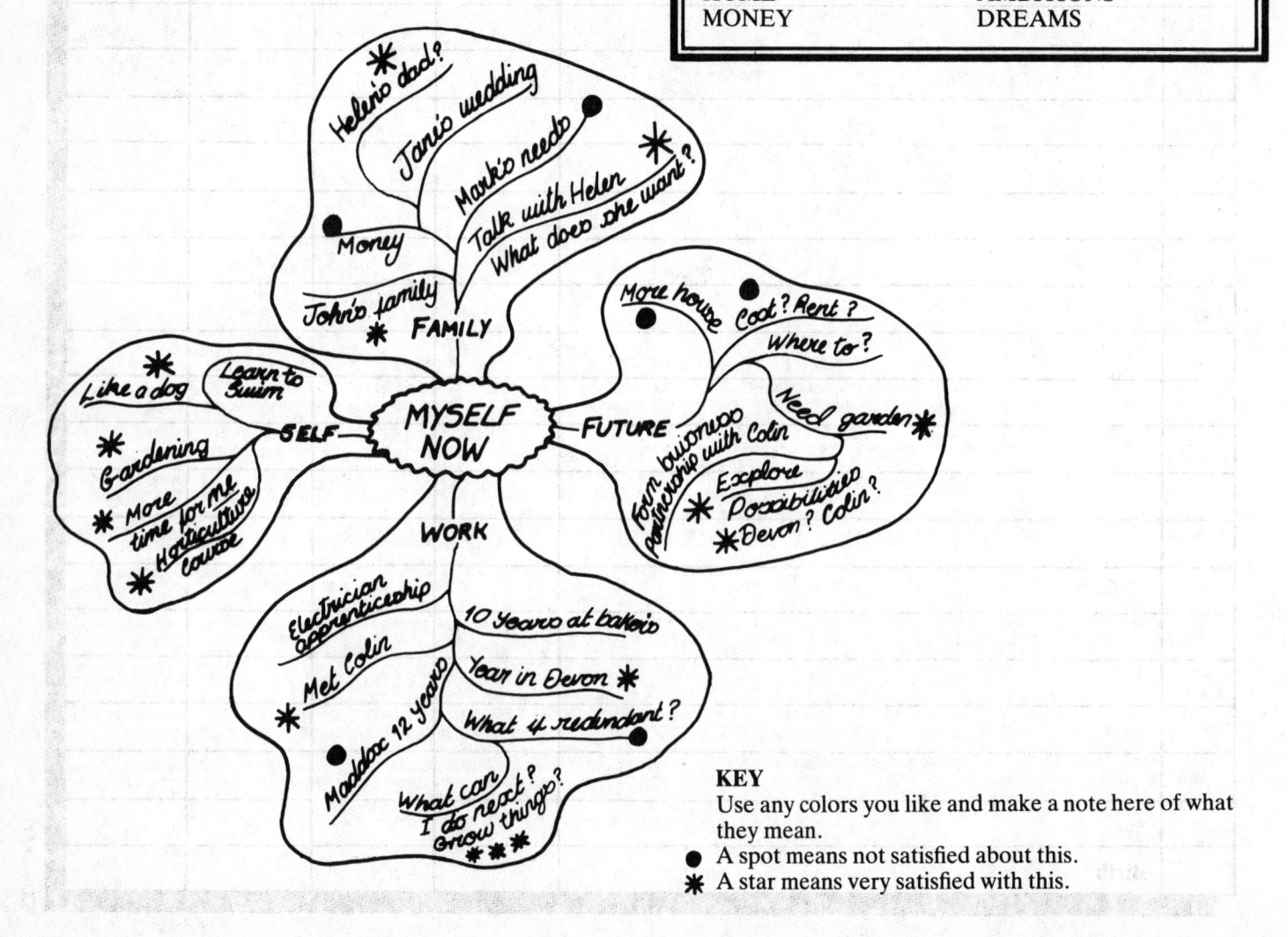

KEY

Use any colors you like and make a note here of what they mean.

● A spot means not satisfied about this.

✱ A star means very satisfied with this.

126

MY FLOWER OF LIFE

MYSELF
NOW

How skilled are you?

You are probably more skilled than you may imagine, in your paid or unpaid occupations, in leisure activities and in personal relationships. On these two pages you can examine more closely skills that you use every day and perhaps give some thought to developing those you didn't know you had, by making a job profile.

Optimists learn to believe in themselves
Having a positive attitude is a skill in itself. If on being asked what you do, you reply, "Oh, I'm only a . . ." then you probably need to do this exercise more than anyone and acquire the skill of believing in yourself, as you do it.

How to fill in the profile
Select the eight work skills you most frequently use and enter them in the work skills column on the page (*opposite*). You will find that two very common skills have already been entered at the end.
If your job has many parts to it, you may like to list all the parts in the list (*right*) and make your selection of eight from that list. A sample list has been given (*below*). You should list exactly **what** you do during the course of your work.

How do you apply your skills?
Write down a brief description of how you apply each skill in the four different areas shown across the top of the profile on the next page. Is the skill used when dealing with people, things or information? How often do you use your own ideas or have to make decisions? A sample list of work skills is shown (*below*), and a partially completed sample profile is given across the bottom of the page to guide you in completing your own job profile on the next page.

MY LIST OF WORK SKILLS

SAMPLE LIST OF WORK SKILLS *Serving in the bar*

Stock up shelves	Unlock store	Give change	Collect glasses
Check money in cash register	Take orders	Handle complaints	Wash glasses
	Serve orders correctly	Make conversation	Take orders for bar food
Turn on all lights	Take money	Keep pumps clean	Balance takings, etc.

SAMPLE PROFILE OF TWO SKILLS   Job: *Serving in a bar*

Work skills	People	Things	Information	Ideas
Take orders.	Giving attention.	Using equipment quickly, holding glasses steady.	Listening and remembering accurately.	Suggesting alternatives, asking if customers would like ice, etc.
Collect glasses.	Moving gracefully, carrying weight and balancing.	Checking if customers have finished with glasses.	How to wash quickly and without breakage	?

128

MY JOB PROFILE   Job:........................

Work skills	People	Things	Information	Ideas
Give appreciation				
Ensure satisfaction				

How does your mind work?

What kind of activities does your mind prefer? For reasons that are not yet understood, some people have a memory for information while others have a very vivid and rich imagination. Some people prefer to work systematically, while others seize-up at the sight of a set of numbers.

Here are five kinds of mind-activities for you to try out. Choose whichever looks most interesting and see if that was the one your mind preferred.
Answers are at the bottom of the page (*opposite*).

DO YOU ENJOY NUMBERS?

Make the square (*bottom*) into a magic square by placing each of the twelve numbers (*below*) in the correct position. When you have solved this one the numbers will add up to 34 vertically, horizontally and diagonally.

1; 2; 3; 5; 6; 8; 10; 11; 12; 13; 15; 16.

9			4
7			14

DO YOU HOARD ENDLESS BITS OF INFORMATION?

Write your answers in the spaces provided.   My Answers

1 In which healing method are fine needles used? _____

2 What is the square root of 225? _____

3 Where would you find the language of Fortran used? _____

4 Which US religious sect can practice polygamy? _____

5 Which is the smallest bird in the world? _____

6 Which branch of science was founded by Mendel? _____

7 Name Mozart's musical rival at court. _____

8 What is the meaning of mendacious? _____

9 Who founded the Muslim faith in Mecca? _____

10 Of which country is Shinto a native religion? _____

11 What color are the flowers of an olive tree? _____

12 Which animal is killed to make ermine coats? _____

13 Who lost his strength when his hair was cut? _____

14 Which shape has sides and diagonals equal in number? _____

15 Who founded the psychology of Character Armoring? _____

16 Name the American who wrote the Tarzan stories. _____

17 Who painted the Spanish village of Guernica? _____

18 Which fish do Polish people eat on Xmas Eve? _____

19 Which Jewish day is Yom Kippur? _____

20 Name the protein that carries genetic information. _____

Total correct [   ]

DO YOU ENJOY CRACKING CODES?

Try decoding this message which has been adapted from an earlier part of this book!

QS LVL DJX KSB IPTF SCXE DJX TSSG SG JVQ MVEDJLZN SE OZQ DJZD Z KZVEN QDSEN DSS?

DO YOU LIKE EXPLORING IDEAS IMAGINATIVELY?

Imagine the world suddenly running out of oil and gas supplies everywhere. Write a brief story here, telling what life would be like. Let your friends read the result; they will tell you if it's good.

_____
_____
_____
_____
_____
_____
_____
_____
_____
_____
_____
_____
_____
_____
_____
_____
_____
_____
_____
_____
_____
_____
_____
_____
_____
_____
_____
_____

CAN YOU REMEMBER BY ASSOCIATION?

Here are two lists of assorted names, events, places, activities, conditions and organizations. Can you pair them correctly? Put the code letter of your choices in the boxes by the numbers on the right.

a Mordillo	Football 1	_____
b McEnroe	Politics 2	_____
c Hitchcock	Films 3	_____
d Sartre	Assassination 4	_____
e Halley	Golf 5	_____
f Mandela	Paris 6	_____
g Armero	Singer 7	_____
h Pavarotti	Comet 8	_____
i Gorbachev	Opera 9	_____
j Berlin	Surrogate birth 10	_____
k Wembley	King 11	_____
l Baby Cotton	Time 12	_____
m Big Ben	Tennis 13	_____
n Live Aid	Wall 14	_____
o Armatrading	Fault 15	_____
p Oswald	Ethiopia 16	_____
q St. Andrews	Apartheid 17	_____
r Pompidou	Cartoons 18	_____
s San Andreas	Volcanic eruption 19	_____
t Martin Luther	Existentialism 20	_____

Total correct [ ]

© DIAGRAM

Magic square solution. The square will be correct when the total is 34 in all directions!

Do you hoard endless bits of information answers
1 Acupuncture, 2 Fifteen, 3 Computer program, 4 The Mormons, 5 Humming Bird, 6 Genetics, 7 Salieri, 8 Untruthful, 9 Mohammed, 10 Japan, 11 White, 12 Stoat, 13 Samson, 14 Pentagon, 15 Wilhelm Reich, 16 E. R. Burroughs, 17 Pablo Picasso, 18 Carp, 19 Day of Atonement, 20 Deoxyribonucleic acid.

Message in code solution
No solution given! But here is a clue; the last word is TOO, so now you know every **D** is T and **S** is O.

Can you remember by association answers
1–k, 2–i, 3–c, 4–p, 5–q, 6–r, 7–o, 8–e, 9–h, 10–l, 11–t, 12–m, 13–b, 14–j, 15–s, 16–n, 17–f, 18–a, 19–g, 20–d.

Are you under stress?

Some stress is necessary in all our lives, but too much can increase the risk we run of becoming ill or having an "accident." It is easy to recognize some of the major – and unpleasant – causes of stress, but we need to remember that it can be caused by the pleasant things we look forward to as well as the unpleasant things we dread. This test will help you calculate the amount of potential stress in your life.

During the last six months, how many of the events listed (*right*) have happened to you? Count up the number of **As, Bs, Cs, Ds** and **Es**, enter them in the relevant boxes, multiply this figure by the value to give a total for each letter, then add up the total score. Finally, read the interpretations for each of the three major causes of stress in our lives.

Interpreting your total scores

0–50
If your total score is less than 50 there is little stress in your life: you are unlikely to become ill or have an accident.

50–150
If your total score is between 50 and 100 your chances of becoming ill or having an accident have increased by 35%.

100–150
If your total score is between 100 and 150 your chances of becoming ill or having an accident have increased by 50%. You should try to reduce the amount of stress in the areas of your life over which you have control.

150+
If your score is over 150 your chances of becoming ill or having an accident have increased by 80%. You should take as much care of yourself as possible and attempt to lead a quiet and unstressed life until your score is reduced.

YOU AND YOUR LIFESTYLE

Statement	Code
You have achieved something outstanding and received recognition for it	D
There have been changes in your daily routine (e.g. the way you travel to work)	E
There have been changes in the amount or type of your social activities	E
There have been changes that affect your leisure interests (e.g. you have taken up a new sport)	E
There have been changes in your sleeping or eating habits (e.g. you have gone on a diet)	E
You smoked more than 40 cigarettes a day and have given up smoking	B
You smoked less than 40 cigarettes a day and have given up smoking	D
You were addicted to or dependent on hard drugs or alcohol and have given them up	A
You have been on holiday or vacation	E
Christmas has taken place	E
You have moved house	D
You live in noisy or stressful surroundings	B
You have suffered a serious personal injury	A
You have been ill (other than minor ailments)	A
You have been in a major accident or undergone a major shock (e.g. car crash, fire, etc)	B
You have received a parking ticket or committed a similar offense	E
You have been convicted of a crime and sent to prison	A

	Number	Value	Total
A		50	
B		40	
C		30	
D		20	
E		10	
Lifestyle: total score			

YOUR FAMILY AND OTHER CLOSE RELATIONSHIPS

You have married or remarried — **A**

There has been an enforced unwanted separation from your partner — **C**

You have had problems with your in-laws — **D**

You and your partner are arguing more — **C**

You have been unfaithful to your partner — **C**

You have discovered your partner's infidelity — **C**

You have had or are having sexual difficulties — **B**

You have been reconciled with your partner — **B**

There have been changes in your family or domestic routine — **E**

You (or your partner) are pregnant (whether a planned or unplanned pregnancy) — **B**

A baby has been born in your immediate family — **C**

One of your children has started school, left home or married — **D**

Your immediate family has gained a new member through marriage — **C**

A member of your immediate family suffers from alcoholism, drug addiction or similar compulsive behavior — **A**

A member of your immediate family has had an accident or been taken ill — **B**

A member of your immediate family has recovered from an accident or illness — **B**

A member of your immediate family has died — **A**

A close friend of yours has died — **B**

	Number	Value	Total
A		50	
B		40	
C		30	
D		20	
E		10	
Family and close relationships: total score			

YOUR JOB AND YOUR FINANCES

You started work for the first time or returned to work after a long absence — **D**

You have a very responsible or very harassing job — **B**

You are constantly overworked — **B**

You have a major anxiety at work (e.g. company failing, staff on strike, etc) — **B**

You have changed or are changing your job — **C**

There have been changes in your job or at your place of work (e.g. new offices, new boss, etc) — **C**

You have been promoted or demoted — **D**

You have had difficulties with your boss or other superiors — **E**

You have retired (whether a planned or unplanned retirement) — **B**

You have been dismissed or made redundant — **B**

There has been a major change in your financial state (for better or for worse) — **C**

You owe more than one year's salary (e.g. on a mortgage) — **D**

You have applied for a large mortgage or loan — **E**

	Number	Value	Total
A		50	
B		40	
C		30	
D		20	
E		10	
Job and finances: total score			

Just for fun...

Try making a scrapbook profile of this fascinating person called YOU. Of course you will need the child-like part of you to enjoy having fun! No matter who you are, think you are, would like to be, etc., there is a very important part of you that must always be given an outlet... the child-in-you that simply enjoys doing things for no reason at all. Pure energy, verve and lust for life. Yes, and speaking of lust for life, do it while your own lusty infant is sleeping (if you've got one).

This is just for you and just for fun. If you can enjoy this, you are also the kind of person who enjoys playing, enjoys doing whatever you do and enjoys loving and making love.

Some things you might like to include:
A photograph of yourself. Quotations, patterns. Pictures of the food, clothes and places you like. Your favorite joke, music, activity. Some cartoons, family pictures, doodles... anything at all that is YOU.
THE SPACE IS ALL YOURS TO FILL!
As with your life: do with it what you will.

Which others?

Who do you know that you like? Write down the names of 25 people you like in the space provided (**A**) at the top of the page (*opposite*). Just put them in any order as they occur. They may include your family.

First find out how much you have in common with the people you have chosen, by doing the exercise (*below*). When you have completed this you will be able to see clearly if you have chosen people in similar situations to yourself, or do your contacts with others spread far and wide? You will also be able to see how geographically close they are.

What characteristics do you value in your 25 people?
Do exercise **B, C,** and **D** together. From your 25,
B choose any 5 you would most enjoy being with for a two-week holiday;
C choose 5 to run a garage sale with you;
D choose 5 you could live with on a desert island for 3 years! Write all the names in the spaces numbered. You might choose the same person 2 or 3 times. Opposite each name write down what you think each person could best contribute in the situation including yourself. Reading these, you will see what it is that you value in each person.

HOW MUCH DO YOU HAVE IN COMMON WITH THE 25 PEOPLE YOU HAVE CHOSEN?

Take each person on your list in turn and check the items (*below*) that apply to that person. You may need to put several checks. Finally, put a small circle next to the items that apply to you.

Family and relatives. _____

Friends on your list. _____

Children up to age 12. _____

Teenagers aged 13 to 19. _____

Younger adults aged 20 to 39. _____

Middle-aged adults aged 40 to 59. _____

Older adults aged 60 to 80 plus. _____

Occupations?

In paid work of any kind. _____

Housewives or house-husbands. _____

In voluntary work. _____

Unemployed. _____

Self-employed. _____

Retired. _____

In full-time education. _____

In care or in an institution. _____

Where do they live?

Close enough to you to visit evenings. _____

Close enough to visit taking a day. _____

Further away than either of these. _____

Family situations?

Married; no children. _____

Married; with children. _____

Living together; no children. _____

Living together; with children. _____

Single parent families. _____

Divorced or separated. _____

Widowed; no children. _____

Widowed; with children. _____

Part of shared household. _____

In a homosexual relationship. _____

In a communal situation. _____

No fixed abode or relationship. _____

Special groups?

Same race or culture as you. _____

Different race or culture from you. _____

Same religion as you. _____

Different religion from you. _____

Same social class or group as you. _____

Different social class or group from you. _____

Have own transport. _____

Are pet-owners. _____

Live in a town or city. _____

Live in suburbs. _____

Live in country. _____

Any other? _____

A 25 PEOPLE I KNOW AND LIKE

_____   _____
_____   _____
_____   _____
_____   _____
_____   _____
_____   _____

B 5 PEOPLE WITH WHOM I'D ENJOY A HOLIDAY   **What could each contribute to make it pleasurable?**

1 _____   _____
2 _____   _____
3 _____   _____
4 _____   _____
5 _____   _____

C 5 PEOPLE I'D CHOOSE TO RUN A GARAGE SALE   **What could each contribute towards its success?**

1 _____   _____
2 _____   _____
3 _____   _____
4 _____   _____
5 _____   _____

D 5 PEOPLE I'D TAKE WITH ME TO A DESERT ISLAND   **What could each contribute to our quality of life?**

1 _____   _____
2 _____   _____
3 _____   _____
4 _____   _____
5 _____   _____

How close to others are you?

The kind of relationship you have with someone does not necessarily say anything about how close you are to that person.

Closeness depends on many things such as common interests, experiences you have had together and how much you know about each other. The length of time you have known each other or the distance between where you live are not necessarily important. Nor is the frequency of your meeting a factor. You may be very distant from someone you contact every day and bonded with someone you see only once a year. Bonds grow between people who never feel out of contact with each other, no matter what happens. Honesty is a very important part of closeness; if you are known by each other very intimately, then you are inevitably close, even when there are problems between you.

Making a relationship pattern can help you to see just how close you are to others in your life and which relationships you want to develop, end or mend.

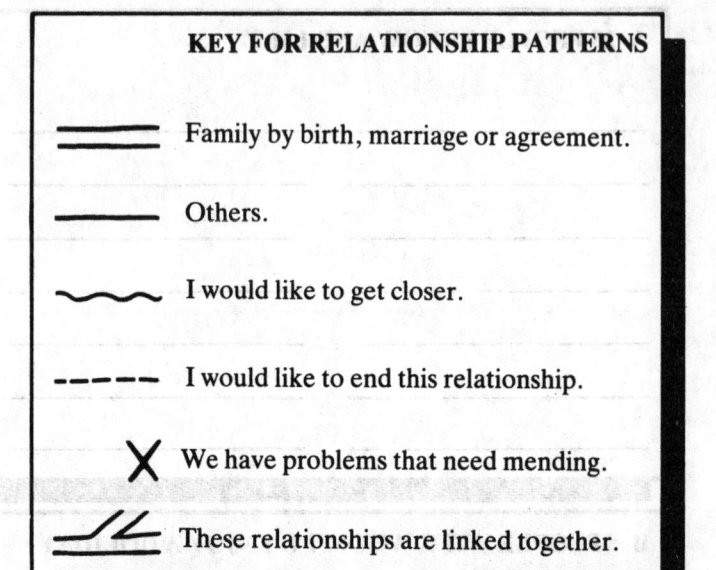

KEY FOR RELATIONSHIP PATTERNS

———— Family by birth, marriage or agreement.

——— Others.

∼∼∼ I would like to get closer.

----- I would like to end this relationship.

✕ We have problems that need mending.

╱ These relationships are linked together.

Making a relationship pattern

Start from yourself in the middle and use pencil so you can make adjustments as you build up the pattern. Every pattern is different. The sample shown is by a fictitious person called Jean, so you can see what it can look like when finished. THE LENGTH OF THE LINES SHOW HOW CLOSE YOU FEEL TO EACH PERSON.

Use the key to decide which kind of lines to draw. You may like to use colors for special reasons, for example circle children in blue, work mates in red, etc.

In the sample Jean feels closer to her friend Mary than to her husband John, but is closest of all to her Dad. More distant from her Mum, Jean feels they have problems. She wants to know Jan better and end contact with Fred. Both she and Bill have problems with Mr. Brown at work.

SAMPLE OF A RELATIONSHIP PATTERN

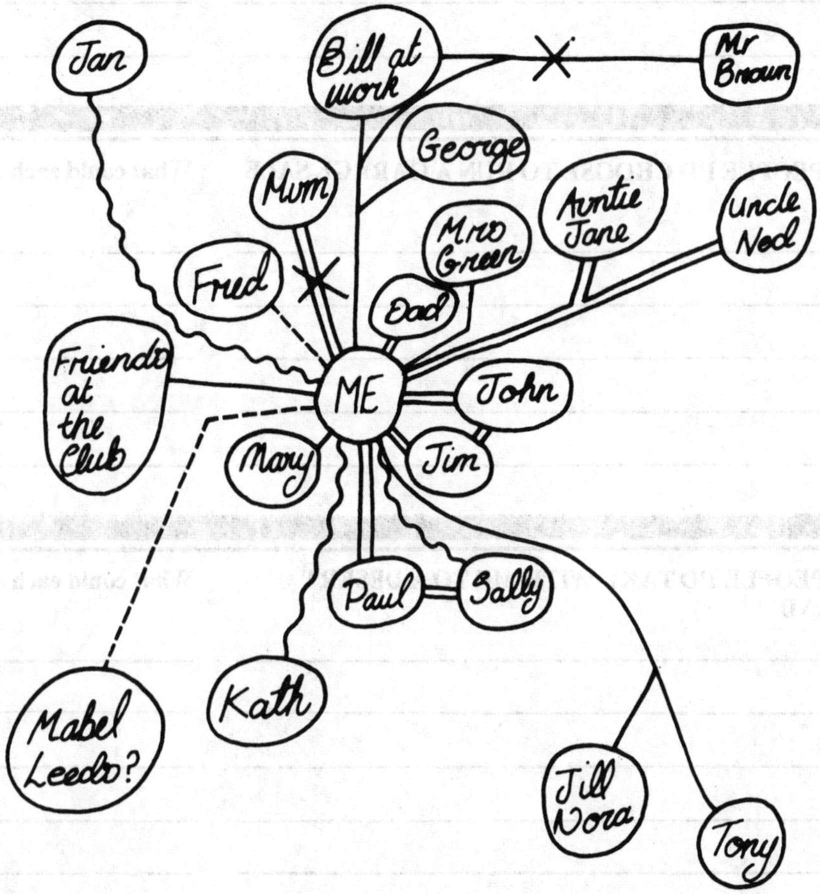

ME

"All the world's a stage...

...and all the men and women players in it." It was William Shakespeare who observed that we all play many parts in life. Different people, changing events and our own fluctuating moods give us opportunities to express the many different parts of ourselves...indeed, this is how we discover our own complexities and develop character, talents and imagination.

Some of the parts we play in life are so well known that they are called roles, but this does not make them any less real. We each fulfil our chosen roles in our unique ways, as do our families and friends.

Which roles do you and the people around you tend to play? If you know the answer to this question, then you could try changing a role in a relationship that has got into a rut. This can be a refreshing and revitalizing experience providing you do it with care and consideration.

Recording the roles used by you and others

Choose six people you would like to include and write their names in the spaces numbered 1 to 6 (**A**). First read the list of roles carefully (*right*). They have all been given familiar names so they can more easily be understood...and make it more fun.

Think carefully about yourself and the people you have chosen, the things you do together and the way you behave towards each other. Fill in the spaces, first with the roles you think you take with them (**B**) and secondly the roles they seem to take with you (**C**). You may like to see if your friends agree with you, but be tactful and gentle.

Finally put YES or NO next to each one, to show whether or not you enjoy the roles you take with each other (**D**) and (**E**). Now you have a record to keep and adjust as time goes by. Do you tend to play one role more than any other? Roles are like jackets and hats; you can change them, yet remain truly yourself, as with any change of clothes.

Which parts do you play?

This small selection of roles is in alphabetical order and there are no right or wrong choices. They mean whatever you think they mean. You may like to add ones of your own devising by letting your imagination run free. These roles, "jackets," "hats" or parts we play, help us to realize how we see ourselves and others.

Admirer	Mickey Mouse
Adviser	Ministering Angel
Appreciator	Mother Earth
Bargain Hunter	Mischief-maker
Big Brother	Mystifier
Big Momma	Nest-builder
Busy Bee	Optimist
Casanova	Paddington Bear
Cheerleader	Peace-keeper
Cinderella	Pessimist
Clown	Peter Pan
Computer	Pollyanna
Conquering Hero	Prince Charming
Cool Customer	Protector
Counsellor	Provider
Cunning Old Fox	Reliable plodder
Crisis-maker	Rescuer
Crusader	Robin Hood
Dreamer	Santa Claus
Emotional Hijacker	Seducer
Fairy Godmother	Sex Kitten
Faithful Follower	Sleeping Princess
Fascinating Witch	Spoiled Brat
Film Star	Sherlock Holmes
Fixer	Shy Violet
Frustrator	Stubborn Donkey
Genius	Starving Artist
Gentle Giant	Sugar Daddy
Gossiper	Tarzan
Guilt-peddler	Teddy Bear
Guru	Tinkerbell
Harassed Executive	Tough Guy
Harassed Housewife	Tragedy Queen
Helper	Turtle
Hippie	Ugly Duckling
Iron Maiden	Very Important Person
Jekyll and Hyde	Walking Disaster
Leader	Walking Encyclopedia
Listener	Willing Horse
Loser	Winner
Lovable Rascal	Wise Friend
Mad Hatter	Zombie

A NAMES	B MY ROLES	C THEIR ROLES	D Do they like my roles?	E Do I like their roles?
1				
2				
3				
4				
5				
6				

©DIAGRAM

141

How well do you know others?

Do you know how your parents met? Have you any idea what your friends think about when they are alone? What was your father's most burning ambition as a young man? When is your great aunt's birthday? Answers to questions like these are not always easy to give, yet we claim to know some people very well.

Here is an opportunity to find out how well you know five adults of your choice; they may be family or friends, but choose at least two people who are not part of your family.
Think carefully about whom to choose. Who do you think you know very well indeed? When you have decided, write their first names, or just their initials across the top of the page (*opposite*), using one column for each person.
Read down the list of items in the left-hand column and write underneath the name of each person your answer, if you think you know it.

How accurate are your answers?
You may need to check with the friends concerned before you can add up a score of right answers for each one. However, looking at it the other way round, how many items could you not answer, including those you really aren't sure about or had to guess. If you were unable to answer more than half the questions, you really don't know that person very well. If you had only three gaps or less, you know the person well. Anywhere in between is average.

Questions about your friends.	Name
Birthday?	
Religious interest?	
Any allergies?	
Any disabilities?	
One personal strength?	
One weakness?	
One secret hope?	
One secret fear?	
One ambition?	
Favorite food?	
Favorite color	
Favorite sport?	
Favorite music?	
One bad habit?	
One good habit?	
One pet hate?	
One irritating saying?	
How sociable?	
How shy?	
What, more than anything, makes your friend angry?	
What, more than anything, makes your friend happy?	
What, more than anything, would hurt your friend?	
Add up the number correctly answered. (Maximum 22.)	
Add up the number you couldn't answer.	

HOW WELL CAN YOU REMEMBER COMPARATIVE DIFFERENCES? Fill in the names in answer to the questions.	
1 Who is the tallest of the five?	
2 Who is the lightest in weight?	
3 Who is the oldest?	
4 Who could lie in the sun the longest without getting badly burnt?	
5 Which of them, if any, is left-handed?	
6 Which of them, if any, has blue eyes?	

Name	Name	Name	Name

How do you handle conflicts?

How do you handle conflicts with people you love? Arguments between friends are not just a matter of getting your viewpoint across, or of getting your way. The friendship may be at stake too.

There are five ways in which people who are close tend to handle conflicts. The outcomes are very different. You can read about them later, but first find out which of the five methods you use most often. You may end

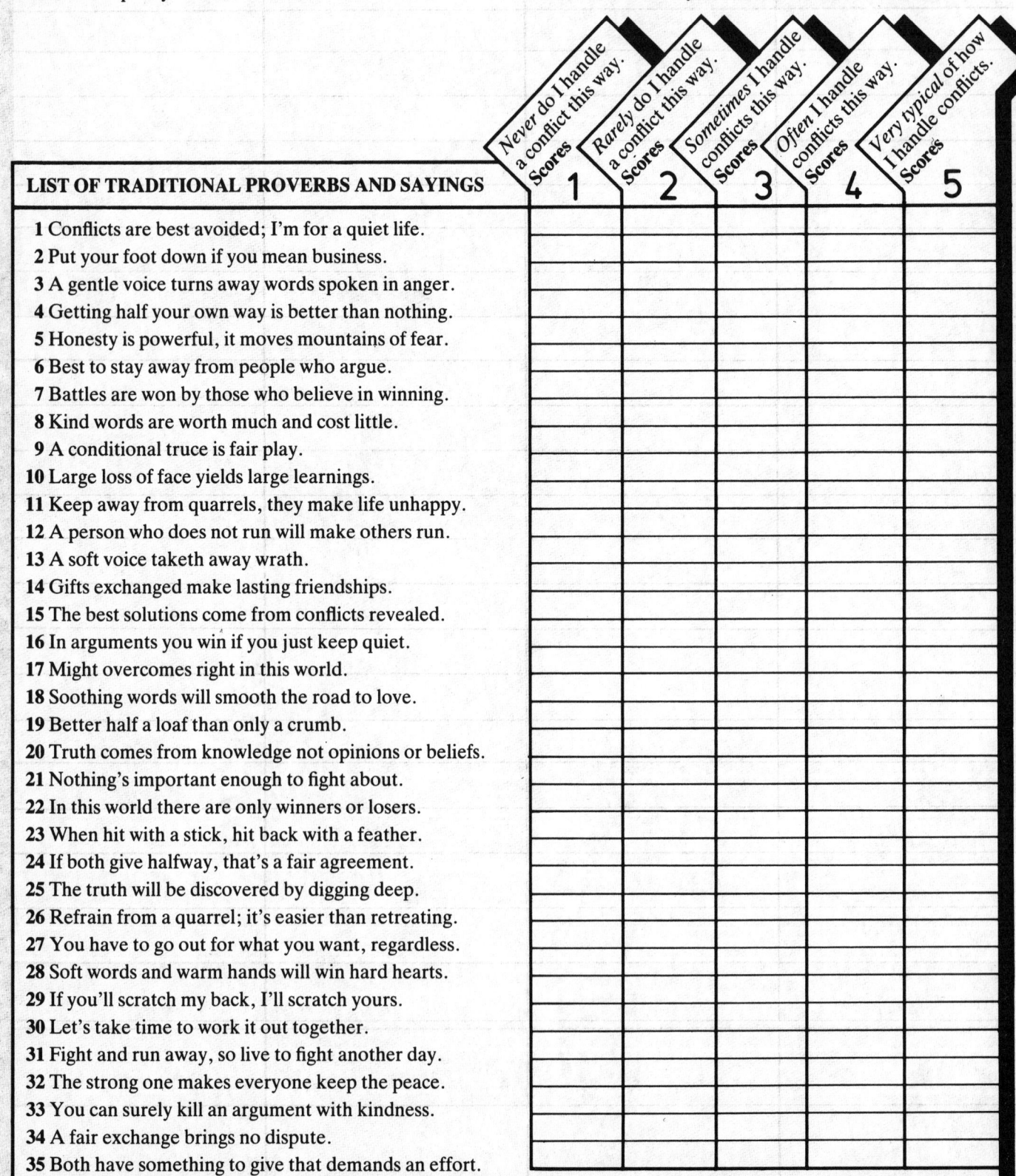

LIST OF TRADITIONAL PROVERBS AND SAYINGS	*Never do I handle a conflict this way.* Scores **1**	*Rarely do I handle a conflict this way.* Scores **2**	*Sometimes I handle conflicts this way.* Scores **3**	*Often I handle conflicts this way.* Scores **4**	*Very typical of how I handle conflicts.* Scores **5**
1 Conflicts are best avoided; I'm for a quiet life.					
2 Put your foot down if you mean business.					
3 A gentle voice turns away words spoken in anger.					
4 Getting half your own way is better than nothing.					
5 Honesty is powerful, it moves mountains of fear.					
6 Best to stay away from people who argue.					
7 Battles are won by those who believe in winning.					
8 Kind words are worth much and cost little.					
9 A conditional truce is fair play.					
10 Large loss of face yields large learnings.					
11 Keep away from quarrels, they make life unhappy.					
12 A person who does not run will make others run.					
13 A soft voice taketh away wrath.					
14 Gifts exchanged make lasting friendships.					
15 The best solutions come from conflicts revealed.					
16 In arguments you win if you just keep quiet.					
17 Might overcomes right in this world.					
18 Soothing words will smooth the road to love.					
19 Better half a loaf than only a crumb.					
20 Truth comes from knowledge not opinions or beliefs.					
21 Nothing's important enough to fight about.					
22 In this world there are only winners or losers.					
23 When hit with a stick, hit back with a feather.					
24 If both give halfway, that's a fair agreement.					
25 The truth will be discovered by digging deep.					
26 Refrain from a quarrel; it's easier than retreating.					
27 You have to go out for what you want, regardless.					
28 Soft words and warm hands will win hard hearts.					
29 If you'll scratch my back, I'll scratch yours.					
30 Let's take time to work it out together.					
31 Fight and run away, so live to fight another day.					
32 The strong one makes everyone keep the peace.					
33 You can surely kill an argument with kindness.					
34 A fair exchange brings no dispute.					
35 Both have something to give that demands an effort.					

up wanting to change your approach to conflicts. A list of traditional proverbs and sayings relating to conflicts with friends is given (*left*). Read each one and decide how applicable it is to you. There are scores of 1, 2, 3, 4 and 5 from which to choose given (*below*). Check the relevant box once you have made your choice. **The five methods for handling conflicts** are shown at the top of each score column: avoiding, pushing, soothing, compromising and resolving, all of which are described at the bottom of the page.

The higher your total score for each of the five, the more you tend to use that method. The lower the score, the less you use that method. Note that the scores for each proverb should be entered horizontally, not vertically, in the score columns.

ENTER YOUR SCORE FOR EACH PROVERB FROM THE LIST (*OPPOSITE*)

AVOIDING	PUSHING	SOOTHING	COMPROMISING	RESOLVING
1	2	3	4	5
6	7	8	9	10
11	12	13	14	15
16	17	18	19	20
21	22	23	24	25
26	27	28	29	30
31	32	33	34	35
Total	Total	Total	Total	Total

THE SNAIL

AVOIDING CONFLICT

Snails withdraw into the safety of their shells whenever a conflict appears, either disappearing or looking so offended the other person feels guilty for even mentioning the subject. Snails feel helpless and are often unhappy as they don't really get what they want. Nor do they get close to people because they stay inside their shells.

THE LION

PUSHING IN CONFLICT

Lions do not like to take NO for an answer. Their goals are so important they are prepared to achieve them at all costs. They believe there is only winning and losing. If they lose they feel weak, so cannot bear to fail.
In conflicts they will use any tactics to win but often lose friendships. Lions are proud, successful and don't care if people dislike them.

THE TEDDY BEAR

SOOTHING CONFLICTS

Teddy Bears value relationships so much they will give up anything to keep a friendship, which is why they get used so much and become tattered. Teddy Bears need to be liked and are afraid that conflict will cause hurt.
They pour oil on troubled waters hardly realizing that oil will kill seabirds and mess-up the shore.

THE FOX

COMPROMISING CONFLICT

Foxes look for a middle ground where both people gain something from the conflict but at the cost of both people giving up something. They dislike extremes and try to find an outcome that is for the common good. Foxes compromise to find a peaceful settlement although it is usually only temporary, since the hunt will begin again later.

THE OWL

RESOLVING CONFLICTS

Owls are wise birds. They know relationships don't thrive unless both people feel satisfied. They resolve conflicts by confronting all the issues involved, which takes courage and time. Thus both people get what they want and grow closer in the process. Owls neither dominate nor cling; they are rare old birds.

145

Getting closer

Some years ago Joseph Luft and Harry Inghams invented the Jo-Hari Window to show people that there are two important parts in the process of getting closer to others. The window has had a curtain and a blind added here, to help you to see how the two parts work in a relationship between YOU (the blind) and THE OTHER (the curtain). The other is a person of your choice, to whom you would like to get closer.

The window represents the relationship between you and the other and the view outside is whatever you build together, i.e. what kind of things you do together, how you make decisions, solve problems and enjoy yourselves.

Read across the top of these two pages first and then try the activities below if you feel like it.

Raising the blind

The blind represents you. In most contacts with friends your blind is about half-way up the window as in diagram A. You have revealed both part of yourself and some of the things you think about your friend. Part of the view from the window is visible; you know what each other looks like, you have conversations together and you may know some of each other's likes and dislikes.

If you tell your friend, Tom, for example, more about yourself, show him what you really think and feel, your blind goes up a little as in diagram B. If you give Tom some feedback about himself, your blind goes up even more. Giving feedback is also part of revealing yourself.

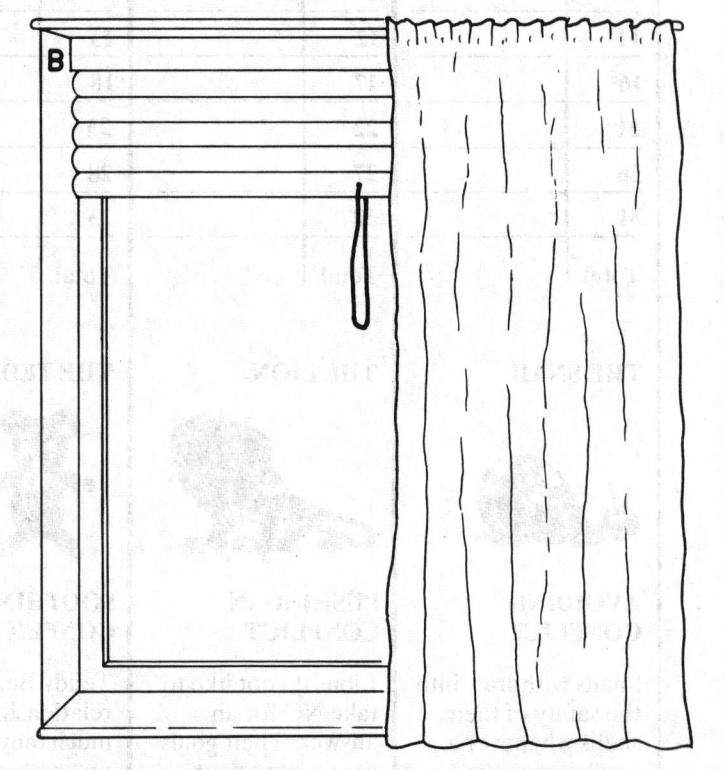

ACTIVITIES FOR SHARING

Before you decide to try and get closer you must first ask Tom how he feels about opening up your relationship.

Secondly, you must be very clear that being close to someone is not all a bed of roses. Thirdly, trust begins with yourself. Do you trust yourself to tell a little more truth about yourself? Can you accept a little more truth from Tom?

Try these activities.

1 Sit opposite to each other and each take five minutes talking while the other listens. As the listener, just accept what the other says.

2 If either person finds talking difficult, then write a letter to each other, which you then sit down and read to each other.

Your list of things to tell

Write down here the things you would like to tell Tom about yourself.

_____

_____

_____

_____

_____

_____

_____

_____

Opening the curtain

The curtain represents Tom. In diagram **B**, the blind is quite high up but the curtain is still half-way across the window. Tom hasn't shown you much of himself and consequently isn't contributing as much to the relationship as you are.

In diagram **C** things are the other way round; Tom has opened his curtain, but your blind is still pulled down. Tom tells you a great deal about himself and about how he sees you, but you stay relatively hidden.

Opening up a relationship

In diagram **D** both the blind and the curtain have been opened to reveal more of the view that has been created by both people. You and Tom have disclosed a lot about yourselves to each other, including your darker sides. You have also given each other some feedback. This has meant telling Tom honestly what you see him doing. It is a sign of inner confidence if you can tell Tom something of your inner truths too. This sharing creates trust and draws people closer to each other. It is also a very risky business, for the view may not be quite so pleasant. Instead you may find there is a rift between you that has to be bridged!

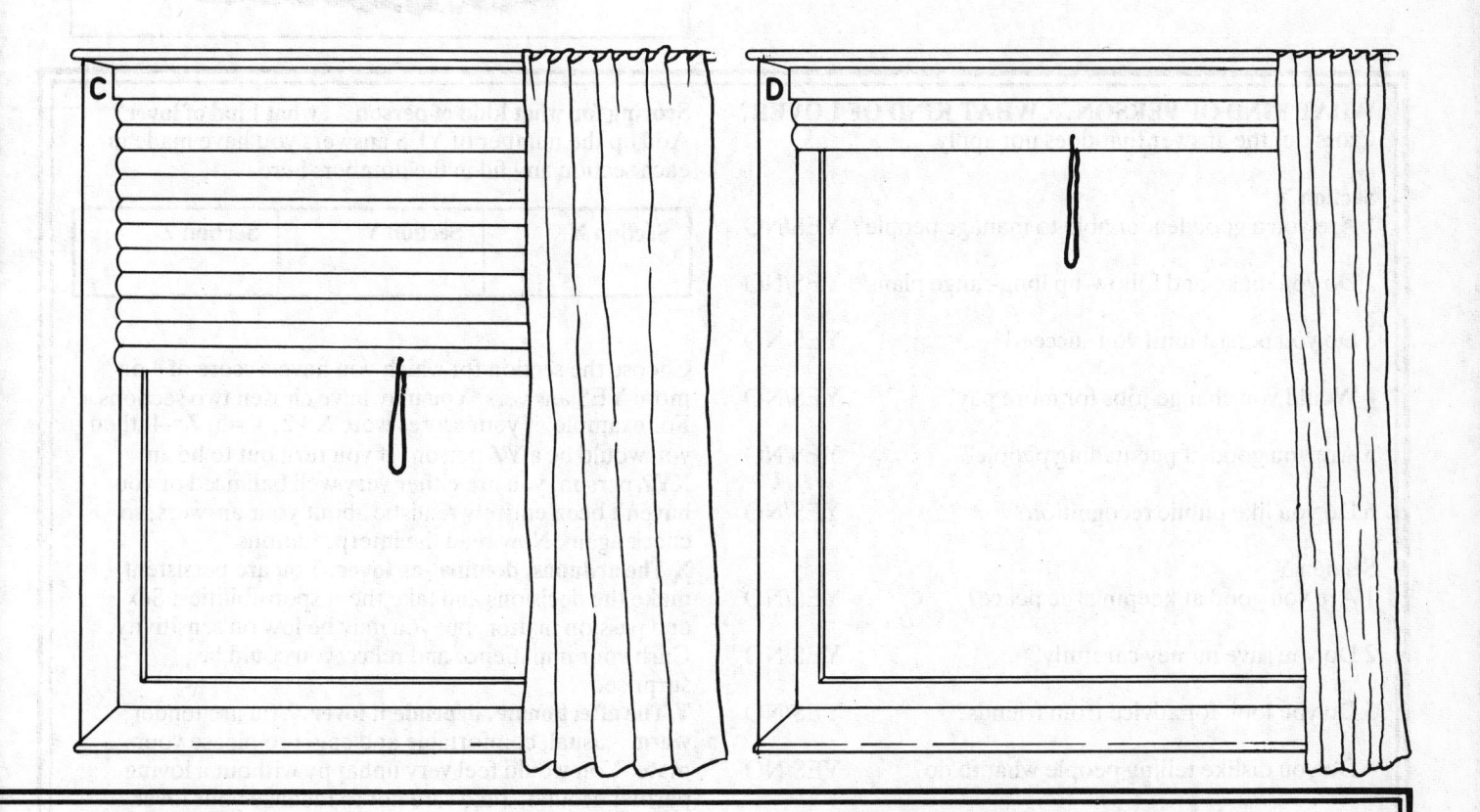

Your list of things to ask

Write here the things you would like to ask Tom about; you may or may not get an answer, of course.

_____

_____

_____

_____

_____

_____

What can happen during these activities?

1 You may feel nervous, tense or anxious. If you feel this way, say so. Just talking about why you feel nervous will relieve the tension.

2 One person may become upset and cry. Part of growing closer is accepting the other person's feelings. A gentle touch or holding hands will help but don't stop the feeling by trying to "comfort" the other.

3 Either of you may become angry. Again, let this happen if you feel able. If you both get into a shouting match that is going nowhere, go away for half-an-hour and then come together, give each other a hug and then try to discuss what made you both angry.

4 One person may "go blank" and not want to talk. Leave it for a few days and agree to try again. Enjoy yourselves getting closer. It can be fun!

© DIAGRAM

147

How good a lover are you?

The kind of person you are, together with your attitude to sexual love will give you an answer to this question. On these two pages are two sets of questions, answers and interpretations. While you cannot change who you are, you can change your attitude, so you may find some clues here that will help you become an even better lover.

WHAT KIND OF PERSON... WHAT KIND OF LOVER?
Cross out the answer that does not apply.

Section X

1 Are you a good leader able to manage people? YES/NO

2 Do you make and follow up long-range plans? YES/NO

3 Do you persist until you succeed? YES/NO

4 Would you change jobs for more pay? YES/NO

5 Are you good at persuading people? YES/NO

6 Do you like public recognition? YES/NO

Section Y

1 Are you good at keeping the peace? YES/NO

2 Do you save money carefully? YES/NO

3 Do you look for advice from friends? YES/NO

4 Do you dislike telling people what to do? YES/NO

5 Does it matter that most people like you? YES/NO

6 Do you prefer company to being alone? YES/NO

Section Z

1 Would you rather watch than participate? YES/NO

2 Are you good at judging character? YES/NO

3 Do you prefer small groups to big parties? YES/NO

4 Are you rather self-critical? YES/NO

5 Do you always avoid tight clothing? YES/NO

6 Do you need to be alone often? YES/NO

Scoring for what kind of person... what kind of lover?
Add up the number of YES answers you have made in each section and fill in the numbers here.

Section X	Section Y	Section Z

Choose the section for which you have a score of 4 or more YES answers. You may have chosen two sections. For example, if your scores were X=2, Y=5, Z=4, then you would be a **YZ** person. If you turn out to be an **XYZ** person, you are either very well balanced or you haven't been entirely realistic about your answers, so check again. Now read the interpretations.

X The arduous, dominating lover. You are persistent, make the decisions and take the responsibilities. Sex and passion matter, but you may be low on sensitivity. Curb your impatience and relax, you could be surprised.

Y The affectionate, dependent lover. You are tender, warm, casual, comfortable and eager to please your mate. You would feel very unhappy without a loving partner around. Take care not to idealize your lover.

Z The charming, reserved lover. You will love and honor your partner but find it very hard to get really emotionally involved and express deep feelings of affection. Rather cool you may feel quite insecure.

XY The arduous, dependent lover. While you like to take the lead you fear really asserting yourself, so you may tend to try hard to please. Tough one minute and soft the next; so try resolving this conflict.

YZ The cautiously affectionate lover. You value love and freedom so it may take you a while to find the right partner. You have patience and sensitivity. Let others see the warmth behind your aloofness.

XZ The arduous and charming lover. Otherwise known as Casanova, both male and female! You have a tendency to love and leave. Reluctant to become deeply intimate, you may need to let go of control.

WHAT'S YOUR ATTITUDE TO SEXUAL LOVE?
Answer YES or NO as honestly as you can in each box.

1 Do you tell your partner what you want during sex?

2 Do you believe that love depends on having good sex?

3 Are there some parts of the body you dislike touching?

4 Do you think a woman can take the initiative in sex?

5 If your partner asks to try something new do you try it?

6 Do you feel disappointed if both of you don't achieve an orgasm?

7 Does being kissed in public make you feel embarrassed?

8 Do you ever lie together and touch each other without having sex?

9 Do you think sex should be at night?

10 Do you think sex should be in bed?

ANALYZING YOUR ATTITUDE TO SEXUAL LOVE
Score 1 for each answer with which you agreed.

1 YES Honesty and willingness to talk openly are part of any good relationship.

2 NO If love depended on sex it would be a very sad world.

3 NO If you dislike any part of your own or your partner's body, you should look carefully at your attitude.

4 YES It is natural that sometimes one partner may take a dominant or leading role, both man and woman.

5 YES If you like to try new ideas you are a creative, adventurous person.

6 NO Orgasm is a state of pleasure, not a goal to be achieved. If sex is truly a pleasurable activity, orgasm will happen, but not always.

7 NO If you don't like being kissed in public, you are rather inhibited.

8 YES Touching is healthy and pleasurable, why deny your partner that?

9 NO Love doesn't have a time-table!

10 NO While privacy isn't always easy to find, there are dozens of alternatives.

SUMMARY OF YOUR ATTITUDE TO SEXUAL LOVE
If you scored less than 5
You have an inhibited and undeveloped attitude to sex. You may be afraid or have inner, hidden negative feelings about physical, sensual or sexual pleasures.
If you scored 5–8
You are still not able to relax fully and may be a little insensitive to your partner's needs and even to your own needs. Do try to experiment a little more.
If you scored 9–10
You are a very mature and caring lover with a very positive attitude to sexual love. You are responsive to both your own and your partner's needs.

©DIAGRAM

Are you a well- informed lover?

Many facts are now known about love and sexuality. Although individual needs vary widely, it is important to know the facts from the fictions. Pleasure grows as two people get to know each other, but maturity comes from being a well-informed lover.
Here are two ways you can test your knowledge of sex, love and sexual love.

DO YOU LOVE THE ONE YOU ARE WITH?
Do you love your partner or are you staying together simply because you need a relationship? Here are some unconscious messages you may be giving yourself to help you distinguish between need and love. Answer YES or NO in these boxes:

☐

1 Have you ever intended to phone your partner but rung someone else instead?

☐

2 If you go away from your partner on a trip do you always want to phone him/her frequently?

☐

3 Have you ever gone somewhere on a date, such as a place where you used to meet a former lover?

☐

4 Do you sometimes leave something behind in your partner's house or car without intending to do so?

☐

5 Do you ever forget your partner's name or refer to him/her by a different name?

☐

6 Do you ever forget to post letters or phone your partner when you have promised to do so?

☐

7 Do you and your partner ever find yourselves dodging round each other to get out of each other's way, but often end up bumping into each other?

☐

8 Do you usually turn over and go to sleep, or move away after having sex with your partner?

☐

9 If you are out with your partner and you are buying the tickets, do you ever forget to buy one for your partner?

☐

10 Do you ever avoid telling your partner things because you think he/she might be hurt?

☐

11 Do you ever have angry arguments with your partner?

☐

12 Do you feel wary or jealous if your partner seems attracted to other people?

READ THESE COMMENTS FOR ANY QUESTION TO WHICH YOU ANSWERED YES

1 You are rejecting your partner. Was it because you had had an argument or are you continuing the relationship out of need not love?
2 You probably need reassurance, a sign you are not certain you can love and let go with confidence. You may be unable to enjoy yourself on your own, away from your partner whom you need.
3 Your new love has not replaced the old one and you probably need rather than love your partner.
4 It shows you want to go back and have a reluctance to leave. Usually a sign of love.
5 It shows you neither love nor need this person and you will not find it difficult to forget him/her.
6 It is doubtful if you really meant the contents, so check out what it was you really wanted to say and say it clearly. If you can't, then it is unlikely that you truly love this person.
7 You want physical contact very much; find out what kind of contact; is it for love and/or sex?
8 It is likely that the attraction is more sexual than loving.
9 You probably wanted to be on your own.
10 You need your partner more than you love him/her. True love can withstand hurts.
11 You probably love each other very much.
12 You probably need your partner's exclusive attention and fail to realize that normal, healthy people can be attracted to others while still loving one person very deeply.

HOW MUCH DO YOU KNOW ABOUT SEX AND SEXUAL LOVE?
Tick whether you think each statement is true or false.

True False

1 Sexual attraction can be the basis of a long-term relationship whether two people love each other or not.

2 Both men and women can enjoy sexual activities in their sixties and seventies.

3 If sex becomes less frequent between a couple who used to have good sex, the cause is usually non-sexual conflict.

4 Rape, sexual demands and pretences often occur in unhappy marriages.

5 Premature ejaculation and failure to achieve erection or orgasm is usually due to emotional problems.

6 The rhythm method, douching and male withdrawal are safe methods of birth control.

7 Surgical sterilization of either sex affects sexual desires and activities.

8 A man who has been circumcised can enjoy sex more fully.

9 Masturbation can be pleasurable at any age to both men and women.

10 Frigidity may have medical and emotional causes and can be helped.

11 It is impossible for a woman to become pregnant during menstruation.

12 Fluid coming from a man's penis before orgasm contains no sperm.

13 A man with large sex organs has a greater sexual capacity than other men.

14 Certain foods, drugs and alcohol are known to increase sexual potency.

15 A woman can stop birth control immediately after the menopause.

16 A woman's desire and sexual capacity decrease after the menopause.

17 Long-term loving relationships are possible without sexual activity.

18 Marriage will change the feelings of a man who is homosexual.

True False

19 Most venereal diseases can be cured but are contagious until treated.

20 Herpes is contagious; it does no harm in a long-term relationship.

21 During intercourse, the position helpful for a woman to achieve orgasm is if she is underneath the man.

22 There are big differences between the sexual desires of women and of men.

23 Shame, or the fear of losing control to pleasure, causes sexual problems.

24 Disabled people are incapable of having satisfactory sex.

25 A penis larger than a woman's vagina can cause pain during intercourse.

26 Sex during menstruation is a matter of personal preference.

27 Retarded children have sexual drives and need sensitive understanding.

28 All normal boys and girls masturbate and it is a natural activity.

29 If a man's testicles have not descended, he is not potent.

30 Touching and caressing should always lead to sexual intercourse.

31 Sex used to relieve tensions and aggressions indicates insecurity and a low self-esteem.

32 Fully relaxed orgasmic pleasure is felt all over the body.

33 Children are often first attracted to the parent of the opposite sex.

34 Incest and child pornography are the inclinations of immature and irresponsible adults.

35 Total honesty between partners is the best way to create a loving and long-lasting relationship.

ANSWERS

1 True	8 False	15 False	22 False	29 False
2 True	9 True	16 False	23 True	30 False
3 True	10 True	17 True	24 False	31 True
4 True	11 False	18 False	25 True	32 True
5 True	12 False	19 True	26 True	33 True
6 False	13 False	20 True	27 True	34 True
7 False	14 False	21 False	28 True	35 True

©DIAGRAM

What's your lovestyle?

Psychologist John Alan Lees has described a whole spectrum of "lovestyles" – the different things people mean by the phrase "I love you." Your way of being in love may involve total devotion to one person, or you may find that you fall in love with several people at the same time. You may be intense or playful, down to earth or over the top, detached or committed – or somewhere in between. This quiz helps you to discover which of the six most common lovestyles is yours.

To discover your own lovestyle, answer all the questions on these two pages, picking the answer from each group that most clearly applies to you. Circle the key letters of your answers in the scoring boxes on the left of the answers – you will find that some answers have more than one key letter. Count the number of key letters you have circled in each column and enter them in the totals boxes.

A	B	C	D	E	F

If one of your scores is much higher than any of the others, you clearly have a preference for one particular lovestyle: you will find it described on pages 154–155 under its key letter. If you have equally high scores for two lovestyles, your own lovestyle may be a blend of the two (read about both of them), or you may switch from one lovestyle to another, depending on the relationship in which you are involved. Remember to answer all the questions before reading the lovestyle descriptions, or you may inadvertently affect your score.

How do you feel about your childhood?

B,C	It was warm and happy
F	It was secure
D,E	It was average – no better and no worse than anyone else's
A	It was unhappy

How do you feel about your life now?

B,C	I'm contented and feel fulfilled
F	It's good, and my friends are reliable
D	It's OK
E	I can achieve what I want
A	I feel lonely and discontented

How important is "love" to you?

A	Life without love isn't worth it
B	It's very important
F	It's an important part of friendship and family life
E	It's a pleasant and desirable part of a well-balanced life
D	Other things are more important
C	It's for fun

If you were to "fall in love" now, how would you feel?

C	I like being "in love" – and I'm often in love with more than one person
E	I could fall in love happily with someone who is really compatible
B	I would like to fall in love, but I don't feel anxious about it
A	I want to fall in love, but I'm worried about what will happen when I do
F	OK, but I prefer friendship to love
D	I'm not ready to settle down

When you begin a new relationship, is your new partner a stranger or someone you already know?

B	A stranger who attracts me strongly
C,D	A stranger who is reasonably attractive and who seems like an acceptable partner
A	A stranger who arouses mixed feelings in me
E,F	Someone I already know

Does a prospective partner's physical appearance matter to you?

B	Yes – I am always attracted to the same physical type
C	I do have preferences, but I'm not too fussy
D	No – I am attracted to a number of different physical types
E	Provided that the other person is suitable, appearances are not very important
F	No – it's more important to get to know the other person
A	I don't know

As a new relationship begins, how do you feel about it?

| A | It's taking over my thoughts |
| B | Very optimistic – my thoughts are pleasant and hopeful |

| E,F | It would be pleasant if we could do more things together |
| C,D | OK – it's not going to change my life |

How much do you want to see of your new partner?

A	I'm worried if we don't see each other every day
B	I'd like us to meet every day
E,F	I'd like us to meet whenever we can find something interesting and enjoyable to do
C,D	I don't want us to be living in each other's pockets

How do you want the relationship to develop?

C	I want it to fit in with the other pleasant relationships that I've got
D	I think we should keep our emotions under control and just enjoy ourselves
E	I want us to have a sensible relationship that suits us both
F	I want us to feel relaxed and comfortable in each other's company
B	I want us to become as close as possible as soon as possible
A	I would like to have some control over how it develops, but my feelings are too intense to allow for this

At what point in the relationship do you want to have sex with your new partner?

F	Only when we have become committed to each other
E	When we know each other well enough
D	When the opportunity presents itself – providing that it doesn't spoil my other relationships
B,C	During our first few meetings
A	I don't know – it's very frustrating

How important is it that you and your partner are sexually compatible?

C,D	Our sexual relationship should be highly enjoyable and good fun
B	Very important – if we aren't compatible the relationship won't work
E	It's important, and we should both make an effort to put right any problems
F	We can work out any problems that arise – there are other ways of showing that we care for each other
A	If we love each other, it's bound to be all right eventually, isn't it?

What's the best way for you and your partner to express your feelings about each other?

F	I think we should know what we feel without needing to talk about it
D	I think we should both play it cool
E	It's nice to express our feelings, but we shouldn't become too intense about it too soon
C	We need to show our feelings for each other – and for other people, too
B	I want us both to be open and sincere in expressing our very deepest feelings about each other
A	I want to talk about how deeply I feel about my partner – I wish my partner felt the same way

Are you possessive?

A	Very
F	To some extent – but it only shows when the relationship is under threat
E	Sometimes – but I don't want to continue a relationship with someone who is unfaithful
B	I want an exclusive relationship with my partner but I'm not frightened of rivals
C,D	No – we should both have other relationships

What will happen if any problems arise in your relationship?

E	I don't continue a relationship where there are problems
D	There will only be problems if my partner becomes too intense or too possessive
B	I don't really expect any – we can deal with anything that comes up
C	All relationships have problems, but they can be dealt with
F	Everything will sort itself out with time
A	I'm anxious about this – I keep thinking that things will go wrong

How do you see the end of the relationship?

A	I don't want it to end – I won't give up trying to make it work
E	We should try to work out our problems – perhaps with expert help – but break it off in a civilized manner if we are incompatible
B,F	Whichever of us ends it, we should try to remain friends
C	Something I can take in my stride – it was nice while it lasted
D	I will be the one to end it – I'll simply find someone else

©DIAGRAM

153

Lovestyles

A THE COMPULSIVE LOVESTYLE

This is possessive, obsessive, tormented love – the lovestyle of grand passions and great tragedy. If this is your lovestyle, you probably feel that you had an unhappy childhood, and you are lonely and discontented with your life now. When you are looking for a new partner, you can fall in love with almost anyone: you may not even like the person very much. You insist that fate brought you together, and blind yourself to your new partner's faults and virtues. In fact, you fall in love with a person you have created in your imagination. Once you fall in love you become impatient, and rapidly try to escalate the relationship to fever pitch.

When you are in love, you veer between extremes of joy and misery, are totally preoccupied with your partner, and find that your feelings are beyond your control. You demand and offer total devotion and expect to possess your partner completely. Your relationships are dramatic – lots of fights followed by lots of passionate reconciliations. If no problems exist, you invent them. If your partner arrives late or misses a promised phone call, you drive yourself frantic with suspicion. You feel insecure, and try to change yourself to please your partner, making great sacrifices to keep the relationship going. You are never the one to end a relationship, and when it does end it takes you a long time to recover.

B THE SENSUAL LOVESTYLE

This is "love at first sight" – the powerful and immediate attraction to a total stranger much featured in romantic fiction. If this is your lovestyle, you probably had a happy childhood and are self-assured and contented with your life now. You are not searching for a lover, but are ready to fall in love if the right person comes along. And the person must be right – you always go for one particular physical type, and are highly critical of any deviations from your ideal. When you meet your ideal, you suffer all the classic symptoms – the sudden shock of recognition, the heavy breathing, the quickened pulse. You want to become emotionally and physically close to your new partner as soon as possible, and you move rapidly to an intense intimacy. Sex is very important in your relationships, both for its own sake and as a means of learning more about and of becoming even closer to your new partner. You see your partner as a real person, and do not blind yourself to his or her faults. You are ready to commit yourself, and you are seeking an equal commitment in return, but without being demanding or possessive. You give and expect complete honesty and sincerity about your feelings. You will end the relationship if you meet someone who comes even closer to your ideal, but however it ends, you will always try to remain close friends with your former partner.

C THE FREEWHEELING LOVESTYLE

This is the Casanova lovestyle, the lovestyle of the open marriage. If it is your lovestyle, you probably feel that you had a happy childhood and that your life now is enjoyable. You are gregarious and meet people easily, not actively searching for love, but if an attractive person (or people) should happen to come along...
You like being in love, and are attracted to a number of different physical types. Sex and sexual intimacy play an important part in all your relationships.
Your lovestyle involves you in a careful balancing act: you want to be intensely involved (both physically and emotionally) but without committing yourself. You can enjoy spending time in close rapport with one partner, and can then go off and do the same with someone else. You are never jealous or possessive, and you expect your partners to be aware that you are not their exclusive property. In fact, you will probably encourage your partners to have other relationships of their own. You do sincerely care about each and all of your partners, and try to avoid causing any pain. When you end a relationship, you try to leave your partner happy and contented, as you may want to return to them in the future. But if you are clumsy or careless – or simply unlucky – you can go through life leaving a trails of broken hearts behind you.

D

D THE LIGHTHEARTED LOVESTYLE

This is love for fun, casual and playful love that is never allowed to get too serious. If this is your lovestyle, you probably feel that you had an average sort of childhood and that you now lead an average sort of life. You do not place a very high value on "love": you feel that other things are more important. You are self-sufficient, rather cool and calculating, almost vain. Your personal involvement in your relationships is limited: you want to play the field, to have several partners at the same time, and to avoid being tied down. You refuse even to commit yourself to definite times and places for meetings, and never make any changes in your life to accommodate a new partner. You enjoy the rituals of love and the thrill of the chase, and are an accomplished flirt. You will flirt with almost anyone, as you have no preference for any particular physical type. You find sex an enjoyable and amusing activity, but treat it as part of the game: you would rather find a new partner than try to solve any sexual difficulties that there may be. You regard your partners as replaceable, and you rapidly drop anyone who becomes too intense or possessive. You expect your partners to understand the rules of the game you are playing, and to be controlled enough to abide by them under any circumstances. You are usually the person who brings a relationship to an end, and any discomfort this causes you is soon forgotten.

E

E THE COMMITTED LOVESTYLE

This is realistic, unsentimental, pragmatic love – the type of love that forms a successful basis for arranged marriages. If this is your lovestyle, you probably feel that you had an average sort of childhood, and you have a very practical outlook on life now, expecting to achieve results by your own efforts. You are not looking for love, but for a partner with whom you can share your life. You require someone with a compatible character and with similar interests and social background to your own – someone who can fit comfortably into your life and be an asset to you. You are not very concerned about your prospective partner's appearance, and you expect to have to work at achieving sexual compatibility.
If you do not happen to meet a prospective partner during your usual social life you will be methodical in your search for one, perhaps using a dating agency or a marriage bureau. When you have found someone you think may be suitable, you will introduce them gradually into your life, being ready to drop them if you turn out to be a less well-matched pair than you had expected. You look on your relationship as an investment, something to which both partners are expected to contribute equal amounts, and you become jealous and possessive only when this investment is threatened. You set out to arrange a satisfactory relationship and you expect it to be long lasting – if problems arise you will sort them out, with expert help if necessary.

F

F THE FRIENDLY LOVESTYLE

This is companionable, affectionate love – love as friendship, the very opposite of grand passion. If this is your lovestyle, you probably had a secure childhood, perhaps as part of a large family, and your friends form an important part of your life now. Your love relationships develop from friendships – in fact, you may not even define yourself as having "fallen in love." You simply begin to include your new partner in more and more of your life. You are the type of person who marries either the boy or girl next door, or someone who could have been the boy or girl next door. Your relationships are undemanding and unspectacular and ripen slowly. You share your interests and activities with your partner in a familiar and companionable way, without being flirtatious or indulging in long, passionate conversations. You are physically reserved – sex is not very important to you and you avoid demonstrative displays of affection. Your partner's physical appearance is also irrelevant, as you are more concerned with getting to know a person's character than with the way they look. You do not expect any problems in your stable relationship, and if any did arise, you would expect them to resolve themselves or to simply disappear if given enough time. If your relationship should come to an end, you would expect to remain close friends with your former partner.

©DIAGRAM

My Findings

Here you can list your discoveries for quick reference and see your general trends while picking out areas of your personality you may like to develop further. If there are some paradoxes you may have to decide which self was answering the questions at the time! (See "Which you?" pages 122-123.)

Remember . . . you are a fascinating and complex person continually growing and changing.

ASTROLOGY

Sun in	Jupiter in
Moon in	Saturn in
Mercury in	Uranus in
Venus in	Neptune in
Mars in	Pluto in
Ascendant in	

ORIENTAL ASTROLOGY

My ruling animal:

My companion in life:

My Moon-Sign animal:

My oriental element:

NATURE OR NURTURE

Some inherited characteristics:

Some acquired characteristics:

My physical coordination:

My body shape:

PHYSICAL TRAITS

My blood sugar score:	Sit ups:
Back Pull:	Push ups:
Spinal Curl:	Kneebends:
Toe Touch:	Stamina:
Toe Flex:	Life expectancy:

BODY BALANCES

1:　　　　　2:　　　　　3:

PHYSIOGNOMY

Face zones:

Face shape:

BODY LANGUAGE

Communication:

Would you believe it:

My action bias:

My physical bias:

GRAPHOLOGY

Color:

Organization:

Character profile:

Rebelliousness:

Assertion:

Aggression:

Ambition:

Originality:

Signs of stress:

Signature size:

Formality:

PERCEPTIONS AND INTERPRETATIONS

Extroverted or introverted:

Value-system:

Pessimistic or optimistic:

Observation score:

Type of dreamer:

PROFILES

Refer to these sections for full information about your personal choices: page 122 onwards.

My stress score:

How I handle conflicts:

As a lover I am:

My lovestyle is:

Index